SMASHING

SMASHING ANDROID UI:

RESPONSIVE USER INTERFACES AND DESIGN PATTERNS FOR ANDROID PHONES AND TABLETS

Juhani Lehtimäki

WILEY

A John Wiley and Sons, Ltd, Publication

PUBLISHER'S ACKNOWLEDGEMENTS

Some of the people who helped bring this book to market include the following:

Editorial and Production
VP Consumer and Technology Publishing Director: Michelle Leete
Associate Director–Book Content Management: Martin Tribe
Associate Publisher: Chris Webb
Acquisitions Editor: Craig Smith
Publishing Assistant: Ellie Scott
Development Editor: Kezia Endsley
Copy Editor: Kezia Endsley
Technical Editor: Sebastian Kaspari
Editorial Manager: Jodi Jensen
Senior Project Editor: Sara Shlaer
Editorial Assistant: Leslie Saxman

Marketing
Senior Marketing Manager: Louise Breinholt
Marketing Executive: Kate Parrett

Composition Services
Compositor: Christin Swinford
Proofreader: Wordsmith Editorial
Indexer: Potomac Indexing, LLC

ABOUT THE AUTHOR

Juhani Lehtimäki is a developer with more than 10 years of experience in consulting and products in various business domains and technologies. He's been working on projects varying from Eclipse plug-in development to backend XML transformation to frontend web development and user interface design.

Recently, Juhani has been concentrating on Android and especially Android user interface design and development. Usability and user interface design has been his passion since early university studies. His interest in user interface design and Android led to the start of a blog about Android user interface design patterns in 2010. He still actively writes about topical user interface issues at `http://www.androiduipatterns.com/` as well as participates in the active discussions around Android in the Google+ social network.

AUTHOR'S ACKNOWLEDGMENTS

Writing this book was a lot of work and a lot of fun. It would not have been possible without the support of my girlfriend who patiently understood why I had to sit inside and type away instead of enjoying her company for the last few months. Thank you for your understanding!

I also want to extend my gratitude to my employer and colleagues at Snapp TV Ltd. for being flexible about work arrangements and letting me spend some of my working hours writing this book. A special thanks to Jasper Morgan for encouraging me to take the time I needed for the book, thus avoiding too much stress in the process.

Also, a big thank you to the awesome Android community that has formed in the Google+ social network. I enjoy reading your posts and comments. Topical matters are discussed in a very informative and friendly matter that encourages everyone to participate. A big thank you to Google's Android developer advocates, especially Nick Butcher, for the active participation in those discussions as well as the encouragement to write about Android.

Thank you to everyone who has read my blog posts and commented on them. It has encouraged me to keep writing and I have learned a lot. Thank you to fellow Android bloggers who have helped to accumulate the amount of information in the online Android community.

Building Android apps would be very difficult without the community of Android library contributors. Thank you to anyone who has built an Android library and distributed it free and Open Source for anyone to use. You all are doing amazing work and making everyone's life easier!

I also want to thank Google for providing tools to build Android apps as well as giving us the Android operating system. Writing this book would not have been possible without the awesome Google Drive (docs) that allowed me to concentrate on the writing instead of figuring out the word processing software. Big thank you also to Herzoglich Bayerisches Brauhaus Tegernsee for giving me energy in the late nights of writing.

Last but not least a huge thank you to Wiley for letting me write my first book. Thank you to Kezia Endsley, Craig Smith, and Sara Shlaer for guiding me in the process and all the help you've given me. A massive thanks to Sebastian Kaspari for being the technical editor of this book and making sure that all the code and examples work and are understandable. Thank you to Kevin Cannon for helping me by providing a designer's point of view for many things.

CONTENTS

INTRODUCTION

Welcome to *Smashing Android UI.*

This book will help you take the next step toward improving your Android knowledge. This book is not meant to teach you Android development from the beginning to the end, but instead builds on your existing knowledge and helps you understand how to build a better user experience for your apps.

For developers who might not be familiar with user interface design, this book gives you an overview of the tools and techniques you can use to determine what your users want and how to evaluate your app's usability.

For designers, reading this book will give a good overview of Android user interface in general. You'll find a comprehensive list of available default components and come to understand how developers use them. This book helps you align your knowledge of the Android platform with your developers to make it easier to work with them to build scalable and responsive user interfaces.

Android fragmentation does not need to be feared; you should think of it as an opportunity instead. This book explains how to approach design and development challenges so that you can build apps that not only run on smartphones but on tablets as well. You'll learn how to adapt your apps to different screen sizes, fully utilizing the available screen real estate and thus providing your users the best possible user experience, regardless of the device.

WHAT IS THIS BOOK ABOUT?

This book explains what is available for you in the Android platform. I'll explain how and when to use the components it provides. The Android platform and its documentation is gigantic. It is often difficult to start searching for information given the massive quantities of it. The goal of this book is to provide you with a good understanding of what information you need and what to look for. You will understand what components others have used to build great apps and learn how and where to use them.

The book explains what you need to do to make your apps adapt to the large number of devices out there, starting from design to implementation. You will come to understand what responsive design means and why it is so powerful on the Android platform.

The book also talks about Android user interface design patterns and anti-patterns. These are the do's and don'ts of the Android user interface design. Design patterns let you learn from others and give you a head start to design and development.

PART I

The first part of this book is dedicated to introducing the user-centered methodology as well as the Android platform as a whole. This part of the book is applicable to designers and developers. Developers might be familiar with the Android platform but might not have a good understanding of the processes they can use to get users involved in the early phases of the app project. Involving users early in your project helps you define what your app should do and how users are going to use it. Getting that part right helps you concentrate on the most important features as well as prevent so-called "feature creep," which can cause your app's scope to become ungainly.

Some designers and developers don't have a clear picture of the Android platform, with its complications like the famous fragmentation and device variety. If that describes you, this part of the book will also paint you a picture of the Android platform in all its glory.

PART II

Part II introduces the Android platform more deeply, explaining how Android apps are structured and how they talk to each other. It also gives you a good picture of available user interface components and how to use them.

PART III

Part III dives into scalable Android design and how to make your apps work on all devices, from small smartphones to large tablets.

PART IV

The last part of this book goes through the do's and don'ts of Android platform user interface design, in the form of user interface design patterns and anti-patterns.

INSTALLING THE COMPANION APP

This book has a companion app, which you can install on your Android device to view the examples in action when reading the book. The app contains all the examples included in this book. Trying out the examples can make the concepts easier to understand and to envision how the examples will work in real life on your own devices.

You can install the app free from the Google Play Store from the following URL or by scanning the following QR code.

`https://play.google.com/store/apps/details?id=com.androiduipatterns.smashingandroidui.examples`

Examples that are available in the companion app have a QR next to the relevant part in this book. To scan QR codes you need to install a QR code scanner on your phone. There are multiple free ones in the Google Play Store. I am using an app called Scan by Scan Inc., which you can download free from `https://play.google.com/store/apps/details?id=me.scan.android.client`.

Once you have a QR code scanner app installed on your device as well as the companion app, scanning the book's QR codes will directly open the corresponding example on your device. Just point your QR code scanner app to the QR code on the page. You can also navigate the examples manually.

Figure 1: This scan app allows you to point at a QR code in this book; it will take you to the corresponding example automatically.

Source: Scan Inc.

APP COMPATIBILITY

Note that not all examples are compatible with all Android versions. Although there are ways to make apps compatible with older Android devices, I have attempted to use only the core Android APIs to keep the examples clean and compatible across versions. If you are using older Android devices, be aware that you might end up on a screen telling you that an example you're trying to open is not available.

APP SOURCE CODE

The companion app is fully Open Source, and you can download it and see the source side of the examples on your own computer. You can find the app source code from github at: `https://github.com/JuhaniLehtimaeki/smashing_android_ui_ example_app/`.

INTRODUCTION TO ANDROID DESIGN

CHAPTER

INTRODUCTION TO USABILITY AND USER INTERFACE DESIGN

USABILITY IS THE most important quality of any app. It doesn't matter how good a feature is if the users don't know how to get to it or can't figure out how to use it. In the cutthroat environment of the mobile app market, users almost always have alternatives. If an app doesn't feel right or if users can't figure out how to perform the main tasks, they will very often uninstall it without giving it a second chance.

The user interface is users use and view your app. Everything that lies beyond is reflected in the UI. If your killer feature provides the next generation cloud communication (or whatever the most awesome capability of your app is) but isn't intuitive, you risk wasting hundreds of hours building something that users won't even try.

Getting the user interface right requires investment into design. This chapter introduces concepts and ideas that make it easier to understand the importance of that investment. It also explains key concepts of the design process and provides some ideas for making users a more integral part of your design process.

CONSIDERING TECHNOLOGY VERSUS DESIGN

User interface design is not an exact science. It also doesn't happen automatically. It requires effort and a budget. In my professional career I've mostly worked for tech-driven companies, so-called developer houses. Almost my whole career I have had to fight to include design considerations in the application-building process. In almost all cases my request for hiring or involving designers has been either rejected or badly misunderstood. In some companies a designer is thought to be a person who draws icons. In some other companies designers are seen as waste of time and money. In these companies, the engineering team or the product management team often created the design; sometimes it was designed by accident. Although various projects lead to various results, the design was always lacking. The products we built felt easy and intuitive to use to the engineering team, but the team struggled to understand why users weren't able to get their work done as they expected. The technical team often said something like the following: "That button is clearly there. The users should be able to figure out how to use it. They must be stupid!"

I've also worked for companies on the other extreme. Everything was design driven. Early customer meetings were attended only by designers, and technologies were selected without properly consulting the technical knowledge of the team. The design was often implemented in Adobe Photoshop and InDesign without much consideration of the technical feasibility, which ended up driving the technology teams into difficult situations whereby they weren't able to provide what the design promised.

Neither of these extremes work. In both cases the result is far from what it could be. I have also had the fortune to work on projects where everything was just about right. Working with a designer or a design team that understands that software engineering is not simply coding and having a developer team that appreciates the craft of user interaction design and visual design can lead to stunning results. A team where designers and developers work together can produce results that are much more than the sum of the components.

My message to developers—Users don't think the same way you do! There are people who have studied user interfaces and have created professional designs. Don't think you won't need them because you do! Knowing how to use a user interface that you've built doesn't prove anything. Users who can't use the same user interface are not stupid. They can't use it because the user interface is badly designed. Designers understand architecture of the user interfaces. They also understand how to test and verify that the design is good. Trust your designers. They don't propose changes to the user interface design because they're mean or want to make you work harder. They want to change the interface because the changes will make the user experience better.

My message to designers—Software engineering is not just about coding. In fact, coding is just a small part of what developers do. Building successful software requires careful planning, architectural design, object relationship design, modular component design, database design, planning for maintainability, deployment, quality assurance, and much more. If you know how to write scripts, that's a good start. But writing scripts is not software development. Building production-quality software based on a Photoshop user interface wireframe is not simple; it takes time, planning, and especially experience! Trust your developers. They are not taking so long to build a screen because they are lazy. They take the time to plan so the application runs smoothly and is maintainable. This way the whole team can keep tweaking and perfecting the app's user interface together, and the changes won't be overwhelming.

UNDERSTANDING THE MENTAL MODEL

It's time to change gears a little bit and think about apps from the users' point of view. What is going on in your users' heads when they see your app for the first time or when they continue to use it? This section introduces a very important concept called the *mental model*.

A mental model is a model that users form of your app's functionality inside their heads. In fact, people do this with everything. When we learn to drive a car we form a mental model of how the car works. The model doesn't have to be technically correct for it to benefit the driver. The fact that in modern cars, for example, the steering wheel is not directly connected to the front wheels doesn't matter. We can keep thinking that it is. We can think that when we turn the steering wheel there are set of gears that turn and make the front wheels turn. Because this model, although technically simplified, helps us understand and simulate how the car will behave when we can use it. Our mental model is consistent with the real-world effect of turning the steering wheel and so don't have any problems with steering the car. We think we understand how it works, and we're happy.

People use apps the same way. It is important for users that they can simulate the app functionality in their heads to predict what happens and when. The mental model is one of the most important concepts of user interface design. The user interface design must support your users' mental model. The app must be consistent and predictable.

The app is easy to use if it consistently corresponds to the user's mental model and the app is intuitive if users have an easy time forming the mental model. Everything in the user interface comes back to the user's mental model, and each problem users experience is because of the inconsistency between the user's mental model (the expectations) and how the app really works.

FORMING A MENTAL MODEL

In the real world, you can infer a lot about the physical functionality of objects simply by looking at them. You know how much they weigh, which way you can manipulate them, and which way you probably can't. With physical objects you can also experiment to determine how they function.

When using software you're stuck with pixels. How do you make sure that all of your users understand which group of pixels can be manipulated in which way? The answer is simple in theory but difficult in practice. You need to guide your users. The interface must be logical and contain visual clues about how things in it work.

You have a lot of tools at your disposal. You can use colors, shapes, textures, 3D effects, and animations. As with any tools, they are helpful only when used correctly and in the right places. That is where the user interface design skill comes in.

Let's look at two examples of Android apps. Google's Play Books is an ebook reader app. Users have a pretty strong image in their heads about how books work and the app helps the users to confirm their mental models by using a transformation animation when they start to swipe a finger across a book page. Figures 1-1, 1-2, and 1-3 display a few frames of that animation.

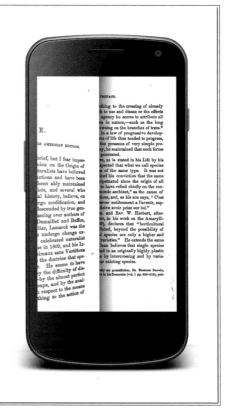

Figure 1-1: User starts to swipe a finger across a page.

Source: Google Inc.

Figure 1-2: User continues the swipe gesture.

Source: Google Inc.

As another example (see Figure 1-4), the Gigbeat app gives users subtle visual clues to help them understand how the interface works and so they can form a consistent mental model. You can see how, at the Gigbeat tour dates screen, the band profile page graphic is also partially visible. Displaying content partially next to the selected content leads users to think that they can view more by moving in that direction. On a touch interface, the navigation is usually done by swiping or tapping.

PLATFORM CONSISTENCY AND USER EXPECTATIONS

An extra challenge comes from the fact that every user forms a mental model differently and expects different things. Some users are familiar with certain user interface concepts whereas other users have never seen them. Users come from different cultures and different backgrounds. They have different experiences in software and software platforms. A life-long Mac user, for example, is going to expect the user interface to work differently from a life-long Windows user.

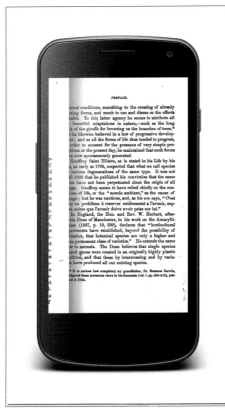

Figure 1-3: User finishes the swipe gesture.

Source: Google Inc.

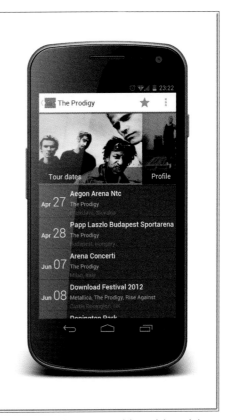

Figure 1-4: The Gigbeat app uses subtle visual clues to help users notice that more content is available.

Source: Gigbeat Inc.

For example, Microsoft Windows users expect that double-clicking a window title bar will maximize the window. The functionality is not intuitive, but users have learned it and now depend on it. It is therefore very important to maintain functional consistency between apps on a platform.

> *Tip: Users expectations are an important part of the mental model-forming process. If your app follows all the platform guidelines, users are much less likely to struggle with your app.*

Let's look at few examples of user interface conventions that make it easier for users to get around in apps because they are widely used on the Android platform. Figures 1-5 and 1-6 show two tabbed user interfaces. Android tabs have a distinct look and feel compared to other platforms. The differentiated look is a good thing as these tabs also function a little bit differently than other platforms. On the Android platform, the main navigation method between tabs is the swipe gesture, although simply tapping on a tab also works. Due to platform consistency users know to use this functionality without you having to design a way to explain it.

Figure 1-5: Android contact app has a tabbed user interface. The tabs can be navigated using swipe gestures.

Source: Android

Figure 1-6: Android dialer app also uses a similar tabbed user interface that allows use of swiping gesture as the primary navigation method.

Source: Android

Another example of platform consistency helping app design is the Android's menu functionality. Apps that have more menu options than can fit on the screen use the Android Action Bar overflow menu. The overflow menu uses three horizontal dots (see Figures 1-7 and 1-8). Users know what the icon means even though it might not be apparent to non-Android users. You will take a much deeper look into different Android user interface conventions and component in the rest of this book.

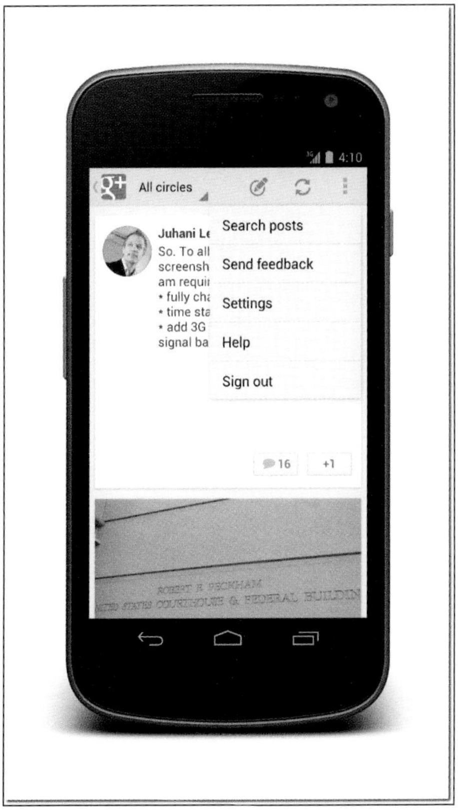

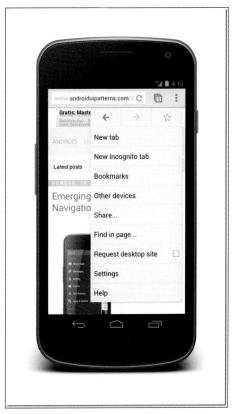

Figure 1-7: Google+ app uses the overflow menu to show menu items that don't otherwise fit on the screen.

Source: Google Inc.

Figure 1-8: Google Chrome browser has many more menu items that would fit on the screen without using the overflow menu.

Source: Google Inc.

DESIGNING FOR USERS

Building usable interfaces to support your user's mental model requires that the user be placed in the center of the design process. The app design must start from the standpoint of the user's needs and keep the focus on the user throughout the whole process. In the software industry, there is a term—*user centered design* (UCD)—that is being thrown about pretty often, but what does it actually mean? How can you put your users in the center of your design efforts?

This section introduces some overall concepts of user-centered design and goes though some of the most important terminology. User-centered thinking is very important for the success of any project, and the concepts described here can be adapted to work in any project. The subject of user-centered design is very large and others have written whole books about it, so there is no shortage of additional sources to deepen your understanding of the subject. I hope I spark your interest in the subject, and I encourage you to seek more information and alternative views from the literature and from the Internet.

USER GOALS

Users don't just want to use your app. They want to get something done. They have goals like "remember to buy milk on the way home" or "buy an Android tablet." Users are going to evaluate your app based on how well it supports them in achieving their goals. If you identify the user goals your app supports and make your user interface support them, your users are going to be happy.

Let's take a little bit deeper look at user goals. What is a user goal and what isn't? In short, a user goal is something the user wants to do but *does not describe any functionality of your application*. For example, the "user wants to save the document" is not a user goal. A user never wants to save anything. Users want their documents to be there when they need them again. This goal might be supported by a save function, but that's not the only option.

For someone coming from a more technical background understanding, user goals are like use cases. A *use case* describes an app's single usage situation. A goal is the description of why the users want to do something.

Table 1-1 shows some examples of how user goals should be formalized using a fictitious college planning app. The table includes badly formalized user goals and reasons why they are bad as well as correctly formalized user goals that match the same situation. Note that the differences in good and bad are subtle, but the bad ones might cause designers and developers to think about features and certain user interface solutions ahead of time.

Table 1-1   Example User Goals for Fictitious College Planning App

Not a User Goal	Corresponding User Goal
User wants to save a document (implies functionality).	User wants to have the same document available when she works on it later.
User wants to see a notification when a new email arrives (implies functionality).	User wants to know when new emails arrive.
User wants to open a calendar view with lecture times (too specific).	User wants to know what time a certain lecture starts.
User wants to see a calendar (too abstract).	Contains multiple user goals.
User wants to use search to find a lecture (describes functions).	Probably contains multiple goals. One of them could be that the user wants to determine whether he knows somebody attending a certain lecture.
User wants to add new reminder to his calendar (describes functions).	User wants to remember an appointment before it starts.

DON'T TALK ABOUT FEATURES

The first thing to do is to change the language and terminology about how you talk about your software project. You must stop talking about features and start talking about user needs. Avoid designing the user interface by accident. If, while still in the concept phase, you start talking about features and how the software should function, you need to take a step back. Users' needs must come first. Be careful to avoid sentences like "Hey, I think we should add a Save button here!" A possible result of that sentence might be a user interface feature that is useless or confusing to users. Think about the user goals first!

DETERMINING USER GOALS

It is easy to say that you should have a list of goals in order to start thinking about the features and the design of your app. But where does that list come from?

User goals should arise from user research, domain expertise, and an understanding of the problem the app is trying to solve. User research is sometimes not possible or not feasible so you might have to rely on more informal means. Consider doing ad-hoc user research by having a short chat with your friends over Google talk or Facebook.

Writing down the user goals you feel are the most important does act as a very valuable discussion starter. A list of initial goals can be an extremely valuable tool especially if you are building an app for a customer. A complete list of user goals is a non-technical description of the app's functionality. It is something that is extremely easy to discuss without any need for technical knowledge or lengthy documentation. A user goal is one or two sentences and a question like "is this important to you?"

To build the user goal list, simply write down what you think is important based on your expertise. Then talk to your customers, domain experts, users, and anyone else you think can contribute. Then you need to reorganize, rewrite, and prioritize your list of goals. By the end of that process you will have something that describes what users can achieve by using your app, even though not a single feature has been designed.

FROM GOALS TO FEATURES

A very important point to understand about usability is how app features relate to user goals. Each feature of any app should cater to something users want to do. Simply adding features without thinking about its user goals is likely to result in a confusing user interface and a lot of wasted hours building features that will never be used.

In theory, every single feature of an app should be traceable to a user goal (see Figure 1-9). In practice that is not always possible but it should be a target for the team. Adding features without thinking about the user goals introduces feature creep to the app. More features don't make apps better especially when the features aren't well thought out. A good example of feature creep is almost any Office productivity suite. The Office suite providers have been piling features on top of features for years, and the apps now require special training to be used.

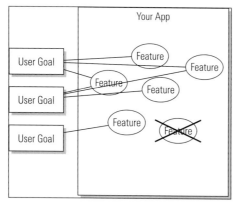

Figure 1-9: In the end your app should not have any features that aren't traceable to a user goal.

NO APP WILL DO EVERYTHING; PICK YOUR BATTLES

Don't try to do everything. Start with key user goals and expand from there. An app that fits perfectly with a smaller set of user goals is much better than an app that tries to do everything poorly. At the start of the project write down what your app is going to do and especially what your app is not going to do.

If you're building a note-taking app, for example, decide what kind of note-taking app it will be. Is it also going to be a to-do-list manager or a word processor? One app can't do all of that. If you decide that no, your app will not be a word processor, write that information down. You won't support users who want to write a book using your app. Your app will help people take basic notes. These kinds of decisions help you concentrate on the key issues and help you build a more focused product that supports your users' key goals. Create a list similar to Figure 1-10 to make it clear to the whole team and other stakeholders what you are doing and what you're not doing.

Tip: Deciding what not to do is as important as deciding what to do.

Figure 1-10: With few written words you can limit the scope of the app and help the whole team understand what the app is going to do and what it is not going to do.

YOU ARE THE EXPERT; USERS ARE NOT DESIGNERS

There will always be someone wanting to tell you which features you should add to your app. User feedback is typically littered with feature requests. Don't assume they are always correct, but don't ignore them either. Simply implementing user-requested features will make your software cluttered and unorganized. Try instead to find the user goal behind each request. Determine if the goal is something your app should support, and, if so, start designing the best possible user interface. Do not let your users design your user interfaces. You are the expert.

An overused quote attributed to Henry Ford goes something like this: "If I had asked people what they wanted, they would have said faster horses." The sentence captures the whole essence of what to expect from users when asking them direct questions about features. Always ask what users want to *do,* not what they want. In this old example, the question is "What do you want to do?" and the answer is something like get from point A to point B faster. A visionary designer can take that information and start to look for solutions that solve the issue in better way (a mechanical car) than the obvious solution (a faster horse).

KNOW YOUR USERS; DESIGN FOR REAL PEOPLE

You are not your app's user. Be wary of implementing features you would like. Don't base UI decisions solely on anecdotal evaluation, yours or your coworkers.

Figuring out for whom you are writing the app is very important. Different kinds of people expect different functionality and need different user interfaces. In some cases you already know your target group, but in other cases you need to do a lot of work to figure this out. People tend to answer that they want everybody to use their software. Even if you did want everyone to use your software, designing for everyone is impossible. You need to decide who your main users are and concentrate on their goals.

USING PERSONAS

Formalizing and communicating who your users are isn't easy, but using personas can help. A *persona* is a made-up person who epitomizes one of your user groups. You could say that a persona is a concrete instance of an abstract group. Creating personas is like creating characters for a play. In this case the play is your app and the character is an example user of your app.

Your personas should be based on user research when possible. Writing down your best guess and having discussions with your customers and other domain experts should get you enough information to build a good set of personas.

Tip: Don't use information from any one real person. It is much easier to talk about fictional persons than about real persons. You also don't want to accidentally insult anybody who was nice enough to participate to your user research.

You don't need to create personas for everyone who is going to be using your app. Each persona represents a group of real users. An average mobile app will probably have between three to seven personas.

Each persona should have the following information (see Figure 1-11 for an example persona):

- A made-up name (look for a random name generator on the Internet if you have problems coming up with one)
- A portrait photo
- A short description, including age, sex, education, and so on
- A list of key goals this persona has relating to your app domain
- Priority describing how important it is that this persona's goals are supported in your app

Torsten Kuster   High priority

Key Goals

Wants to be available via phone 24 / 7.

Wants to be able to read and write work emails wherever he is.

- Lives in Goettingen, Germany
- 37 years old
- Financial consultant
- Father of two, married
- Hobbies: football, reading
- Drives about 45 minutes to work every day
- Has a Galaxy S smartphone which he uses to check work and private emails, take photos and talk to friends and family

Figure 1-11: An example persona.

Source: http://www.flickr.com/photos/yuri-samoilov/4105603525/copyright Yuri Samoilov

Once you have your personas laid out you will have a very good and concrete picture of your target users. You don't have to think about your users as abstract stereotypes; you have people with names and personalities instead. You can use the personas to simulate your app functionality as well as decide who are the important and who are the not-so-important people for your business goals.

Now you have the personas and user goals. Use them! If it helps, print out the persona descriptions and hang them on the office walls to remind you and the team that these are the people who are going to use your app.

GETTING INTO YOUR USER'S HEAD

Once you reach the point whereby you have your personas and user goals listed you're pretty well positioned to start thinking about features and design. You hopefully have a great understanding as to what you want the app to do and who the users are. Your whole team and stakeholders have a good agreement about what needs to be achieved. Now all you need to do is create the actual design. I'd like to tell you that it is the easy part but I would be lying. The design and development is the hard part.

Build the information architecture and visual design to cater to the user goals. Make sure that all the important goals are easy to achieve with the design you're doing. Keep testing your designs with the mindset of the personas, and simulate the app with the user goals in mind. Ask a lot of questions like "Would persona X understand this?" and "How about persona Y in this situation?" Stay in the mindset of your users when thinking about using your app. This way you will avoid designing the app for yourself.

There will be moments in the design process when brilliant feature ideas pop up. They might not fit into the personas or user goals but might feel like great ideas nonetheless. Be wary of those situations. Sometimes the idea might lead to real innovation and is worth pursuing. Whenever a feature doesn't fit the user goals, though, be extra critical of it and evaluate it twice.

SUMMARY

The actual design work requires skill and experience. The rest of this book talks about designing for Android and the things you should know about the platform. It discusses platform-specific problems and opportunities. It explains what is possible and what is difficult to implement. It also talks about tools like prototyping and Android user interface design patterns that can help you get the design details right.

A big part of building a great user experience is getting to understand how users think. Once you can think like your users or understand how they think you are in a good position to design user interfaces for them.

If you invest time to do the research and design you will save a lot of time in the long run. Do your legwork; bug your friends and family. Make sure you understand who your users are and what they want to do. Make sure that your team knows which user goals are the important ones and which personas are the high-priority ones.

DON'T START CODING JUST YET

ONCE YOU HAVE a good understanding of your users and what they want, it is tempting to start coding. You probably already have an idea in your head how the app will look and function. But don't jump into coding just yet! Code is rigid and difficult to change. It is better to use more flexible ways to think about the design first.

The app-building process is a continuum from low-fidelity ideas on paper to high-fidelity designs and working prototypes toward the final product. This chapter introduces some tools and ideas that will help you on the way.

PROTOTYPING

Draw your design ideas on paper first. Getting ideas from your head to paper will make them concrete and much easier to discuss with the rest of the team. This phase of app building is called prototyping. *Prototyping* is an essential part of the design process. It provides a way to test ideas without having to implement them, therefore giving the team greater creative freedom.

The purpose of a prototype is to simulate the functionality of the app you are building. The simulated functionality will let you experiment and expose problems that you and your team might not have thought about. A prototype can be a low-fidelity paper drawing that doesn't have any real functionality or a high-fidelity functional prototype that can actually be used and experienced—or anything in between.

> *Tip: The best place to start prototyping is on paper. Paper is virtually free and paper prototypes can be modified with an eraser and a pencil. Paper and pencil prototypes also aren't limited by the technology. Go crazy! Don't let the technical limitations get in your way. Sketch out your ideas and discuss them with the team.*

WIREFRAMES

App structure is the big picture of the design. Thinking about what kind of screens are needed and how they relate to each other is a good place to start. Ignore interface details first. You don't want to be spending time designing visual details or thinking about exact wording of controls before you can be sure that those details will be needed.

Drawing wireframes is a good way to get the app structure on paper. A *wireframe* is a blue-print of your app. On a wireframe you describe how your app's screens are composed and how they relate to each other without many details about visuals or content. A wireframe is usually a black-and-white line drawing that contains rough component descriptions, symbols for images, and filler text for text blocks. Figure 2-1 shows an example of a very simple wireframe that has a list of items on one screen and an item details screen.

Wireframes are very fast to build and painless to modify. They are not meant to fully specify the app user interface. They do, however, make ideas more concrete and testable. They also make it easier to discuss ideas with other team members. You have something concrete you can show instead of trying to explain abstract ideas verbally.

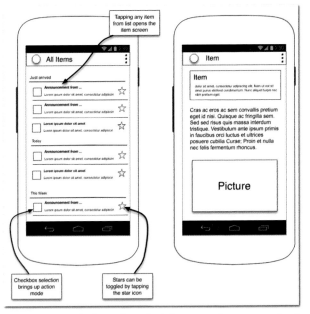

Figure 2-1: An example of a wireframe sketch for an app with two screens, a list of items and an item detail screen.

The effortlessness of wireframe drawing also makes it easy to test your ideas. If you have a crazy idea that just might work you probably won't be able to convince others that it should be used in code without any proof. Building a wireframe is worth the time and effort. You can wireframe and demonstrate your ideas in a relatively short amount of time.

HIGH-FIDELITY PROTOTYPES

Not everything can be prototyped using simple wireframes. Can you be sure that the screen transition you've been thinking about will work the way you want it to? Once you are certain that this transition is needed it is time to get coding involved. Building a functional prototype of part of the app makes sense when a concept is complex, and there is uncertainty as to whether it will work in practice.

A high-fidelity prototype might not be a throw-away prototype. Sometimes it is possible to build the prototype using reusable components and implementing functionality that can be utilized in the final product. The reusable components might even save you some time in the implementation phase, but that should not be the priority at this point of the project. The priority should remain strictly in producing the best possible user interface in the final product, and that should guide the decision.

PROOF OF CONCEPT

Sometimes the technical feasibility of a new design is uncertain. This might be because designers want to use existing components in a way they have not been used before or maybe even use a new component. In this kind of scenario a proof of concept should be built. A *proof of concept* is a piece of working software implemented with enough details that it can be verified to work in practice. A proof of concept gives the team confidence that the design they are proposing will work in practice or clarifies that the approach is not feasible and should be redesigned. A proof of concept doesn't need to be a fully functional app but instead concentrate on a single design idea like a novel interaction method on a list or even just to test the effectiveness of certain graphics.

TOOLS FOR DESIGN

Paper prototyping is all well and good, but at some point in the process it is useful to start using digital tools. Once the big picture design is clear, digital tools can really help you fine-tune it. Other obvious benefits of using digital tools include easy distribution even when team members are not located in the same physical space.

Whenever people talk about design software, Adobe's name pops up. They produce multiple tools that are very widely used but are also very expensive. This section introduces a few tools that are maybe less known but also much cheaper. Each of these tools has good support for the Android platform and can be very useful for drawing Android app wireframes.

OMNIGRAFFLE AND STENCILS

The OmniGraffle wireframing tool (see Figure 2-2) is my personal favorite. With a great user interface, great Android support, and reasonable price I do wholeheartedly recommend OmniGraffle to anyone who is using a Mac. Unfortunately it is not available for Linux or Windows.

OmniGraffle is also one of the few applications that Google has released the official Android design stencil of (downloadable from Android design guidelines web page). The stencil is very helpful for drawing more detailed user interface designs. It contains all standard Android user interface components and many helpful composite controls like action bar and keyboards.

WIREFRAMESKETCHER AND TEMPLATES

WireframeSketcher (see Figure 2-3) is a multi-platform wireframing tool that can be installed to Eclipse or as a standalone installation. It is available for Linux, Mac, and Windows. It also has multiple community-provided Android stencils that can be helpful during the wireframing process. This tool, however, is not well suited for detailed user interface design.

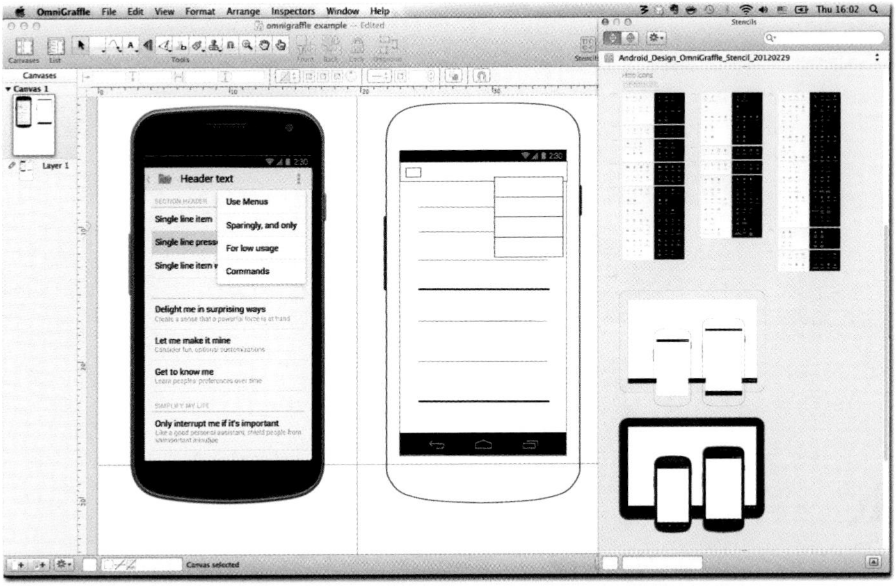

Figure 2-2: The OmniGraffle wireframing tool is a great Mac tool.

Source: The Omni Group

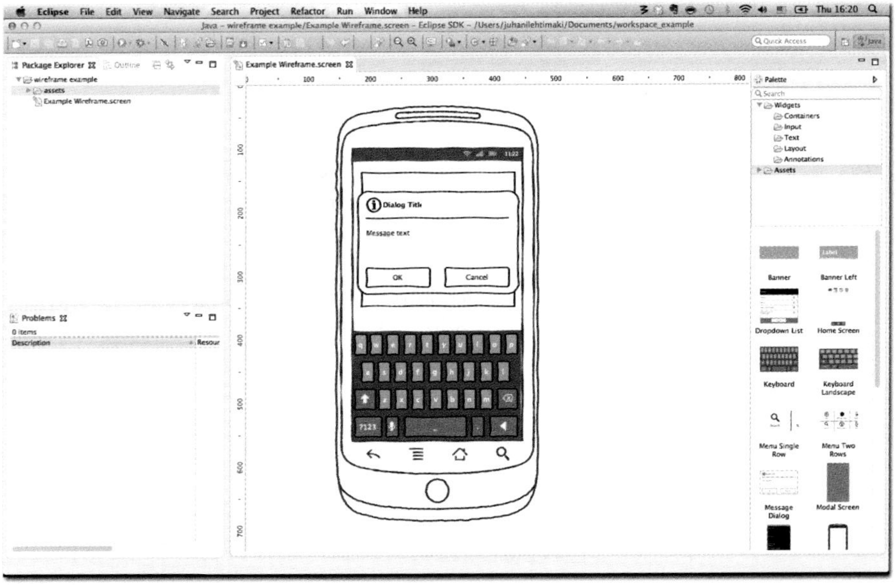

Figure 2-3: WireframeSketcher is a multi-platform wireframing tool.

Source: WireframeSketcher.com

BALSAMIQ

Balsamiq (see Figure 2-4) is a multi-platform wireframing tool that can run on a browser or as a standalone app on Linux, Mac, or Windows. It also has community-provided stencils for the Android platform.

Figure 2-4: Balsamiq is another great wireframing tool.

Source: Balsamiq Studios, LLC

What Is Eclipse?

For those of you with your heads in the sand, Eclipse is an Open Source IDE that runs on OS X, Linux, and Windows. It is currently the most popular tool for building Java applications. It also has a very good support for third-party plug-ins. It's no surprise that Google chose Eclipse as the platform for Android tools.

Read more and download it at http://eclipse.org/.

ANDROID ECLIPSE PLUG-IN GUI BUILDER

Android SDK ships with a user interface builder. Although its primary purpose is user interface development it can also be used for prototyping. The interface builder is constantly getting updated, and it is likely that Figure 2-5 will be outdated by the time you are reading this. Check out `http://tools.android.com/` to see what's new in the Android tools.

Using a development tool for design brings extra challenges, and I would not recommend this approach unless you are already very comfortable with the tool. The obvious benefit of using such a plug-in is, of course, that the resulting prototype can be run on real devices.

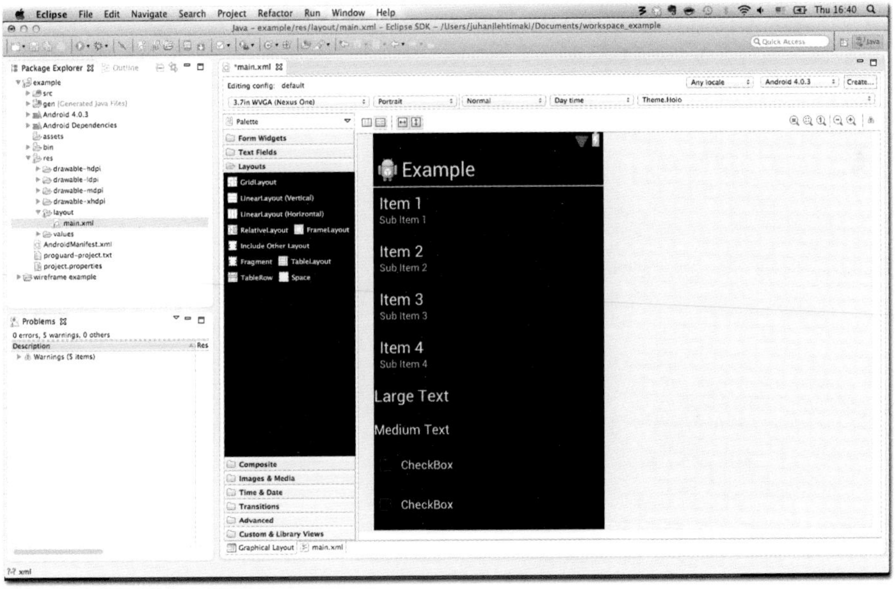

Figure 2-5: The Android Eclipse plug-in.

Source: Android SDK

PENCIL

Pencil (see Figure 2-6) is a free standalone app or an add-on to the Mozilla Firefox browser. Although some features are missing, the app is free so trying out Pencil is risk free. Community-provided Android stencils are available for Pencil.

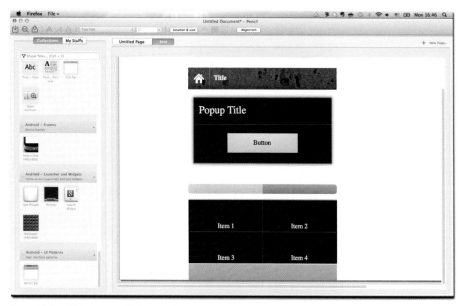

Figure 2-6: Pencil helps you quickly draw wireframes.

Source: Evolus

ADDITIONAL UTILITIES

Android Design Preview is a handy little utility that allows you to display part of your desktop on any connected Android phone or on the emulator. You can test out designs directly from your computer drawing app on a real device without having to copy anything over to the phone. You can download the Android Design Preview from `http://code.google.com/p/android-ui-utils/`.

Android Asset Studio is a handy web app that can help you generate different icons for launcher, menu, action bar, tabs, and notifications. You can use graphics or text as the basis, and the web app will generate icons for all required densities and different Android versions. You can download Android Asset Studio from `http://android-ui-utils.googlecode.com/hg/asset-studio/dist/index.html`.

USER TESTING

As mentioned in the previous chapter, you are not your app's users. A typical developer is very bad at guessing how their users will understand the user interface and how they will use it. That's why actual users should test the design.

In a user test you put your design in front of real users. In a formal user test the users are typically invited to visit the testing facility—maybe your office or some other neutral place, although remote user testing technologies also exist. They are then presented with the prototype or functional app and asked to perform simulated real-world scenarios. The users are asked to think aloud while performing the tasks to get a better understanding of their thought processes. The test is usually videotaped for further review and then observed by a few people.

Although a formal user test is the best tool you have for uncovering usability problems it is not always possible, either due to financial or time limitations. In that case try to find alternative methods for getting feedback about your design. Your coworkers probably aren't the best source for representative feedback, so it is better to go outside the office. Even testing the design with your family and friends is valuable. Performing a formal testing can be difficult, but asking questions like "How would you send this document via email?" or "What do you think this button does?" can provide you with valuable insight to your design.

User testing has the same philosophy as any other testing. A user test is successful if it uncovers problems. Be aware of the normal tendency of falling in love with your own creations. If you spend a lot of time building something, you want to see it succeed. If the app has problems, they will pop up at some point—either in testing or when the app is published. The sooner the better.

SELECTING YOUR PARTICIPANTS CAREFULLY

Remember the personas discussed in Chapter 1? You should have already chosen whom you are writing your app for. Those are the people who you should try to use during user testing. Of course, you can do dry runs and even additional testing with your friends and coworkers, but you should always give more weight to tests with users from your target group. Use the personas you created in Chapter 1, and seek out people fitting your high-priority personas.

PLANNING FOR A USER TEST

Remember what you designed your app to do. Try to formalize the bulk of the user test scenarios based on the core functionality of your app. Go through your user goal definitions and make sure that the high-priority user goals are covered. Follow the same rules when writing the user test scenarios that you did when writing user goals. Do not include technical features in your scenarios, and let users figure out which features they want to use. A bad user test scenario would be something like "Open a document and press Save and add it as an attachment to email," while a good scenario could sound something like "You remember writing a document about your friends before. You want to refresh your memory about the content of the document and send it to your friend via email."

Tip: Try to use real data as much as possible. If your app has, for example, contact lists, you should populate them with real-looking data. Don't use clearly fake data like "contact 1," "contact 2," but instead create names that look real. Avoid situations where users have to imagine pieces of the app if possible.

It can be a good idea to write scenarios to test features you're not sure are going to work. If your team is planning to build something that isn't typically supplied on the Android platform, for example, you certainly want to test that feature. If none of the test subjects touches on the features you wanted to test, you can add questions to the end of the user test to ask the users how they think the specific features work.

STAY NEUTRAL; DON'T GUIDE THE USERS

People are naturally reluctant to criticize work done by others they don't know. The test participants might think that they are offending you and your work. It is some times a good idea to present the app as something that was done by someone else to get more honest feedback.

Be neutral during the testing, and don't argue with the test subjects. If they don't understand some user interface paradigm, or they criticize parts of the user interface, don't try to justify or defend the design. The test subject is always right.

Try also not to lead the users. If the users are lost and are unable to perform a scenario move to next one. Explaining how the user interface works in this situation is not useful. Try to figure out why this happened instead.

DON'T OVER-CORRECT; ARE THE FINDINGS REAL?

Pay careful attention to all usability problems the test subjects bring up, but note that not all of them require action. Look for patterns and problems that seem to be present with more than one test subject. Not every issue a single test subject encounters is real. The situation in which your app is tested doesn't correspond fully with reality. The test subjects are under pressure and might encounter problems they wouldn't if they were trying the app alone.

FIVE USERS ARE ENOUGH

Then there is the question of how many users should participate in a usability test before any findings can be seen as meaningful. The fact is that each individual user test is expensive. The optimal number of user test subjects has been studied a lot. Findings from different studies are not unanimous. Probably a safe bet is to test with five people at a time. After five tests the number of new usability problems uncovered starts to drop and the investment is no longer justified. On the other hand fewer than five test subjects is too small a set to tell if the individual problems are problems that will affect a large number of people or just issues that a single user encounters.

MOBILE USER TESTING

As this book is about Android and mostly about apps that are used on the go, it is worth mentioning that *use context* (the environment in which the users are using your app) matters. If you test an app in a quiet office meeting room, the problems you encounter might be very different from the real use context. This is not an easy problem to solve, but it is something you should keep in mind when interpreting the test results.

USER TESTING WITH PAPER PROTOTYPES

As already established, paper is the best medium to work in during the early stages of the design process. As it turns out paper prototypes also function very well in user testing. Although it might sound crazy at first, running paper-based user tests is easy, valuable, and fun.

Building a paper prototype that can be used in a user test requires a bit more preparation. You need to be able to simulate app functionality on paper. In practice this requires use of paper, scissors, glue, and imagination. Back to kindergarten!

Once you have set the scenarios you want to be tested, think how they would be performed with your design. Print out or draw the screens those scenarios cover. You might also need to create individual components and component states that can be used to simulate the user interface functionality.

In the testing situation one person will act as the computer and update the paper prototype user interface based on user actions. The users will use the paper prototype the way they would use a real device. After the initial laugh while explaining this to the test subject, the test usually works very well.

BACK TO THE DRAWING BOARD

Finding usability problems won't help your design unless something is done to fix them. You must schedule time to react to the findings after each user testing round. Be prepared to change the user interface. Sometimes, especially in the early phases, the problems are so apparent that even after a few tests it is clear that the user interface must be changed. If you are working with a paper prototype and sometimes even with a functional app you can decide to make changes between tests to try out something new.

SUMMARY

It is very important to try out designs before coding. Do not lock yourself into a design before you are sure that the design works. Work your way up from low-fidelity paper prototypes to a concrete design and finished app.

Remember that you are not your app's user, and acknowledge that developers are generally very bad at guessing how users see the user interface. Put your design in front of real users. Aim to do formal user testing, but if that is not possible, ask your friends and family to help you evaluate the design. Getting outside views and opinions is very valuable.

CONSIDERATIONS IN DESIGNING FOR MOBILE AND TOUCH DEVICES

MOBILE DEVICES ARE very different from desktop or laptop computers. They differ in both the way they are used as well as where they are used. Phones and tablets are mostly used to consume information, whereas computers are also used to create information.

Modern smartphones contain some of the most advanced technology available for consumers, including very high-density displays and sensitive multi-touch capable touch screens. On the other hand, the devices still fall short in many other aspects like available memory and CPU power.

The device capabilities bring both opportunities and challenges when it comes to user interface design.

It's not all about technology, either. Mobile devices serve a different purpose in their users' lives. They are also used in very different surroundings than the more traditional computing devices. Without understanding the limitations and opportunities of both the technology and the use context, creating good user interfaces is difficult.

DESIGNING FOR MOBILE

Not all Android devices are mobile phones, but the vast majority is. It is safe to assume that if you are building an Android app it will be running on a phone. In order to successfully target phones, it is necessary to look into the limitations that mobility brings into the game.

USE CONTEXT OF MOBILE DEVICES

Mobile devices are used, as the name suggests, on the move. The environment is noisy and users are interrupted all the time. Often, an app on a mobile device is one of many stimuli fighting for the user's attention. They might be walking in a busy city pedestrian area, driving a car, or listening to a school lecture. In most cases the mobile app design cannot demand the user's full attention.

To support users without forcing them to concentrate requires a good user interface. The interface must be intuitive, and all the controls must be clearly visible. Navigating a complex menu structure won't be possible when you're distracted.

When you're designing your app's user interface, do not overestimate the importance of your app to the users. Think about your app as the secondary function, and keep asking yourself if the app's interface is usable even if the users only glance at the screen.

MOBILE MULTITASKING

Sometimes users will interrupt the use session just to pick it up few minutes later. Think about a scenario where a user is reading a newsfeed from a mobile app in public transportation and must transfer from one vehicle to another. The user is likely going to be in the middle of reading something when she arrives to her stop and places her phone into her pocket or purse. She is likely to pick the phone up again once the transfer is complete. The app must remember where the user was and allow her to continue as if there were no pause.

A similar situation is when a user receives a phone call. Imagine if you had to start a game from the beginning just because your gaming session was interrupted by an incoming phone call. It would not be acceptable. Apps must remember their state and prepare for interruptions. Again, don't think that your app is the only one the user is going to be using or even the most important one.

DEVICE CONSTRAINTS

Mobile devices suffer from many constraints. They have small screens and limited controls. The devices don't have much processing power or a lot of memory. Even on the latest generation smartphones with more powerful CPUs and more memory, running apps is very different from doing so on a desktop or laptop.

In a low-memory CPU environment a badly designed app will stand out and not in a good way. An app performing CPU-heavy operations in the background will cause other applications to become non-responsive.

It is worth taking the time at the beginning of the project to think about your app's hardware requirements. Could you, for example, move some tasks to a server and use the mobile app only for displaying the results?

BATTERY POWER IS NOT ENDLESS

Mobile devices run on batteries, and that battery power is limited. People rely on their phones, and the phone must have power when it is needed. In some cases not having sufficient battery power can lead users into serious or even life-threatening trouble.

Apps must be optimized to conserve battery life. Any app that drains the battery will quickly be thrown out and very likely receive harsh ratings in the app market. And don't think that users are not going to notice; they are. The Android operating system provides a very handy way for users to check what is going on if they suspect that something is draining the battery faster than it should be (see Figure 3-1). You can find this screen on any Android phone running 4.0 or newer.

Figure 3-1: Android battery status screen, including battery consumption per app.

Source: Android

Different apps consume battery differently. When starting to design an app take a moment to think about what kinds of tasks your app is going to perform in order to satisfy the user's goals. Table 3-1 shows an overview of the relative battery consumption of different operations. I'm leaving games and gaming technology out from this consideration, as they are totally different beasts when it comes to battery consumption.

> Tip: For more information about gaming and other more power-hungry apps, look at the Android NDK documentation online at `http://developer.android.com/tools/sdk/ndk/index.html`.

Table 3-1   Different Operations and Their Estimated Effect on Battery Consumption

Operation	Battery Consumption
Using a network when connected to WiFi	Medium
Using a network when on a good coverage cellular network	Medium
Using a network when on a bad coverage cellular network	High
Using a Bluetooth	Medium
Using a GPS	Medium
Using a cellular location	Low
Using an NFC (near-field communication)	Low
Preventing the screen from turning off	High
Using a microphone	Low
Using the camera	Medium
Waking up the phone when in sleep to perform any operation	High (not including operation cost)

RAPID INNOVATION

Even with these limitations, the smartphones and tablets on the market today represent some of the latest and best innovation available to consumers. Mobile technology is also one of the fastest moving technology fields. Nokia N95, a popular smartphone released in 2007, had a 2.6-inch display with a 320x240 pixel display. Samsung Galaxy Nexus, released in 2011, has an impressive 4.65-inch HD display with 1280x720 pixels. The Nokia N95 shipped with a 332MHz processor while the Galaxy Nexus ships with a 1.2GHz dual-core CPU accompanied by a 304MHz GPU.

It is a full-time job to keep up with all the new technology introduced into mobile devices. A mobile app project starting now and shipping in six months might need more than one change on the way to support new operating system versions or even new technologies.

Tip: The mobile market is a land of opportunities. All the change might feel intimidating, but the fact is that you don't need to worry about building support for many of these new technologies right away, and the user device base is replaced relatively slowly. It is worth it, however, to keep your eyes open and follow the news. Some new innovation might solve the problem you have been struggling with.

NETWORK CONNECTION WILL DROP

Most mobile devices have one or more ways to connect to the Internet. Many modern phones also support multiple generations of cellular data connections. Although the newer networks provide faster data speeds they often offer smaller coverage while the networks are still being built. By default phones usually try to use the most modern technology they support and drop back to the older networks if the coverage gets too weak.

To an app a change of network appears as a short connection drop. Mobile network coverage is inherently unstable due to varying traffic load and connection drops and your app must be prepared to handle them.

Think of the different ways you can help users with connection problems without requiring actions from them. If your user wants to download a large file, for example, make sure the app will automatically try again later in case of a network connection drop and will continue the download instead of restarting it.

If your app deals with any kind of media, this connectivity problem is emphasized. Take care to design your buffering algorithms and caching to support an optimal user experience.

DATA IS NOT FREE

An important point to keep in mind when designing mobile apps is that data transfer is not free. Many, if not most, users have limited data plans. Going over the data limits either lowers the users' data speed or ends up costing dearly. Your app should try to limit data transfer only to necessary operations. Because the data-carrier plans have become more and more complicated and the risk of getting massive bills is getting higher, users are becoming more aware of app data usage. Google has reacted to this by providing users a way to view and control their data usage per app (see Figure 3-2). If your app appears on this list without an obvious reason, it is likely that users will uninstall it and rate it poorly in the Google Play.

For any long-running data downloads you must provide the users with a way to cancel them. Users must feel like they are in control. You will learn about managing background tasks in Chapter 9.

Many, in practice almost all, phones have support for a WiFi connection. A WiFi connection is more stable, cheaper, and faster than a cellular connection. If your app does data-heavy operations you should let users decide if they're performed on WiFi only or also on the cellular networks. It is possible to detect when a user enters or leaves a WiFi network, and start and stop operations accordingly.

Figure 3-2: Users can view data usage per app and restrict the apps using Android tools.

Source: Android

Even on WiFi, you should use data operations carefully. Remember that data transfer bandwidth is shared between all apps. Whenever your app is using part of it, other apps won't be able to utilize it fully.

PASSIONATE USERS AND OPPORTUNITIES

Techies have always been passionate about their particular choice of technology. It has always been Amiga vs. PC, Windows vs. OS X, Xbox vs. Playstation, and so on. Mobile ecosystems are no different. Mobile fans are even louder and more active. They love to show off their device of choice and the coolest apps they have. People wear clothes with operating system logos and line up outside stores for days to be the first ones to get their hands on the latest release. I am one of those people. I have an Android logo on my laptop cover.

This user passion creates great opportunities for app designers and developers. Create a unique app with an exceptional UI and the users will do a big part of the marketing for you. Popular apps spread like viral videos on the Internet. Mobile news blogs are hungry for topics, and one of the great topics is a new app that is worth talking about.

On the other hand, users are very demanding. They know what they want, and they're not happy with badly built apps. If your app's design doesn't fit on the Android platform, users are going to reject it. Users will frown upon an iOS design on an Android app.

Mobile operating system blogs have thousands of followers, and they are all hungry for big headlines. The best blog posts, from the blog's profit point of view, always puts at least two mobile operating systems head to head. Anything with "Android vs. iOS" in the headline is guaranteed to bring in a lot of viewers and inbound links. Understanding the user passion and everything that relates to it is vital.

NATIVE APPS VERSUS WEB APPS

Writing a platform-specific app is not the only way to reach mobile users. Although this book covers native Android apps (*native* meaning that they are built using Android SDK or NDK), another very good approach is to build a mobile web app. A web app runs in the user's browser and is, therefore, much less tied to the platform. iOS and Android use the same WebKit-based browsers, so building a web app that works well on both of the largest mobile platforms isn't impossible.

The mobile web app sounds great! Why not simply forget the native app idea and write web apps and target all platforms at once?

The choice between native and web is a very important and should be carefully considered at the beginning of any project. The answer to this question depends a lot on the type of project. There is a place for each solution. As a rule of thumb an app that is used fairly irregularly is best implemented as a web app, and any app that is going to be used very frequently will be better as a native app.

A regularly used service that has two competing service providers, only one of which provides a native app, is most likely going to see the most Android users moving toward the service provider that has taken the time to implement a platform-specific Android app.

There are also technical issues that can affect the decision. A web app won't have access to all the platform APIs and, therefore, won't be able to utilize all device capabilities. Although HTML5 APIs are catching up, they still lag behind. A web app won't be able to use Android notifications and will have limited offline capabilities.

HYBRID APPS WITH HTML WRAPPERS

PhoneGap, Titanium Appcelerator, and few other frameworks provide a way to build something that is between a web app and a native app. They let developers write the app code using web technologies like HTML and JavaScript. Some frameworks then try to compile the code into a native app code and some other frameworks simply wrap the web app into a web browser container, in essence turning the web app into an app that looks like it is running natively.

Although there's a promise of a platform-independent solution I advise a careful evaluation of this kind of framework. Even if the code runs on iOS, Android, and other platforms, it doesn't mean that the apps are good. User experience guidelines of each platform differ greatly. You'd still have to design and implement the app for each of the target platforms separately to reach an acceptable result.

I advise caution with these multi-platform frameworks. Delivering acceptable application quality might be more difficult than you expect.

DESIGNING FOR TOUCH INTERFACES

Users have been using their computers with a mouse and keyboard for a long time now and have became very good at it. Users have learned that double-clicking icons launches apps, right-clicking things pops up menus, and holding the mouse button allows them to select areas or drag things around. Power users have learned to use keyboard shortcuts to operate without having to move their hand off the keyboard.

Things have been changing lately. Mouse and keyboard interaction is nearing the end of the road. A new primary control paradigm has taken the smartphone industry by storm. Nearly all smartphones now ship with touch screens as the main user interface. A touch screen is a much more immediate control mechanism. On a touch screen, you no longer have a disconnect between the physical controls and the UI itself. On a touch interface, you can directly touch the items you want to manipulate. That's why touch interfaces are sometimes also referred to as *natural interfaces*.

IMPLEMENTING GESTURES

Users control touch-based interfaces with gestures. A *gesture* is like a drawing on the screen that the operating system or the app interprets as a command to perform an action. Gestures vary from very simple one-finger gestures to complex multi-finger gestures. Simple gestures include tapping a user interface control and panning or scrolling a screen by dragging a finger on a control surface. More complex gestures including tapping and holding or drawing by dragging letters. Multi-touch gestures include a two or more finger swipe or multi-finger pinch or spread.

Table 3-2 describes the basic gestures supported by the Android platform. The icons in this table are used in later chapters to refer to these touch gestures.

Table 3-2   Android Touch Gestures

Gesture Name	Description	Icon
Tap	User touches the screen.	

Gesture Name	Description	Icon
Double tap	User touches the screen twice quickly in the same location.	
Swipe (sometimes also called fling, flick)	User drags finger across the screen swiftly into one direction.	
Drag	User drags finger on screen. The motion is slower than swipe and doesn't have to be into one specific direction.	
Pinch, close	User drags two fingers on screen towards each other in a pinching motion.	
Pinch, spread	User drags two fingers on screen away from each other.	
Tap and hold	User taps the screen without lifting the finger.	

GESTURE DISCOVERY

A touch-based interface creates a new set of usability problems. How do users discover gestures that you put into your apps? Basically, there are only two naturally discoverable actions on a touch UI. Users tend to tap on things that look like buttons or links, and they drag UI components so make them pan or scroll. Everything beyond these two must be learned.

Take pinch-to-zoom as an example. It feels natural now as you have seen and used it, and you have started to understand that you probably can use the gesture to zoom maps or large documents in and out. But how do you know that this is possible without trying it first? Imagine having a new app that you have never tried before in front of you. The app has a map component as part of a screen. Will you be able to use the pinch-to-zoom gesture, or will you have to use some other method? Lack of visual clues makes it difficult to understand what your options are.

Pinch-to-zoom wasn't always the way developers controlled zoom on touch devices. Before multi-touch capable devices, users did something else. Sony Ericsson used a novel zoom control on their devices before Android gained multi-touch support. On the Sony Ericsson device a user first had to long press the image he wanted to zoom and then without lifting the finger move it up to zoom in and down to zoom out. On Nokia's Maemo, the operating system zooming was also done with one finger. In their approach zoom was done by moving a finger in a spiral pattern either clockwise to zoom in or counter-clockwise to zoom out.

I bet that both of these methods made perfect sense to the team who came up with the idea and implemented it. Neither of them felt natural, and they didn't catch on. Pinch-to-zoom, on the other hand, feels natural, and that is now the de-facto standard for the zoom gesture.

What will happen if you take the gesture interface even further and keep inventing new ways to use gestures? What if someone decides to implement pinch-to-zoom on a list component? How would users find out how to use it without the developer having to tell them?

Probably the best way to get users to understand available gestures is by convention. Although new conventions arise slowly, it's better to use existing and established conventions when possible. For example, maps should always allow pinch-to-zoom. Tabbed user interfaces should let users navigate between tabs by swiping. You'll learn more about Android-specific user interface paradigms in Chapter 11.

GESTURE CONFUSION

As designers keep inventing new and more creative ways to use gestures in apps, developers run into another problem. How does the app detect the correct gesture? Some gestures are very similar. The best example of two gestures that can cause confusion when used on the same app are *swiping* and *panning*.

Consider an ebook reader app as an example. The app supports two gestures that are relevant in this example. One gesture is the horizontal swipe to change to the next or previous page. The other gesture involves panning by dragging when a page doesn't fully fit on the screen.

Let's assume that a user is reading a page and zooms in. Now, a full page of the book doesn't fit on the screen, and the panning gesture can be used to reveal different parts of the page. What happens if the user uses a swipe gesture instead? The swipe gesture and panning gesture are identical at the start. Only after the user has performed the gesture beyond the start can the gestures be differentiated using velocity and direction. How can the app differentiate between the user's intention to pan the page and swiping to change the page?

The short answer is that you should try to avoid using conflicting gestures in same component. Take gestures into account early in the design process and prototype them.

REACT TO GESTURES IMMEDIATELY

Your interface must react to its users' gestures immediately. The users must have immediate visual feedback that the gesture is working. It will make the user interface feel more responsive but also helps both with gesture discovery and avoid gesture confusion.

A bad, and unfortunately common, example of implementing gestures is waiting until the user finishes a swipe gesture before performing the action. In other words, consider an ebook reader app whereby the users must finish swiping horizontally before the app shows the page change animation. Users will have hard time finding the gesture and learning how to use it. A better and correct way to implement the same gesture would be that the page change animation follows the user's finger from the start of the gesture to the end. In other words, when the user starts moving his or her finger on the page, the page starts changing. The page moves with the same pace as the user is moving his finger. This way there's no room for misunderstanding; your users are more likely to figure out this gesture on their own.

TOUCH INTERFACE, NOT SO NATURAL INTERFACE

As discussed in the previous sections, providing a touch interface doesn't mean that users will have any easier a time figuring out how to use it. Calling it a natural interface is a bit misleading. Human beings are used to manipulating three-dimensional objects that have different weights, sizes, textures, and many more properties they can sense. Touch screens still lack most of these properties, and users struggle to understand different metaphors. Touch interfaces do require the same amount of design work as any other interaction method. Be careful not to think of the touch interface as a shortcut.

SUMMARY

Mobile devices are used differently and in different settings than computers and laptops. When designing a mobile app, you must always remember that your users probably won't give your app their full attention.

Mobile devices also have limitations that computers don't have. Limited computing power and battery life, as well as connectivity problems, all bring challenges to the design process.

The main control interface of most mobile devices is the touch screen. The touch screen creates a new set of challenges, but also provides many design opportunities. Touch-based user interfaces can be very powerful as long as you take their limitations into account from the beginning.

CHAPTER

EXPLORING THE ANDROID PLATFORM

ANDROID IS A PLATFORM of opportunities. It has a massive user and fan base. It is the worldwide leading smartphone platform, and there's no end in sight for its growth. Android can be found running on hundreds of different devices and many different device categories. With massive success comes lots of challenges. How do you write apps that run on all of these devices? How different are these devices?

This chapter explains what you can expect from the Android devices. It explains what Android fragmentation means and puts this idea in context. The chapter also talks about the opportunities created by the open Android ecosystem and Open Source community.

CHALLENGES OF THE ANDROID PLATFORM

You must have heard about Android fragmentation. It seems to be a buzzword of bloggers and journalists trying to get more interest in their articles. This term is often thrown around without any true understanding of what it means and how it affects developers and users. People often say fragmentation when they actually mean the variation in devices that Android runs on.

There's no need to panic. The Android platform was built from the ground up to give developers good tools to support multiple different devices. Utilizing the platform tools correctly will help you to support most, if not all, the devices out there. That is not to say that supporting all these devices is free. It requires work and planning but can be done with reasonable effort, if you approach it correctly.

But what does fragmentation mean in practice, and where does it come from? If you walk into a mobile carrier store and look around, it is nearly impossible to recognize which of the phones on the shelves are Android phones and which aren't unless you're an expert. Android phones are not built by a single manufacturer, and Android also doesn't have strict limitations about the hardware it runs on. This means that almost all manufacturers have created their own design language for the software and hardware.

The Android platform is also very open for customization by its users. Users don't need to hack or jail-break their phones to replace the home screen, app launcher, or keyboard. Replacements for al of these features can be downloaded from Google Play. They are just apps that connect different platform *intents* (more about intents in Chapter 6).

This chapter covers how Android devices differ from each other—in terms of hardware and software—and seeks to give you an understanding of what a true Android device is.

HARDWARE

It all starts with the hardware. There is no such thing as standard Android hardware. Android is Open Source, and nobody can stop anyone from putting Android on anything they like. I have seen Android running on washing machines, ski goggles, and wristwatches. These are the extremes, though. Although a correctly written Android app will probably be usable on a wristwatch, it probably won't be very good. I think that in this context it is pretty safe to exclude the extremes and concentrate on the more normal devices.

Even if you talk about mass-produced devices, the variation in hardware is massive. Android runs on very low-end smartphones with small displays, barely any memory, and cheap (and slow) CPUs. It also runs on the latest super phones with high-density displays, high-end multi-core GPUs, CPUs, and large memories. But it doesn't stop there. Android also runs on tablets and even on TVs.

There you have it. It is surely impossible to build software for the Android platform. There's no way the same app could run on a 2-inch cheap phone screen, on a 10-inch tablet screen, and on a 55-inch TV screen. Fortunately things aren't as bad as all that. The variety of devices does present a challenge. However, with a right approach, it is possible to support most, if not all, of the devices.

Open Source Software

Open Source software is distributed under various Open Source licenses. These licenses vary from strict licenses that require any derived software to be distributed under the same license to more permissive licenses that allow the license terms to be changed when derived software is distributed. GPL, which is used in the Linux kernel, is a common example of a stricter Open Source license. Everyone distributing software based on the Linux kernel must distribute their work under GPL. The Apache license, on the other hand, allows people to take Apache-licensed software and distribute derived work under any other license. The Android project is distributed under the Apache license. All Open Source licenses allow users to modify and redistribute the code. Read more at `http://opensource.org/`.

GOOGLE'S CONTROL

As mentioned earlier, Android is Open Source, so the license permits anyone putting it on any device they want. Google doesn't force any control on Android devices. They do, however, have something called the *Android Compatibility Program*. The program defines a large number of hardware and software requirements. A device will ship with Google apps and especially Google Play, if has passed the compatibility requirements.

TABLETS

Tablets seem to be the latest boom in the mobile market. Every manufacturer is building its own tablet devices. How can you prepare for tablets in Android design?

Let's draw an analogy from iOS. Those guys have it easy. They either target the iPad or the iPhone and that's it. Can you do the same? The answer is no. Android devices cannot be categorized to tablets and phones so easily. Where does a tablet start and phone end? If you have a phone with a 5-inch display, will a phone user interface be better for it than a tablet user interface? What about a 7-inch tablet and a 13-inch tablet? Is there a tablet design that works on both?

Android devices are a continuum instead of a clear separation between two device categories. You should try to avoid talking about designing for tablet or designing for phones. Android apps should not have a separate tablet-user interface. This doesn't mean that a user interface designed for phone screens will work perfectly on a larger screen. Due to the lack of clear separation between device categories and big difference in devices in each category, it is important that Android user interfaces are scalable. This situation is very familiar to any web designer or developer. Web designers have solved the same problem using something called responsive design. Responsive web pages rearrange their components when necessary to create optimal performance for any screen resolution.

OEM DISTRIBUTIONS, SKINS, AND THEMES

Android devices are manufactured by hundreds of different manufacturers. These devices are then marketed by dozens of carriers all around the world. Both the manufacturers and carriers often want to make their own modifications to the operating system. Many of the larger manufacturers have created fully themed Android distributions featuring original equipment manufacturer (OEM) skins. Probably the best known examples of these are HTC Sense and Samsung TouchWiz. The OEM skins add their own features and functionality on top of the default Android experience. The main home page of phones is often altered drastically to make the phone's branding stand out. See Figure 4-1 for examples of three manufacturer home screens.

Figure 4-1: Home screens from left to right by HTC, Samsung, and Sony on their Android 2.3 devices.

Sources: HTC Corporation, SAMSUNG, and Sony Mobile Communications AB

Although the OEM skins rarely break compatibility, they can make detailed visual design more difficult. A typical change the manufacturers tend to make is to change the system default colors. For example in Android 2.3, the default highlight color for buttons and text fields is orange, but on HTC devices it is green, and Sony devices use blue. In Figure 4-2, you can see how much the manufacturers have changed the default component look and feel; it shows a window from three different manufacturers. Buttons on the top part are in their default states and in the bottom part the OK button is in its pressed state. All of these screenshots are from Android 2.3. This demonstrates how much Android visuals can vary even inside one Android version. Especially noteworthy is that on Sony device the window has a header part whereas on other devices it does not.

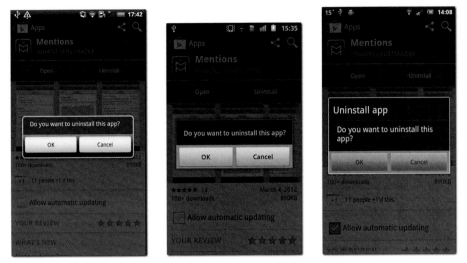

Figure 4-2: A window and buttons with default themes from HTC, Samsung, and Sony.

Sources: HTC Corporation, SAMSUNG, and Sony Mobile Communications AB

In addition to visual changes, manufacturers tend to bundle their own versions of Android default apps. Often, the dialer, messenger, or contact app is replaced. Although they do good work ensuring compatibility by making the intent interface the same (intents are explained in more detail in Chapter 6), there can be some nasty surprises on some devices when they are depending on the default Android apps. In Figure 4-3 you can see the dialer apps manufacturers have used to replace Android's default dialer.

Figure 4-3: Manufacturer dialer app replacements from left to right: HTC, Samsung, and Sony. All screenshots are from Android 2.3.

Sources: HTC Corporation, SAMSUNG, and Sony Mobile Communications AB

HOLO THEME UNIFIES ANDROID APP LOOK

Starting with Android 4.0, all manufacturers are required to include Android Holo themes in their Android distribution to fulfill the Android compatibility requirements. In practice this means that developers and designers can depend on the default themes and define their user interfaces by using the default themes or extending them. The apps will look the same on all Android 4.0 or newer devices. Figures 4-4 and 4-5 show two example apps using the two default themes—one light and one dark. Note that developers must set their app's target SDK level to Android 4.0 or newer for the apps to utilize this new look.

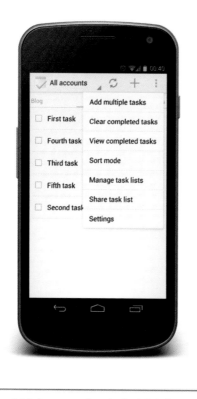

Figure 4-4: Tasks app using the Android Holo light theme.

Source: Tasks app

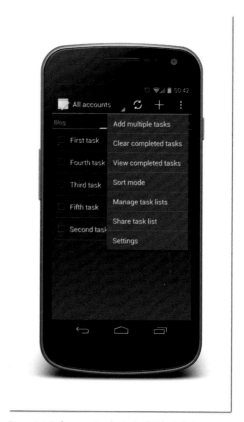

Figure 4-5: Tasks app using the Android Holo dark theme.

Source: Tasks app

KEYBOARD REPLACEMENTS

All Android released APIs are open to every application. Everything Google is doing in their apps can be done in any other app. The open APIs leave the door open to third-party replacements for everything, including the keyboard.

As a designer you cannot assume that the user is using the default keyboard. It is possible that the user has replaced the keyboard that was shipped with their phone with something they got from the Android Market. The third-party keyboards can differ radically from the default keyboards. The user might not be typing in one key at time but instead using a cluster of keys. So don't rely on individual key presses on any design. In fact, the users might not be pressing any keys at all. Figures 4-6, 4-7, and 4-8 show different keyboards.

Figure 4-6: When using the 8pen keyboard, users drag their fingers in circles to select letters and form words.

Source: Dasur Ltd.

Figure 4-7: Siine Keyboard provides icons that can be used to form sentences with a few taps. Each tap will add one or more words to the text field.

Source: Siine Ltd.

Figure 4-8: This is the standard Android voice input mode.
It is used instead of a keyboard.

Source: Android

Given the changes in this field in the past few years, it's hard to even imagine what kind of
keyboards there will be in the future.

THIRD-PARTY HOME SCREEN REPLACEMENTS

Users can replace the Android home screen (OEM or Google). Replacing the home screen
and the app launcher is literally as simple as installing an app from Google Play.

The home screen is a central app of the phone, and replacing it can change the phone's
behavior and feel radically. The home screen or app launcher changes are not visible to
normal apps though. Once an app is launched, its behavior stays unchanged no matter which
home screen or launcher you used to start it.

Although most of the home screen replacements support standard Android home screen
widgets, they often provide extra APIs that developers can use to build home screen widgets
for that home screen replacement. Some popular launchers have managed to gain enough

momentum to create mini ecosystems of people building and distributing apps and themes that work only on that home screen replacement.

Go Launcher (see Figure 4-9) is probably the most popular home screen replacement ecosystem in current circulation. The core app itself has more than 10 million downloads from Google Play. There are hundreds of themes, widgets, and plug-ins for the Go Launcher. Users can use them to make their home screen much more interactive than the default Android APIs allow.

Other popular and noteworthy home screen replacement is the ADW Launcher (see Figure 4-10). ADW Launcher is noteworthy because of its popularity, but also because it is the default home screen on the most popular third-party ROM, CyanogenMod (more about ROMs later in this chapter).

Figure 4-9: The Go Launcher home screen with some Go widgets.

Source: Go Launcher

Figure 4-10: ADW Launcher home screen replacement.

Source: ADW Launcher

Home screen replacements don't end here. At the time of this writing, there are nearly 150 home screen replacement apps available for Android phones.

ANDROID VERSIONS

An Android OS version has a name and version number. Google uses dessert names in alphabetical order. Not every new release receives a new name though. For example, both 2.0 and 2.1 are release Eclair and 3.0, 3.1, and 3.2 are Honeycomb. Versions without a new name can be seen as minor updates, and it is fairly safe to assume that all devices will get updates to the largest version number of a named release. The Android update cycle is about six months.

Technically Android versions are differentiated with number code called the API level. API levels run sequentially from API level 1 upward. Whenever there's a change in Android API the number is increased.

Every Android version has a name, version number, and API level. Table 4-1 shows a list of Android versions released so far. As you see, there are some missing versions like Android 2.0. That is a version that was updated to Android 2.1 so soon that no devices have it anymore, so there is no point listing it. Android 3.0 – 3.2 Honeycomb is likely to have the same fate. I believe that all Honeycomb devices will be updated to Ice Cream Sandwich or above very soon.

Table 4-1   Android Versions, Their Names, and the API Level Code

Android Version	Name	API Level
Android 1.5	Cupcake	3
Android 1.6	Donut	4
Android 2.1	Eclair	7
Android 2.2	Froyo	8
Android 2.3 – 2.3.2	Gingerbread	9
Android 2.3.3 – 2.3.7	Gingerbread	10
Android 3.0	Honeycomb	11
Android 3.1	Honeycomb	12
Android 3.2	Honeycomb	13
Android 4.0 – 4.0.2	Ice Cream Sandwich	14
Android 4.0.3	Ice Cream Sandwich	15
Android 4.1 – 4.1.1	Jelly Bean	16

Google releases accurate numbers of Android version distribution on devices on the Android developer website. The numbers are updated relatively often and are usually very current. The version distribution numbers are based on Android devices that access Google Play within a 14-day period. The version distribution chart can be found here: `http://developer.` `android.com/resources/dashboard/platform-versions.html`.

ANDROID ON TABLETS

Android Honeycomb was an exception to the normal release cycle. It was a tablet-only Android version. It was only ever released to selected manufacturers to be put on tablet devices, and the source code was never released. It is safe to assume that a large majority of devices that shipped with Honeycomb will be updated to Android 4.0 Ice Cream Sandwich or newer. I recommend ignoring Honeycomb and targeting the Ice Cream Sandwich instead.

ANDROID JELLY BEAN, THE LATEST ANDROID RELEASE

At the Google I/O 2012 conference Google announced the Android 4.1 Jelly Bean. At the time of writing this it is the latest Android version. The Jelly Bean release follows the visual guidelines set in the previous Android 4.0 Ice Cream Sandwich release. The Android 4.1 added only few new features, but it improved a lot on some existing features, like adding expandable notifications and offline voice input. The latest version greatly improved Android user interface speed and responsiveness. In the last two releases Android has truly matured as an operating system.

NEXUS DEVICES

Usually, Google releases an updated Android version in cooperation with a device manufacturer. This device acts as a reference implementation of the new OS version. This line of devices is called the Nexus devices.

A Nexus phone always ships with vanilla Android (which means no manufacturer skins or any other third-party customizations). Some carriers still put their own apps on them, though. Nexus devices are also updated directly by Google, which in practice means that they get new Android version updates before other devices. This makes them ideal developer devices.

Previous Nexus devices have been Nexus One built by HTC, Nexus S, and Galaxy Nexus built by Samsung. Other devices that basically belong to this same series but don't carry the Nexus name are the very first Android phone HTC G1, Motorola Droid, and Motorola Xoom tablet. They also were used to release a new Android version and shipped without any manufacturer customization.

UPDATES TO OLDER DEVICES

Android has become infamous for not updating old devices to newer OS versions. Some manufacturers do a better job than others maintaining their older devices, but many of them simply ignore all devices that are older than one year.

Manufacturer unwillingness to support old devices hinders Android version propagation. Historically, it has taken at least a year from a new version release for it to gain significant enough market share to be viable target to be developed for. It is safe to assume that this trend will continue.

WHICH VERSION SHOULD YOU TARGET?

Selecting the minimum Android version to support is tricky, but here are few guidelines. As a rule of thumb you should try to support all Android versions. In practice this is not always possible. New versions bring new APIs and new features that are often very desirable. If you find that you need some of the newer features, you might have to start raising the minimum supported Android version of your app.

First, take a look at the latest Android version distribution numbers from the Developer Dashboard mentioned previously. At the time of this writing, it is clear that Android versions 1.5 and 1.6 can be ignored without much thought, as their distributions are 0.4% and 0.8%, respectively.

Secondly, determine whether the features you need are optional or mandatory. Features that only improve your app's functionality are optional, for example. You can use simple coding tricks to enable them on devices that support them and leave them out of older versions.

A good example of this kind of functionality is multi-touch gesture support like pinch-to-zoom. On an Android web view pinch-to-zoom works, but users can also zoom using the standard on-screen controls. Using multi-touch gestures on Android 2.1 requires a lot more work than on 2.2, so adding multi-touch gesture support to your app only when it is running on 2.2 or a newer Android version is possible. This way you still allow users with Android 2.1 devices to install your app but enable users with newer devices to fully enjoy their device capabilities.

Only when the user experience is unacceptable without a newer Android version should you raise the minimum supported version. You will have smaller target group of users but the ones who do use your app will be getting the most out of it.

ANDROID APP DISTRIBUTION

Some other mobile operating systems have become famous about their so-called *walled garden* approach to software installations, whereby any software must be installed only from official software distribution channels. Android is very different in this sense. Google doesn't force any limitations to the operating system.

Some carriers have enforced stricter app installation policies by preventing app installation from sources they have not approved. Fortunately, this has happened only in very rare cases. In general users can install apps from different app stores or directly by downloading the app package (APK) from the Internet. Installing apps directly is called *side loading*. Side loading isn't enabled by default, but any user can enable that function in the Android Security settings (see Figure 4-11).

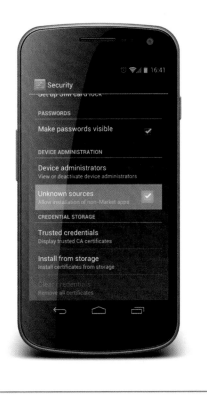

Figure 4-11: To side load an app, users must first enable it from the Android settings.

Source: Android

THE APP STORES

As already mentioned, there are multiple ways users can download apps to their devices. Besides side loading users have a choice of multiple app stores. The most prominent app store is the Google's Play Store. By far the most Android devices ship from the Play Store, and many users are happy with it and don't search for alternatives.

Another very popular app store is the Amazon Android App Store. Amazon's entry to tablet market has sparked an interesting situation in the Android ecosystem. Although Amazon bundles its own app store with its own devices, it is also available with any other device.

In addition to these two big app stores, there are many smaller ones. Barnes & Noble has its own store that serves apps only to their own devices. GetJar is a popular multi-platform app store as well.

APPLICATION SAFETY AND APPROVAL PROCESSES

Different app stores have different approaches to app security. Google's Play Store doesn't require developers to put their apps through any kind of approval process to get their apps into the store. But that doesn't mean that anything is allowed into the store. There are guidelines the developer must agree to before uploading the app. Apps breaking the guidelines are removed from the store and violating developers might end up losing their account. Google Play developer program policies can be found at `http://www.android.com/us/developer-content-policy.html`.

The lack of approval process has caused controversy and malware found from Google Store has been visible in news and blogs. To help to prevent malware getting into Google Play, Google has implemented an automatic virus scanning system called *Bouncer*, which scans all uploaded apps for known viruses.

Lack of an approval process does have positive implications to app quality on the market. Developers are free to upload patches to their apps without having to go through complex processes. Android apps generally receive small patches fairly regularly on Google's Play Store and therefore detected bugs get squashed faster than on app stores that require approval processes.

WHICH APP STORE TO USE

Selecting the app store to use is an important decision. Uploading your app to all app stores might sound like the obvious choice but could end up not being the best approach after all. There are so many apps on all the app stores nowadays that gaining visibility can be very difficult.

App store ranking algorithms are closely guarded secrets to prevent people from gaming the system. Some things that affect the app rankings are clear, though. One of them is the download number and the number of active users. Concentrating all downloads to a single store might be smart. If your app is available from multiple sources, the users are also spread between them. Instead of having 6,000 downloads in two stores, you have 12,000 downloads in one store, which might make the app much more visible in that store and cause an exponential trend in downloads.

MAKE USERS FEEL SAFE

Especially in Google Play, malicious imitation apps pop up all the time. Popular iOS app knockoffs that are not yet available on Android are used to lure unsuspecting users to install the app and then give their login credentials, personal information, or email addresses to the malicious app developer.

Incidents like those cause users to mistrust such app stores. Users are starting to understand that mobile app stores are very similar to the Internet, and not everything is always the way it seems. The users start to look for signs of legitimacy before installing an app. Make sure that all the marketing graphics you have provided to the App Store are high quality and correspond to your app's general theme to create a more polished impression.

What can you do to make your users trust the app you upload? Although this isn't much you can do that hasn't been done by malicious app developers, one way to assure users is to provide a legitimate website. On Google Play, developers always must provide a link to their website. Make sure that the website you provide is the official site of your company. Also make sure that the website links back to your app on the market. Users have already learned how to recognize a trustworthy website and link between the site and the app will make the users feel safer. Never use a Google+ site or a Facebook page as your developer website.

WHAT DOES OPEN SOURCE MEAN?

Android is Open Source. But what does that mean to developers and designers? First, it is good to understand what Open Source software is and what it isn't. This topic could fill multiple books, so I'll try to simplify things here. Basically, Android consists of two distinct components. The core of the operating system is the Linux kernel. The kernel is built by a massive Open Source community and distributed under the General Public License (GPL). The GPL says that anyone can take the Linux code and redistribute it, modify it, and even sell it as long as any derived products are also distributed under GPL and the source code of the new product is distributed alongside any binary distributions. The second part of Android is the Android framework itself. This part is built by Google and distributed under the Apache license. The Apache license isn't as strict as the GPL. It allows distribution of binaries without releasing source code.

ACCESS TO SOURCE CODE

Although Google doesn't allow feature contributions to their code base directly, they do allow developers to download the full Android code base. You can see how Android internals work and, in some cases, even fix or tweak functionality you need on your applications. This approach should be left as the last resort, but sometimes it can save a feature that is too difficult to build otherwise. You can, for example, make a copy of Android's Button class, change the internal functionality of it, and then use it to implement some or all of your buttons in your application.

ANDROID COMMUNITY

Although the Android project is not a community-driven project, there are multiple community-driven library projects that support Android development. A search in GitHub reveals more than 15,000 repositories with the word Android. Not all of them are useful projects, but many of them are. Some libraries provide useful front-end functionality like pull-to-refresh or a back-ported Action Bar, some provide easy access to third-party systems like Facebook or Twitter, and others are helpful in other ways.

The best place to reach the Android developer and hacking community is the XDA Developers website and the related forums. The site has a massive registered community of people who are building apps, creating custom ROMs, unlocking and rooting phones, and much more. It is a very good and mostly reliable source for anything technical about Android.

The Android community isn't just for coding. There are many forums dedicated to helping Android users with their problems of everyday use. Presence on some of the larger ones can be very helpful for promoting your apps.

CUSTOM ROMS

Anyone can take the full Android stack, build it, and redistribute it. This has spawned multiple custom ROM projects. A *custom ROM* is a full replacement for the operating system that was shipped with the device. Installing (or flashing) a custom ROM to a device is the equivalent of reinstalling an operating system to a computer. Probably the best known ROM project is the CyanogenMod (`www.cyanogenmod.com`).

Although custom ROMs are not going to gain popularity with average Android users, they are a small but meaningful part of the Android ecosystem. Projects like CyanogenMod often bring newer Android versions to devices that are no longer supported by the manufacturers or enable users to remove manufacturer customizations from their devices.

SUMMARY

The Android platform, with all its openness and flexibility, might feel overwhelming at first glance. The truth is that it is manageable. Understanding the limits and challenges early in the project planning will help you overcome them.

The same flexibility that creates challenges provides opportunities. In an open ecosystem the opportunities are limitless. If you don't like something you can change it and so can your users.

Don't be afraid of the Android fragmentation. It is manageable if tackled correctly. It is as much an opportunity as a challenge. Make sure you understand the platform before building apps for it. Otherwise, you might end up in a difficult place and might have to work much harder to reach the Android masses than you'd hope for.

PART

ANDROID PLATFORM FEATURES AND UI COMPONENTS

ANDROID APP STRUCTURE AND ONLINE GUIDELINES

THIS CHAPTER INTRODUCES terms and technical concepts used later in this book. This chapter gives you an overview of the Android app structure, general components used to build an app, overview of the development processes, and available online documentation. The goal of this chapter is to make sure that you understand the terms used in the following chapters but not to teach you Android development from the ground up.

If you are familiar with the Android platform already you can skip this chapter or skim through it.

ANDROID APP STRUCTURE OVERVIEW

This section gives you an overview of how Android apps are structured. Understanding some of the concepts discussed later requires you to understand the technical concepts at some level. The level of required understanding depends on whether you are a designer wanting to learn about designing for the platform or you are a developer implementing designs. For a designer, the level of understanding that this section provides is most likely enough. Developers should also look at more technical books for a deeper understanding of each of these topics.

The Android app structure is well defined, and the app framework supports developers very well as long as they build the apps as intended. The Android platform is much stricter about the way components should be used than many older platforms.

ANDROID APP BASIC BUILDING BLOCKS

The Android app is assembled from a set of ready components and custom made components. It's helpful to look at the components that are used to build user interfaces from largest to smallest. Figure 5-1 shows an abstract representation of Android components and their relationships.

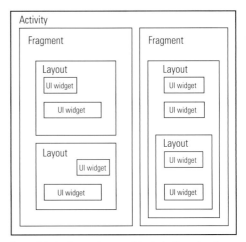

Activity

Activity is the core component of Android apps. An activity often represents one screen. Although it is possible to add more screens than just one to an activity (or some activities don't have a user interface), thinking about activities as single screens and related functionality is the easiest way to understand the app structure.

Figure 5-1: An abstract diagram of the Android user interface structure.

Activity is the controlling instance that handles what is visible on the screen at any time. The activity can be used to remove and add new components as well as trigger intents to start new activities.

Activities form the core of the Android app navigation structure called the *back stack*. Whenever a new activity is brought to the front, the previous one is placed to the back stack. When users then press the Android Back button, the current activity ends and the topmost activity from the back stack is brought to the front.

You'll read more about activities and the back stack in the following chapters.

Fragments

A fragment is a newer user feature that was introduced in Android 3.0 Honeycomb to make applications more scalable between smartphones and tablets. You can think of fragments as sub-activities. A *fragment* is an independent part of a screen that can be placed on-screen either alone or with other fragments.

Let's look at an example to get a quick understanding of what fragments are and how they relate to activities. The Gmail app is a very well implemented app that scales perfectly from smartphone screens to tablet screens. The app on tablets and smartphones is the same one. Figures 5-2 and 5-3 show the Gmail app running on a smartphone. In both screens, the app is running a separate activity, which both have a single fragment visible on them. Figure 5-4 shows the same app running on a tablet. In this case there is now a single activity that displays two fragments. The fragments that are visible are the same ones that are used on the smartphone in two separate screens.

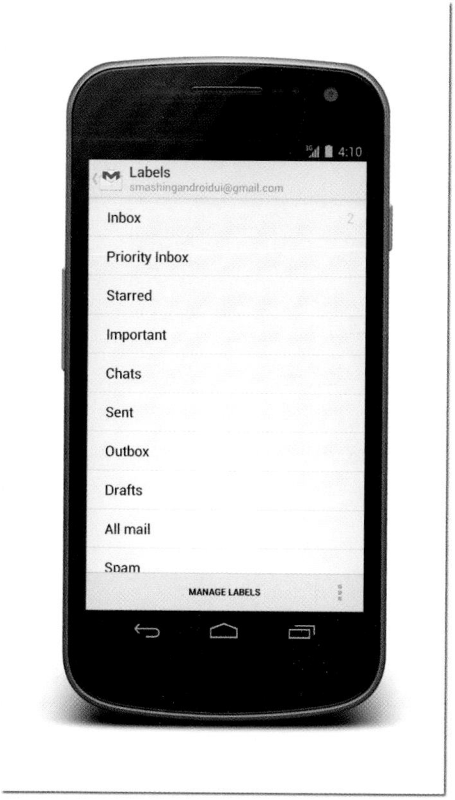

Figure 5-2: The Gmail app label list on a smartphone display.

Source: Google Inc.

Figure 5-3: The Gmail app email list on a smartphone display.

Source: Google Inc.

Figure 5-4: The Gmail app on a tablet combining both label list and email list into
a single screen.
Source: Google Inc.

You'll learn much more about fragments in Chapter 15.

Layouts

Layouts are collections of user interface widgets. An activity or fragment has one layout as the root container that is used to fill in the rest of the content into the activity screen or fragment. Layouts can also contain other layouts forming hierarchical structures. The Android framework provides multiple layouts and are all that most apps need. In a case where the platform layouts aren't enough, developers can implement their own. Layouts are also handled in much more detail in Chapter 13.

User Interface Widgets

User interface widgets are individual components like buttons and text fields that are used in Android user interfaces to represent functionality. The Android platform provides a large selection of user interface widgets that can be used but it is also possible for developers to implement their own.

The user interface components vary from simple text labels to complex gallery widgets, list widgets, and tab containers. Most of the components are very flexible and can be customized by simply changing their parameters. Most of them can also be skinned and themed almost limitlessly.

Interface widgets are discussed in more detail Chapter 11.

INTENTS AND BROADCASTS

Intents are the glue that binds Android apps together internally as well as externally. Activities are started by triggering intents.

Intents can either be implicit or explicit. With *implicit* intents the intent defines which component should handle it. With *explicit* intents the operating system picks the best suited one or presents the users with an option to select which app should handle it.

Intents are also used by the operating system to notify apps about changing the environment and other events in the device. Apps can subscribe to receive these events. These kinds of messages are called *intent broadcasts*. This broadcast mechanism is not only reserved for operating system broadcasts but can also be used by apps.

Intents are fairly complicated but also a very powerful and important mechanism. You'll learn much more about intents in Chapter 6.

SERVICES

Services are tasks that are running in the background. They can be long running or short-lived. A service never has a user interface. They take care of tasks like fetching new information from the server, polling to check for new information, and so on. This book doesn't cover much about services, but it is good to know that they exist.

APP WIDGETS

Android app widgets are small layouts that users can place on their home screens. The app widgets provide limited app functionality by, for example, displaying some relevant data or providing direct access to some of the most important app functionality.

Home screen app widgets are one of the identifying features of the Android powered devices. They can be very powerful when used right in the right kind of apps. Not all apps need to implement an app widget.

ANDROID PROJECT STRUCTURE OVERVIEW

The Android project structure is well defined. The Android SDK expects certain things to be in set places. The structure of the project allows the SDK to build apps in a way so that they function well in many different devices. Although developers need to be very aware of the project structure, designers don't need deep knowledge of the subject. This section gives a very short overview of the subject, which can lead to a better understanding of some terms introduced later in this book, even for the less technical readers.

COMPONENT FOLDERS

An Android project consists of source code, resource XML files (layout definitions, text files, and so on), resource graphics, and libraries. Each of these file types must be placed in the right folders under the project structure, or they won't be detected by the Android SDK and will not be included in the app. See Figure 5-5 for an example project folder structure.

Figure 5-5: An example project structure.

Source: Eclipse

Code files on the project are placed into the `src` folder. The Android SDK generates a lot of source code and all that generated code is placed in the `gen-src` folder.

For all resource files, the folder structure is a bit more complicated. Each of the folders can have extra attributes in their names to tell the SDK what kind of device or execution environment the files inside that folder are meant for. You'll learn much more about the folder structure in the sections about scalable design, as the folder structure is the key for supporting different screen sizes and densities. The same approach also allows developers to specify separate language files for devices with different locale settings.

LIBRARIES

Android projects can take advantage of multiple community maintained and commercial libraries. Many third-party Java libraries are compatible with Android projects and can be used to implement functionality that doesn't have a user interface, such as streaming or encryption libraries.

Android also supports special Android library projects that allow developers to organize functionality and use third-party libraries that do implement user interface functionality. Probably the best-known third-party library is the ActionBarSherlock that provides back-port of the Action Bar user interface pattern to older devices (see `http://actionbar sherlock.com/`).

OFFICIAL ANDROID GUIDELINES

Android has a lot of great online resources that can be used to dive deeper into the platform's secrets. Google is constantly improving their documentation and it is worth taking a look. You can often find solutions to technical problems directly from the developer documentation, including working examples.

Google has also released documentation for official design guidelines. At the time of this writing, the documentation is pretty thin but is likely to grow over time.

ANDROID DEVELOPER DOCUMENTATION

The Android developer documentation should be the first place to look when you run into problems. This is also where to go to get your development environment to set up. You can find the official Android developer documentation at `http://developer.android.com`.

Dev Guide, Training, and Videos

The developer documentation consists of different guides like managing virtual devices, handling USB connections, and hundreds more. Google has also set up multiple online training courses with topics varying from simple to advanced.

Google has also gathered all of the Google I|O conference (the yearly conference for different Google technologies, including Android) Android presentation videos into this site. Although the older ones might not be up to date, the newer ones are very informative and a very good source for additional information.

Reference Documentation

The most important part of the developer documentation is the Android reference documentation that specifies every single Android framework interface that is available to Android developers. Every class, method, and parameter is defined here.

Android Developers Blog

If you haven't done so already you should subscribe to the Android Developers blog. This is a place where Google's own staff posts topical and informative posts about Android development. Most of the posts are very technical, but design topics are also often discussed. You can find the blog at `http://android-developers.blogspot.com/`.

ANDROID DESIGN GUIDELINES

The Android Design web page is a great place to get an overview of the Android user interface design. It does lack details in many places. It is also targeted only for Android 4.0 Ice Cream Sandwich or newer. You can find the Android Design page at `http://developer.android.com/`design.

GOOGLE PLAY GUIDELINES

The Android Developer page also has guidelines for publishing your apps to Google Play. Although the guidelines are good to read, the best way to see what you actually need to do is to go to Google Play's developer console. You can access the developer console at `https://play.google.com/apps/publish`.

To access the developer console, you need to create a Google developer account. The account creation is not free but it's inexpensive. At the time of this writing, the account creation requires a one-time payment of $75.

SUMMARY

Android apps are constructed using sets of building blocks provided by the platform. This book does not require you to understand every component, but you should have an overview of the kinds of components that exist and how they relate to each other.

This chapter explained Android component hierarchy from a user interface point of view. You should now understand how activities relate to layouts and how layouts relate to user interface widgets.

This chapter also took a quick look at the available Android online documentation and resources. The official documentation is always a great place to learn more about the platform.

ANDROID INTENTS

ANDROID'S INTENT SYSTEM is probably the most powerful platform feature that the Android has. The intents tie apps together internally and externally. The intent system makes it possible for developers to call functionality from the Android platform and from any other installed apps. It also allows your app to provide functionality to other apps.

This chapter explains what Android intents are and where they are used. The goal of this chapter is to give you a good understanding of how the intent mechanism affects Android user interface design. This chapter explains some examples but does not cover the full intent specification and all use cases. I encourage you to see Android documentation for deeper technical information (see `http://developer.android.com/reference/android/content/Intent.html`).

INTENTS ALLOW APPS TO WORK TOGETHER

In short, an *intent* is a technical and formally defined message sent to an application component. The message can be internal in one app or sent between different apps or even between
the operating system and apps. An app can, for example, message the operating system that it
wants to dial a phone number.

The most powerful implication of the intent mechanism is that the apps are all capable of
working together and sharing each other's functionality in a very easy and seamless way. Any
app can ask the platform to identify other apps that provide certain functionality, and then
use one of them or let the user pick one.

One of the most common use cases for intents is an app wanting to share something, an
image for example. Regardless of whether your app is a photo editor, a camera app, a drawing
app, or anything else, it can let the Android system know that it has an image to share. The
operating system knows which other installed apps can help your app with this request.

Let's look at an example. The following sequence of figures illustrates a series of actions by a
user, utilizing the functionality of four different apps to produce a picture and then share it to
a social network. In Figure 6-1 the user takes a photo with the Android camera app. Next the
user shares the photo to an editor app, Skitch, where he adds a text overlay to the photo (see
Figure 6-2). Finally, the user shares the completed picture to Twitter (see Figure 6-3).

Figure 6-1: User taking a photo with the Android camera app.

Source: Android

Figure 6-2: User adding text overlay to the shared picture with Skitch app.

Source: Skitch, copyright 2012 Evernote Corporation

Figure 6-3: User sharing the completed picture to Twitter.

Source: Twitter

Noteworthy in this sequence is that the user at no point has to save the picture to a gallery or file system to continue to work with it. The image file is moved seamlessly by the Android operating system without the user having to know about it. The last step, Twitter sharing, is performed by the Twitter app and, therefore, the user doesn't have to perform a separate login to ensure that everything is ready for sharing.

USING SOCIAL NETWORKS AND SHARING

Mobile apps and social networks go hand in hand. People love their phones, and they love to share everything they see, hear, and eat to their social network of choice. On some platforms Facebook and Twitter integration has risen to be a sales pitch and a marketing tool. On an Android device, you can share from all apps to any social network that had an Android app from the start, including Google+, LinkedIn, Orkut, and of course Facebook and Twitter. A new social network only has to provide an Android version of their app using the correct intent filters (explained later in this chapter), and they are done. After installing the app, users can share directly from a gallery, all correctly implemented photo apps, postcard apps, drawing tools, or text editors to the new social network. For the same reason, users aren't tied down to only to the official client app. In Figure 6-4 you see an example of a user wanting to share an image. Note that Seesmic, Plume, Tweet Lanes, TweetDeck, and Twitter are all Twitter clients and the user is free to use any of them for sharing to Twitter.

When building an Android app you don't have to worry about social network integration—the platform takes care of it for you. You don't have to pick the apps you think should be supported or build any functionality for sharing to a specific social network. The only thing you need to do is to implement your sharing intents according to the specification. Note that the list of apps shown in Figure 6-4 is automatically provided by the operating system, so you don't have to build anything even for that. The operating system takes care of everything. Also noteworthy in Figure 6-4 is that it only shows apps that are able to handle image sharing. The user will never see apps in the list that will not know what do with the type of data that is shared.

Now take a look at Figure 6-5. In this figure the user has triggered a similar sharing intent, but this time she is sharing not an image but a URL from her browser. Android's intent resolution system automatically figures out which apps it should provide in the list. You will take a better look at intent resolution later in this chapter.

WORKING WITH BROWSERS

Browsers are an essential part of smartphones and tablets. They probably are the one of the most used apps of any Android device. The intent system allows your app to hook into them too. Android browsers, at least the ones implemented correctly, use intents to open each link as the user taps it. Typically the intent is handled by the browser itself, but sometimes the target URL could viewed better by another app. An app can tell the operating system that it can handle URLs with certain patterns, for example a domain name. When a user taps a link that matches the pattern, the operating system presents the user with the familiar choice. In Figure 6-6 you see an example of what happens when a user taps an ordinary HTML link that points to Google Play. The Android operating system recognizes that the link is a special case and that a Google Play app could also handle this request, so the operating system lets the user choose the app she prefers to use. In addition to the two browsers the user has installed, the Google Play app is also presented as an option to complete the action.

Figure 6-4: The user has selected to share a file from within the Android gallery app. The Android OS then asks the user to pick which app she wants to use to complete the operation.

Source: Android

Figure 6-5: The user has selected to share a URL. The Android OS no longer shows image manipulation apps, but only apps that know what to do with a URL.

Source: Android

Figure 6-6: The user clicked a link that points to the Android Market in an Android browser. The operating system recognizes that there is another app that can handle the URL and presents the user with an option to select which of the apps should handle the request.

Source: Android

What makes this particularly powerful is that there's no special syntax required on the website's side. The website contains a perfectly normal link that would take the user to the Android Market website if the user were using a normal desktop browser or didn't have the Google Play app installed on their device.

> *Tip: If your app is an alternative for viewing content that is also available online, you should make sure that it subscribes to URLs that fit the corresponding domain pattern. There really is no reason not to do it. The app is supposed to be a superior way to browse and interact with the content. If it isn't you should either rethink your app strategy or improve your app.*

Note that URL intents do contain the full URL including all parameters. This means that your app can directly open the right content. In the preceding example, selecting the Google Play app would lead the user directly into the correct app page inside the Google Play app. Similarly, a YouTube link opened using the YouTube app will directly play the correct video.

HOW DO ANDROID INTENTS WORK?

Let's take a look under the hood and see how Android intents work. Even if you are not interested in the deep technical details, it is useful to get an overview to better understand what is possible and what isn't. There's also some terminology that can be useful to know. The examples in this chapter are very basic; if you're not a developer, you can just jump over them.

TYPES OF INTENTS

There are two kinds of intents: activity intents and broadcast intents.

- *Activity intents:* Activity intents always have exactly one sender app and one handler app. The handler app can be an activity or a service. Activity intents are divided into two further categories: explicit and implicit intents.
  - *Explicit intents:* If an app knows exactly which activity or service class it wants to handle the intent, it can trigger an explicit intent. The intent will be directly handled by the given activity or service and that's it. This is how apps typically communicate internally. While a very important construct, explicit intents aren't very interesting when considering user interfaces.
  - *Implicit intents:* Implicit intents are used when the triggering app doesn't know which app will handle the request. The triggering app creates an intent describing what kind of action it wants to be performed and includes data with the intent and sends it to the operating system.

    This implicit intent mechanism creates a loosely coupled relationship between the calling app and the responding app. The interface between them is specified but neither of the apps need to know anything about each other. Keeping components loosely coupled will make your app much easier to maintain as changes in other components or other apps won't break anything as long as the interface stays unchanged. Also being agnostic about the other apps means that apps you didn't even think about during your app's development might later provide shared functionality to your app.

    Implicit intents are very interesting and relevant from a user interface design point of view. Understanding how to work with them is a must if you want to build great apps for Android.

- *Broadcast intents:* Broadcast intents are, as the name suggests, sent by one app but can be received and handled by many. Activity intents always have only one app sending the intent and only one handling it. But sometimes one-to-one communication isn't suitable solution. Some events, such as a device's battery running low on power, might interest more than a single app. For such situations you need broadcasts. Broadcasts use the same intent mechanisms as explicit intents but broadcasts are handled not by activities or services, but by broadcast receivers.

TECHNICAL EXAMPLE OF SENDING INTENTS

In this example, you'll see how to make the example app allow users do more with a postal address. This functionality is widely used in the Android default apps like Android calendar and Google Maps. It is a good example of the power of the intent system. Let's say that your application has postal address information. It can be a good idea to provide your users with a map view or even with a navigation option to the address. Note that you don't have to know what the users will do with the address information. It is up to them to pick the app they want.

The great benefit of using intents here is that you don't have to write any of the map or navigation code into your app, but you can let other apps handle it. Sending this intent is very simple. Take a look at the following code sample. This code can be anywhere, but in this example it is in an activity class. The intent is triggered when users tap the UI button.

```
sendIntent.setOnClickListener(new View.OnClickListener() {
  @Override
  public void onClick(View v) {
    Uri geoUri = Uri.parse(„geo:0,0?q="+ addressField.getText().toString());
    Intent mapCall = new Intent(Intent.ACTION_VIEW, geoUri);
    startActivity(mapCall);
  }
});
```

When the intent is sent, the users will be shown the already familiar app selection dialog box, as shown in Figure 6-7. If the user selects, for example, Google Maps, the app will open and directly display the correct address, as seen in Figure 6-8.

INTENT FILTERS: ACTIONS, DATA, AND CATEGORIES

How does the operating system know which activity, service, or broadcast receiver should receive the intent? How do you know that an intent you send will be handled only by activities that can perform exactly what you want. You are giving control out from your own app to some other application. You must be able to rely on the operating system to take care that you don't lead your users into trouble.

Figure 6-7: The app selection dialog box after the app sends the intent.

Source: Android

Figure 6-8: Google Maps opens the sent address.

Source: Google Inc.

Here is where you need to peek under the hood and understand how Androids intent resolution works. There are two main components in the system. Any activity, service, or broadcast receiver can have a set of intent filters associated with them in the application's manifest file or dynamically in runtime code. The intent then contains an action definition and data field, and possibly categories and some extra data. When the operating system receives an intent, it compares the action, data, and categories with the intent filters of all apps and picks the ones that match.

Actions and categories are simply names. Nothing more complicated there. Data and extra data are a bit more complex. Data is defined either as a URI or a mime type. A URI is composed of two parts separated by a colon. The first part defines the data type or scheme. The second part identifies the data. For example, the URI `tel:123456789` means that the data type is `tel` and the data is `123456789`. In intent resolution the meaningful part is the data type.

Android APIs define a number of standard actions, categories, and extra data keys. These standard intent definitions are used throughout the Android platform. Some are triggered by the operating system while others are used by the default apps that ship with the Android system. The standard actions include send (or share), dial a number, call a number, view, and many more.

Table 6-1 shows a list of standard activity actions, and Table 6-2 shows the standard broadcast actions. For a full list of actions used in the Android SDK, see the intent documentation at `http://developer.android.com/reference/android/content/Intent.html`.

Table 6-1   Android Standard Activity Actions

Action Name	Action Description
ACTION_ANSWER	Handle an incoming phone call.
ACTION_ATTACH_DATA	Indicate that some piece of data should be attached to some other place.
ACTION_CALL	Perform a call to someone specified by the data.
ACTION_CHOOSER	Display an activity chooser, allowing the user to pick what they want to before proceeding.
ACTION_DELETE	Delete the given data from its container.
ACTION_DIAL	Dial a number as specified by the data.
ACTION_EDIT	Provide explicit editable access to the given data.
ACTION_FACTORY_TEST	Main entry point for factory tests.
ACTION_GET_CONTENT	Allow the user to select a particular kind of data and return it.
ACTION_INSERT	Insert an empty item into the given container.
ACTION_MAIN	Start as a main entry point, does not expect to receive data.
ACTION_PICK	Pick an item from the data, returning what was selected.
ACTION_PICK_ACTIVITY	Pick an activity given an intent, returning the class selected.
ACTION_RUN	Run the data, whatever that means.
ACTION_SEARCH	Perform a search.
ACTION_SEND	Deliver some data to someone else.
ACTION_SENDTO	Send a message to someone specified by the data.
ACTION_SYNC	Perform a data synchronization.
ACTION_VIEW	Display the data to the users.

Table 6-2   Android Standard Broadcast Actions

Action Name	Action Description
ACTION_BATTERY_CHANGED	This is a sticky broadcast containing the charging state, level, and other information about the battery.
ACTION_BOOT_COMPLETED	This is broadcast once, after the system has finished booting.
ACTION_PACKAGE_ADDED	A new application package has been installed on the device.
ACTION_PACKAGE_DATA_CLEARED	The user has cleared the data of a package.
ACTION_PACKAGE_REMOVED	An existing application package has been removed from the device.
ACTION_PACKAGE_RESTARTED	The user has restarted a package, and all of its processes have been killed.
ACTION_POWER_CONNECTED	External power has been connected to the device.
ACTION_POWER_DISCONNECTED	External power has been removed from the device.
ACTION_SHUTDOWN	Device is shutting down.
ACTION_TIME_CHANGED	The timezone has changed.
ACTION_TIMEZONE_CHANGED	The time was set.
ACTION_TIME_TICK	The current time has changed.
ACTION_UID_REMOVED	A user ID has been removed from the system.

In addition to data type and action, the operating system looks into category of the intent and the intent filter. In most cases, the only relevant category is the *default* category. Whenever intents are sent from your code, the operating system automatically adds the default category to the intent. For the same reason you should always add a default category to your intent filter.

Intent categories become relevant only when you want to replace the home screen activity, car dock, or table dock activities. One exception is category launcher. All activities that have an intent filter with launcher category will be displayed in the application launcher.

Intents can also transmit more data than just the URI. Each intent can have extra data fields that are not formally specified and are not part of the intent resolution. The extra fields are related to different actions. Activities handling certain types of actions expect extra data with certain keywords. Some examples of standard extra keys are email, title, text, subject, stream (used in image sharing) and many more. A complete list of standard extras can be found in the Android documentation at `http://developer.android.com/reference/android/content/Intent.html`.

TECHNICAL EXAMPLE OF RECEIVING INTENTS

Receiving intents isn't technically much more complex than sending them. Let's use the same example but from the receiving end. Imagine that your app can provide some useful service to users when they want to view an address. This service could, for example, be anything from special navigation instructions, like biking or public transportation, to a novel way of displaying the address information.

Receiving intents need two components. First, you need to add an activity to your manifest file. In the activity entry you must also define the intent filter to let the Android system know what kind of intents your activity can handle. In the following code sample you see how you can define an intent filter to handle actions to view an URI with geo scheme. The geo URI scheme is a formal specification for describing geolocations.

```
<activity
  android:name=".intents.ReceiveIntentExampleActivity"
  android:label="Smashing Android UI" >
  <intent-filter>
    <action android:name="android.intent.action.VIEW" />
    <category android:name="android.intent.category.DEFAULT" />
    <data android:scheme="geo" />
  </intent-filter>
</activity>
```

Scan the QR code with your Android phone to open the companion app and try out a functional example. Of course, make sure you have the Smashing Android UI companion app installed on your phone first. See the Introduction for more information.

In the activity code you can read the attached geolocation from the intent. In the following example the geolocation URI is read from the intent data and simply displayed as such. In a real app you would have to parse the URI content to perform something meaningful with it.

```
@Override
protected void onCreate(Bundle savedInstanceState) {
  super.onCreate(savedInstanceState);
  setTitle("Receive Intent Example");
  setContentView(R.layout.receive_intent_example);
  TextView addressText = (TextView) findViewById(R.id.example_address_field);
  addressText.setText("" + getIntent().getData());
}
```

CREATING YOUR OWN ACTIONS

You don't have to settle for the predefined standard actions. Nothing prevents you from creating your own. Maybe you provide a service in your app that could be useful for other developers, or maybe you have multiple apps and you don't want to build a tight coupling between them.

Your own actions are simply names for actions that you've defined. As a general guideline it is good to always prefix your actions with your app's package name to keep them from getting mixed up with actions defined by others.

The following example of an intent filter definition is for a custom action that was defined by me. If I now would publish this action name—com.androiduipatterns .smashingandroidui.examples.EXAMPLE_ACTION—on my app's website, other developers could use it to integrate their apps specifically with this activity.

```
<activity
 android:name=".intents.ReceiveCustomIntentExampleActivity"
 android:label="Smashing Android UI" >
  <intent-filter>
    <action android:name="com.androiduipatterns
        .smashingandroidui.examples.EXAMPLE_ACTION" />
    <category android:name="android.intent.category.DEFAULT" />
  </intent-filter>
</activity>
```

INTENTS ARE EVERYWHERE

Almost everything on Android is triggered using intents. Whenever you start an app from a launcher, you have used an intent that was triggered by the launcher or home screen. In fact, you start the home screen by triggering an intent. If you want to replace your home screen all you need to do is to make another suitable app handle the home screen intent. The Android home screen and app tray is just an app with specific intent filter.

Even the default phone application is started with an intent, and a phone call is dialed with an intent. Both of them can also be implemented by an app. If you want to write an app that replaces the dialer you can do so.

On Android there's no such thing as *the* Android browser. Well, strictly speaking there is an app that is called Android Browser, but what I mean is that Android includes multiple browsers on the platform, and you cannot know which one a user is using. Any app that handles URLs can become the user's default browser by simply implementing an activity with a corresponding intent filter.

The flexibility of the Android platform opens a lot of opportunities for your app, but it also creates challenges like not being able to rely on the user using the default address book, home screen, dialer, or browser.

INTENTS VERSUS THIRD-PARTY APIS

When it comes to sharing, using intents is not the only option you have. Many social networks and other services provide APIs you can use to integrate their functionality directly into your app. While in some cases this is a good way to go, you should evaluate it carefully. In many cases you will have to implement many features that you could otherwise get for free by using the intents. Also, whenever any of the social networks add more functionality, your app will fall behind until you add them to your implementation. If you are using the intents you will get the new features automatically when the client app is updated.

Another big downside of using tight integration is that if the part of the API you're using requires user authentication you must implement it into your app. You must either ask users for their credentials or open an embedded web view that does the authentication. Either way the user must trust your app. They either give their login credentials to you or authorize your app to perform operations with their account. Would you want to give a random app your Facebook login credentials or authorize it to post to your Facebook wall?

SUMMARY

I hope I have convinced you about the power and flexibility of the intent mechanism. When thinking about your app's design, take a minute to think how your app could be a more integral part of your user's device. Is there some functionality you could share with other apps as an intent? Could you use functionality offered by other apps instead of writing them yourself?

This chapter wasn't intended to teach you the full technical side of intents. For more details about that side of things I recommend checking out Reto Meier's *Professional Android 4 Application Development* book (Wiley, 2012) or Google's Android developer documentation at `http://developer.android.com/reference/android/content/Intent.html`.

For intents provided by third-party apps, take a look at the Open Intents website at `www.openintents.org/` and especially at the intent registry they maintain.

CHAPTER

ANDROID APP NAVIGATION STRUCTURE

NAVIGATION STRUCTURE IS A CRITICAL aspect of an app's usability. Get the navigation wrong, and the app is useless. Getting the navigation structure right requires careful planning and a good understanding of the platform. I have seen examples whereby developers ported an app designed for another platform over to Android, unchanged. Results are mostly disastrous in these cases. Navigation must work consistently in all apps on Android platforms. Users learn to use Android apps a certain way and expect the same behavior.

Navigation structure is all about presenting your content in a meaningful and intuitive way. Users must be able to determine where to find the content they are looking for and how to navigate the app without getting lost. It is important to let the users feel like they are in control all the time. Making users feel lost in your app is a sure way to get your app uninstalled.

Navigation is not just about your app's internal structure. On Android your app is part of the platform. You must plan how your app integrates with other apps and understand the different ways your users can enter and leave your app.

This chapter explains what you need to take into account and know to be able to design and implement good Android app navigation.

COMPONENTS OF ANDROID NAVIGATION, ACTIVITIES, AND INTENTS

To understand how Android navigation works, you need a good understanding of what's going on under the hood, so to speak. This section explains some of the most important technical navigation concepts.

The two main components of Android navigation are intents and activities. An *activity* is the core component of the Android app user interface. An activity very often corresponds one-to-one to a screen. Although this is not always true and there are many situations where this isn't true, you can think about activities this way for now. The way activities are called and closed form the bulk of the navigation structure of an app.

As explained in the previous chapter, activities are started by triggering intents. By default, each intent creates a new activity, which is then activated. If another activity is already active it is moved to a structure called the *back stack*.

Users can then navigate backward by closing the active activity, for example by pressing the Back button. Whenever the active activity is closed, the topmost activity from the back stack is brought to the front and activated. If no activities are found from the back stack, the user is brought back to the home screen.

MODIFYING BACK STACK BEHAVIOR WITH INTENT FLAGS

In most cases the default behavior of back stack is enough, but sometimes using the default behavior would lead to situations where the back stack structure doesn't make sense. It is possible to tell the operating system to handle the activity stack differently by adding control flags to the triggered intent.

There are more than 20 intent flags that can be used to launch activities. Most of them are useful only in very rare cases. Three of the intent flags are important and used very often, and are listed here:

- **FLAG_ACTIVITY_NEW_TASK**—An activity started with this flag will start a new task. Later in this chapter, you'll see an example of this flag in practice.
- **FLAG_ACTIVITY_CLEAR_TOP**—If an instance of the new activity is already running in the back stack, the instance is brought to the front and all the activities on top of it are cleared. This intent flag is especially useful with notifications. You'll find an example of this later in the chapter.
- **FLAG_ACTIVITY_SINGLE_TOP**—If the topmost activity in the back stack is an instance of the activity that is being launched, that activity is brought to the front and no new activities are launched. This intent flag is very useful for preventing the same activity from getting started over and over again when it is not needed.

Scan the QR code with your Android phone to open the companion app and try a functional example. Of course, make sure you have the Smashing Android UI companion app installed on your phone first. See the Introduction for more information.

TASKS

Whenever an app is launched from the home screen it has its own back stack and does not interfere with other apps' back stacks. Two apps that are launched from the home screen can, therefore, be thought of as separate tasks. *Tasks* are collections of activities in the back stack. You can manually start a new task inside your app by using intent flags. This feature is not needed that often when navigating within one app, but sometimes you can make better use of the other intent flags if you use tasks to group activities in your app. Tasks are an important concept when you are launching other apps from your app.

ANDROID NAVIGATION CONTROLS

Android provides a set of standard navigation controls to the users. The Back and Home buttons have become identifying hardware features of all Android phones. On top of these two navigation keys is the Up button, which is sometimes used to help users navigate in the screen hierarchy. Users can also directly switch between apps by using a dedicated multi-tasking button on newer phones or holding down the Home key on older phones. All of these controls have dedicated roles and all app designers must understand them.

THE HOME BUTTON

All Android phones have a Home button. Older ones have a physical one and newer ones often have a software-rendered one. The Home button serves a critical purpose, and the Android platform prevents you from overriding its functionality. Pressing the Home button will always trigger an intent that opens the user's home screen. Any running app moves to the background. The current activity doesn't end, so the user can return to the app using Android's multi-tasking controls. Always keep in mind that the user might choose to press the Home key at any time.

THE BACK BUTTON

Users navigate backward in the navigation hierarchy by pressing the Android Back button. In older devices the Back button is a physical button, and in newer generation devices it often is a software key rendered by the operating system. Developers can trust that the Back key is always available.

> *Tip: By default, pressing the Back button will end the active activity and return users to the previous activity. In the vast majority of cases, this is exactly what should happen and what users expect. As a rule of thumb, do not override the Back button's functionality unless you have a very good reason for doing so!*

For developers, having the Back button terminate the current activity makes sense. It is easy to understand and logical. For users, Back button functionality can be more confusing. They don't understand or care what activities are, what their lifecycle is, and what happens under the hood. If you use more complex activity structures, always make sure that the Back button functionality looks correct to the users regardless of the underlying implementation.

Although the Back button typically exits the active activity, its functionality has been overridden in many places. All of the following examples might look different to phone users, although to a technical person they all make sense. More importantly, the behavior under the hood is consistent.

- Go back to the previous screen (activity).
- Exit the running app when on the last activity.
- Return to the previous app when on the last activity and when the app was launched through an intent from another app.
- Dismiss a pop-up.
- Terminate a long-running process.
- Close the on-screen keyboard.
- Go to the previous page on a browser.

You must keep in mind that the Back button is probably the most popular user control on the Android platform. Users use it without thinking. It should always be clear to the users what is going to happen when they press it. If users have to think about what is going to happen even a bit, it will make the app feel cumbersome and difficult to use.

THE UP BUTTON

With the release of Android 3.0 Honeycomb, Google introduced a new navigation concept, the Up button. The Up button is derived from a concept that is very common on the web. On many web pages, the top-left corner contains the website logo. Users can click the logo to go to the front page of the website. Before the 3.0 Android release, an emerging pattern on Android apps was to place the app logo in the top-left corner, which always took users to the app front page.

Unfortunately, Google decided to change this concept and replaced the functionality of the top-left button. The top-left button, which is part of the Action Bar pattern (more about the Action Bar in Chapter 18), is now the Up button. Although developers don't have to use this feature in their apps, it is encouraged as it has become a pervasive feature and users are starting to expect it.

Visually, the Up button is the application icon with a left caret when it is active. Figure 7-1 shows an example of the Up button from the TED talks app.

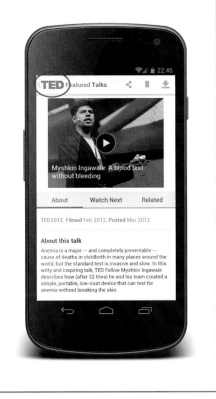

Figure 7-1: The Up button is a left-pointing caret.

Source: TED CONFERENCES, LLC

In theory, at least, the purpose of the Up button is simple. Whereas the Back button takes the users back to the previous screen, the Up button takes the users to the screen that is one step higher in the hierarchy. Figure 7-2 shows a simple example demonstrating the difference between the Up and Back buttons. In the example, screen A, a list screen, is higher in navigation structure than screens B and C, which are item details screens. The user first navigates from the list screen to the first item details screen B, and then to another item details screen C. If she is on the item details screen C, pressing the Back button would take her back to the previous item details screen B, whereas pressing the Up button would take her to list screen A.

USER CONFUSION

The Up button can easily confuse users. For technical people it is easy to understand and once the difference between the Back button and the Up button is explained, it's usually clear. Unfortunately, nobody is going to be explaining the difference to most users. Users historically have a hard time understanding the difference between Up and Back. Google's unfortunate choice to use the left-pointing caret as the Up symbol doesn't help. The Back button icon also points left.

The iOS Back button is often placed very similarly as the Android Up button. This is guaranteed to cause even more confusion for people using both platforms.

Due to the possible confusion it is very important to follow the guidelines carefully. Consistent functionality in all Android apps is the only way to combat user confusion.

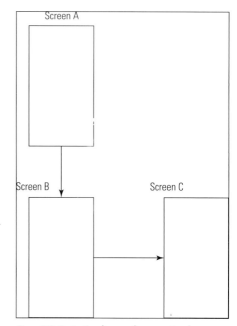

Figure 7-2: Navigation diagram demonstrating the difference between the Up and Back buttons.

Up Button Rules of Thumb

Clearly, the functionality of the Up button versus the Back button can cause some confusion for users as well as developers. Here are some rules of thumb you should follow when using the Up button (unless you have a very good reason to break them).

- The Up button should never lead the user to the home screen.
- The Up button should never lead the user to another app.
- Disable the Up button when there are no more levels for the user to go up. The left caret must not be visible when the Up button is disabled.
- The Up button should always lead to the same screen from one screen regardless of how the user navigated to the screen (in-app navigation, from notification, and so on). A screen can exist only in one place in the screen hierarchy.

You should familiarize yourself with the latest navigation guidelines in the Android Design guidelines online at http://developer.android.com/design/patterns/navigation.html

NAVIGATION IMPROVEMENTS IN ANDROID 4.1

In the Android 4.1 Jelly Bean, Google has added many features that help developers build the back stack and Up button functionality more easily. Probably the biggest improvement is the addition of the `android:parentActivityName` attribute for the `activity` tag in the Android app manifest file. You can now define the parent activity of any of your activities there and the operating system will take care of the navigation for you.

They also added convenience classes to help you manage your back stack and activities. Take a look at the online documentation of the `TaskStackBuilder` class at `http://developer.android.com/reference/android/app/TaskStackBuilder.html`.

MULTI-TASKING

Android is a true multi-tasking operating system. Users can switch between apps seamlessly at any time by tapping the multi-tasking button on newer generation phones or holding the Home button on older phones. Figure 7-3 shows an example of the multi-tasking menu on Android 4.0.

Figure 7-3: Android 4.0, ICS, multi-tasking menu.

Source: Android

A true multi-tasking environment is challenging to its developers. The Android operating system can kill any activities and apps that are not active at any time. The operating system does this to clear up memory that is needed for other operations. Android APIs provide developers ways to save the activity state before it is killed by the operating system. You should make sure that your app's state persists, especially when your activity holds data that is difficult to fetch again. This kind of data could be, for example, retrieved from a server or data that required heavy calculation to obtain. Write this kind of data to long-term memory whenever the operating system is killing the activity. Read more about activity lifecycle from the Android documentation at `http://developer.android.com/reference/android/app/Activity.html`.

WHERE DOES AN APP START?

Although using an application icon is a common place to start an app, it isn't by far the only option. In fact, many apps are rarely launched from the launcher icon. Some apps are more commonly opened using intents from other apps or from status bar notifications.

In either of these cases, it is likely that the app should not be opened from its landing screen. Tapping notification should always take the users directly to the corresponding info and an intent from another app should initialize the app with all the data from the intent. Should the back stack be empty in these cases? What does the user expect to happen when he or she presses Back?

This begs a question or two. Where does an app start? Or, what is the app's starting screen? Consider an email app as an example. The app has a launcher icon, but when is it used? Let's look at the following three use cases:

- A user wants to be notified when a new email arrives and read it if he so decides.
- A user wants to write a new email.
- A user wants to send a photo she just took to someone using email.

When a user wants to be notified when a new email arrives, the app is most likely going to use a status bar notification to let him know that there's a new email. The user can then tap the notification, and the app should take him directly to the corresponding email screen, where he can read the message if he chooses.

When the user wants to compose an email, the app is triggered by the user and he is likely to use the launcher icon to start the app. Most email apps open to a message list, which also has an action link for composing a new email.

When the user wants to send a photo she just took to someone using email, the user will start the app from another app using Android intents. The email app should open in the email compose screen and attach the image automatically.

In all three examples, the app opens from a different screen and from a different place within the app. The app must function logically in each of these cases, and the user must easily be able to navigate within the app. Android apps have multiple entry points.

EXITING AN APP

As explained previously, pressing the Back button in normal cases terminates the active activity. When there are no more activities left in the app's back stack, the app exists. The user will return to the device's home screen. Or, if the app was launched from another app using intents, the user will return to the previous app.

But what is the difference between the Android Home button and pressing Back on the last activity? To users the functionality looks exactly the same and they won't be able to tell the difference. What is happening under the hood is vastly different, though. The Back button terminates the app, but the Home button leaves it running.

As the users won't be able to tell the difference, you must make sure that they don't have to. An app must save all the data and be able to continue where the user left off.

MAKING SURE THAT USERS KNOW WHERE THEY ARE

The user must always know where they are in the app screen hierarchy by glancing to the screen. You must not require users to remember how they navigated to the screen to know where they are. Each screen should have clear labeling or other methods helping users to remember. Users won't always remember what they did last time they were using the app.

NAVIGATING TO ANOTHER APP

A well designed app takes advantage of services provided by other apps by using intents to call functionality from them (see the previous chapter). If you simply trigger an intent to, for example, view a web page, the browser activity is placed on your app's activity stack. This will be confusing to your users, and multi-tasking won't work the way they are expecting. They won't be able to navigate back to your app in any other way than pressing the Back button in the browser to close it. Or if they leave the app at this point and return to your app using the multi-tasking menu, they will be presented with the browser page.

The solution is to start a new task. Telling the operating system that viewing the web page is a new task will place the browser activity in a different activity stack. Your user can now return to your app with the multi-tasking menu. Then, if they return to the app after viewing the website, they will be presented with the last screen of your app that was visible when the browser was launched.

See the following code example for how to trigger an URL view intent as a new task.

```
Intent browserIntent = new Intent(Intent.ACTION_VIEW,
    Uri.parse("http://twitter.com/lehtimaeki"));
browserIntent.setFlags(Intent.FLAG_ACTIVITY_NEW_TASK);
startActivity(browserIntent);
```

Consider an example. An example app lets users tap a button to open a tweet in a Twitter application. Figure 7-4 shows how I have modified the code and removed the intent flag. After tapping the button and opening the Twitter app, I press the Home button and open the multi-tasking menu. As you can see, there's only one active app. The open app has the name and icon of the example app, but the screen capture is from the Twitter app. Selecting that app would open the Twitter app.

Figure 7-4: An example of multi-tasking menu after opening an app from another app without the new task intent flag.

Source: Android

Figure 7-5 shows how I have fixed the problem by adding the new task flag to the intent and performing the exact same actions. Now you can see that there are two separate apps in the multi-tasking menu. Users won't be confused when they return to the original app.

Figure 7-5: App opened correctly from another app. The two applications are separate.

Source: Android

NAVIGATING FROM NOTIFICATION

If your app uses notifications, you need to make sure that the back stack is correct when the user enters your app by tapping the notification. Even with very simple apps it is easy to get this wrong. Consider for example an app that has only two screens—a list of items and an item details screen. The app notifies the users using the Android notifications whenever new items are added to the list and the notification will trigger an intent to open the list activity. What happens when the user taps the notification? Every time a new list activity is created, the old one is placed in the back stack.

To users this will seem right until they press Back and end up in the same activity as before. It is possible to create a situation whereby you have many of the same activities in the back stack, causing users to have to press Back multiple times to exit the app.

For notifications, it usually makes sense to use the FLAG_ACTIVITY_CLEAR_TOP intent flag to make sure that the activity is not recreated. This also takes care of situations where users have the item detail page open, as in the previous example, and then tap the notification. The operating system will activate the list activity from the back stack and close all activities on top of it, including any item details activities. Now the Back button behaves as users expect.

See the following code for an example of creating a notification with the clear top activity flag.

```
Intent notificationIntent = new Intent(this.context, BlogTrackAddictActivity.class);
notificationIntent.setFlags(Intent.FLAG_ACTIVITY_CLEAR_TOP);
PendingIntent contentIntent = PendingIntent.getActivity(this.context,
    NOTIFICATION_ID_GOOGLEPLUS, notificationIntent, 0);
```

NON-ACTIVITY NAVIGATION

Not all on-screen user interactions cause new activities to be created. Probably the best example is the tabbed user interface. All tabs are on the same activity. From the user's point of view, this can cause problems. Using the Back button is an unconscious action for most users. If your app's root activity has a tabbed view, users who tap the Back button because they're trying to return to the previous tab will exit the app instead.

Users are not going to use the Back button to move back in navigation when they use gestures to move between content of same level. There are no easy answers for this conundrum. One way to think about user expectations is that if your navigation is something users can do by accident, they are probably going to use the Back button to remedy their error without thinking about it.

STOPPING RUNNING PROCESSES WITH THE BACK BUTTON

An important special function of the Back button is to terminate ongoing operations. Knowing when the Back button should stop the operation and when it should navigate to the previous screen is important.

The Back button should not terminate the running process when the corresponding user interface component is not the dominant component of the screen. If the process indicator is part of the screen design, the Back button should take the users to the previous screen and leave the process running in the background. Figures 7-6 and 7-7 show examples of processes that should not end when the Back button is pressed.

Figure 7-6: Google Play displays an installation progress bar as a small part of the user interface. Users won't expect the Back button to terminate the progress, but to navigate to the previous page instead.

Source: Google Inc.

Figure 7-7: The Twitter feeds process indicator in the Twitter app is just a small part of the screen and should therefore not be terminated by the Back button.

Source: Twitter

When the process indicator dominates the user interface, users will expect the Back button to end the process. Especially when there's a pop-up dialog box indicating the running process, the Back button should dismiss the pop-up and end the process. Figure 7-8 shows an example of a pop-up dialog box progress indicator.

Figure 7-8: A pop-up progress indicator is used to log in to the Twitter app. The Back button should terminate the process and dismiss the pop-up window.

A bit more on the fine line are progress indicators that are on the screen but are a dominating feature of the screen. This can be a confusing situation to users and should be carefully considered. The best approach in general is not to end the process and navigate to previous screen. If the process is something that consumes a lot of data or time, you should add a notification that users can use to get back to the screen where they can terminate the process. Figure 7-9 shows an example of a screen that is dominated by the progress indicator. In this case, users are likely to expect the Back button to terminate the process.

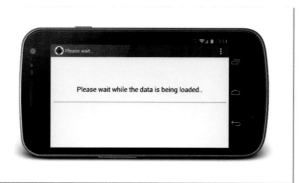

Figure 7-9: An example app downloading a large file. The dominating component on the screen is the progress indicator. Users are likely going to expect the Back button to terminate this process.

USING TRANSITION ANIMATIONS

The Android operating system has a built-in mechanism to enhance users' mental models and make it easier to understand how screens relate to each other. When new activities are launched, they are not simply placed on the screen, but an animation is played. The function of the animation is not just to make the app look and feel nice but also to give subtle clues to users as what is happening. The default transition animation for animations is defined by the system. Different Android versions and different manufacturer phones have different animations. Early Android versions had a simple sliding animation from right to left when a new activity was started and vice versa when Back button was pressed.

Developers can replace the transition animations, but doing so breaks the platform consistency. Even if users don't pay attention to the transition animations they probably associate them unconsciously to navigation actions. They know that if the correct transition animation plays, it is likely that the Back button will take them back to the previous screen.

> *Tip: In Android 4.1 Jelly Bean, the activity transition animations can now be made to easily appear to start from a source view. For example, selecting an app from the multi-tasking menu animates the app in a way that it appears to zoom in from the selected app preview. The same applies to starting apps from shortcuts from the home screen or app launcher. You can utilize this same improvement on your apps when running on Android 4.1 or newer. See the Android documentation for more details at* `http://developer.android.com/reference/android/app/ActivityOptions.html`.

Use animations carefully. Always think about what you want to convey with the animation. Do not add animations just to make the user interface look "cool." Excessive use of animations can make the app perform poorly and consume more battery due to added CPU consumption as well as make it look restless and unnecessarily flashy or even confusing.

SUMMARY

On the simplest level, Android navigation involves starting activities. Although many apps can get by with that level of simplicity, more complex apps need more careful navigation design. You must understand all the different entry points and know how to properly handle communication with other apps. The Android platform provides a lot of tools. When you use these tools correctly, your apps will be easy and intuitive to use.

The Back button forms a core of navigation controls in any Android app, whereas the newer Up button tries to improve the distinction between in-app navigation and navigating between different apps. The complex interaction between activities in one app and externally with other apps can create difficult-to-navigate hierarchies as well as confusion with users. It is important to design the navigation carefully and follow the platform guidelines to make apps behave consistently. Consistent use of navigation controls will make it easier for your users to understand how to reach their goals.

HOME SCREEN APP WIDGETS

APP WIDGETS ARE small apps that can run inside another app, called the *widget host*. Although developers can create widget host apps, the most common use for app widgets is on the home screen.

App widgets on home screens have become one of the key differentiating features of the Android platform, separating it from the other mobile operating systems. App widgets make Android home screens more than just a collection of app icons.

This chapter explains how to make useful and scalable home screen app widgets. It doesn't cover other types of widget hosts, as they are very rarely used.

USES OF HOME SCREEN APP WIDGETS

A typical app widget is usually an extension to an app that provides users with more direct access to the app functionality or information. Users don't have to start the application to interact with the app widgets. These types of widgets are called *companion* widgets. Another type of widgets is the app whose main functionality is the widget itself. These could be, as examples, clocks and settings toggles.

Weather widgets are currently the most popular type of widget. The best example of such a widget is Beautiful Widgets by LevelUp Studio (see Figure 8-1). It also was the first paid app on Android that reached one million downloads. That happened in December of 2011.

Device manufacturers use app widgets heavily on their marketing and branding. The HTC sense clock is an iconic mark of their brand and makes HTC sense user interface instantly recognizable in any HTC marketing material.

The potential for app widgets is huge, but the field where they are useful is pretty narrow. Users do use widgets but only in fairly limited situations. Not all apps benefit from having companion widgets.

Launching an app on Android is simple and most well built apps launch in no time. The decision to build an app widget should be carefully considered, as in many cases it can be just wasted development time that could be used elsewhere.

The following sections look at some features that can make building a widget worthwhile.

DISPLAYING RELEVANT UP-TO-DATE INFORMATION AND BEING CONTEXT AWARE

Some information is so valuable to users that they either look at it multiple times a day or need to have access to it, when needed, as fast as possible. A good example of this kind of app widget is the weather widget described previously and app widgets like Öffi, which is a timetable app. The Öffi app widget (see Figure 8-2) is context aware and always shows public transportation departures from the closest favorite station.

When it comes to displaying data on an app widget, the most important things to remember are the following:

- Be context aware. Display information that is relevant to the user's current location, current time, locale, and so on.
- Think about ways to reduce the amount of information is in the app widget to include only the most relevant bits.
- Make sure that the information is always up to date. If that is not possible due to app widget limitations, an app widget might not be a good idea. You'll read more about app widget limitations later in this chapter.

Figure 8-1: Beautiful Widgets by LevelUp Studio is the best-known widget app on Android.

Source: LevelUp Studio

Figure 8-2: Öffi app widget shows next departures from the closest favorite station.

Source: Öffi.

PROVIDING EASY ACCESS TO SIMPLE FUNCTIONS AND TOGGLE CONTROLS

Some apps have functions that users want to access directly and that don't require the app to be opened in order to be completed. The best example of this kind of app widget is Google Play Music controls widget (see Figure 8-3). Playing, pausing, and skipping songs are functions that users are likely to perform often. Having to open the music player app to pause a song makes the app seem cumbersome. Figure 8-4 shows examples of app widgets that let users toggle device features like WiFi, Bluetooth, and more. These are valuable shortcuts, as opening an app to do the same thing would introduce a lot of overhead.

When it comes to designing these simple-function app widgets, the most important things to remember are the following:

- Functions that can be completed with a single tap and that do not require the app to be opened make good candidates for app widgets.
- Keep the app widget simple and small so users can easily fit it on their home screens.

Figure 8-3: Google Play Music controls app widget provides users with direct access to the basic player controls.

Source: Google Inc.

Figure 8-4: App widget that allow users to toggle functionality like WiFi and Bluetooth, on and off.

Source: Android

PROVIDING SHORTCUTS TO APP FUNCTIONALITY

App widgets can also act as app navigation aides by providing shortcuts to app functionality. Some apps have functions that users use more often than others, and so it can be a good idea to provide users with direct access to that functionality. A good example of this is an email app, whereby the compose email functionality becomes an app widget. Due to the app widget limitations composing emails inside an app widget is impossible. Users must open the app to do that. The Gmail app widget has a list of emails and also a button that opens up the message compose screen directly. The saves users time by allowing them to navigate directly to the desired functionality without first having to open the app and then tap the compose email link (see Figure 8-5).

Figure 8-5: The Gmail app widget provides a shortcut to the compose email functionality.

Source: Google Inc.

DEVELOPING APP WIDGETS FOR TABLETS

Many home screen widgets that aren't useful on a small smartphone display can be very useful on a larger tablet screen. A tablet display allows much more room for app widgets, and you can use the larger size to display richer information. Figure 8-6 shows a few examples of widgets that work very well on a large tablet display.

Figure 8-6: The Android calendar and the Google RSS reader are examples of widgets that work very well on a large tablet screen.
Source: Google Inc.

UPDATING APP WIDGET DATA

In many cases the app widget shows some current data like weather, latest news, and so on. Information like that is not very helpful unless it's up to date. As with everything on a mobile device, you need to consider battery life impact with every action. Anything that is on the home screen has an especially high risk of impacting the battery life, as it is potentially visible all the time.

On runtime, Android app widgets are technically part of the home screen process and not your app's process. This has some implications as to the way the app widgets can interact with the rest of your app. The normal memory management of the operating system does not apply to the app widgets, as they are not part of your app and cannot be stopped if resources are running low. That is why the operating system limits the updates any app widget can do and the way they can trigger user interface updates.

AUTOMATED UPDATES

A home screen app widget can initialize an update only every 30 minutes or more. This limitation is set to limit the amount of battery drain caused by the home screen widgets. You can define the update interval in your app widget configuration file. Any value less than 30 minutes (180,000 in milliseconds) is converted to 30 minutes.

There are ways to get around this restriction, but it's not a good idea to do so. In addition to the battery drain concern, badly implemented app widgets can cause the device's home screen to become unresponsive.

> *Tip: Update your widgets more frequently only if they are useless without the update. For example, an email widget reacting to new email would need frequent updating.*

When the app widget triggers the update, a broadcast intent is sent that your app can react to. You can then update any of the user interface widgets on your app widget.

UPDATING UPON USER INTERACTION

Due to the automatic update limitation, many widgets offer a manual Refresh button to its users. You can always react to user's interaction and call updates to your widget regardless of the automated time interval.

Updates triggered by clicking a button on your app widget are handled through the Android intent system. Your app provider will receive an intent asking you to update the widget. The best way to handle it is to start a service to do the work. Note that the service must complete its task within five seconds or the operating system deems it to be too slow and it might be killed off by the system.

Note that the user interaction is sent to your app but it is not always immediate. There can be a short delay between the user interaction and your app receiving the intent. In normal circumstances, the delay should not be noticeable.

DESIGNING SETUP ACTIVITY

With some apps it is not clear what data users want to have in the app widget. Fortunately there's a ready mechanism you can use to let users define that data when the app widget is added to a home screen. A good example of this is adding the Gmail app widget to a home screen. The Gmail app launches an activity and asks the user which label he wants to have in the app widget (see Figure 8-7).

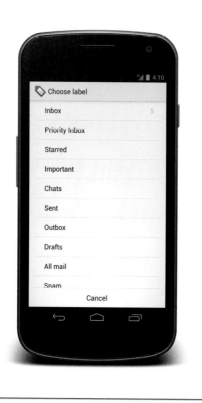

Figure 8-7: The Gmail app widget setup activity asks the user which label to include in the app widget.

Source: Google Inc.

APP WIDGET LAYOUT AND FUNCTIONALITY

So what can the app widget actually do? As mentioned, the app widget's functionality is more limited than an app. Due to the limited tools it is even more important to use the tools correctly.

USER INTERACTION WITH APP WIDGETS

Most of the rich gesture support and interactions are not available with app widgets. Users cannot do more than scroll scrollable containers and tap buttons. That is all. No swiping, pinching, or long pressing. As a developer, the only thing you can react to is a user tapping on a view (most of the time a button).

UNDERSTANDING THE HOME SCREEN GRID

Android home screens are grids. Your app widget will occupy a number of grids instead of any number of pixels, unlike layouts in your app. Even though you define the minimum width and height in pixels (density independent pixels), the home screen lays out your app widget into the grid and uses the grid sizes.

Most smartphones give app widgets a grid of 4×4 and tablets can go as high as 8×7 (a 10-inch range tablet) or even higher for a larger tablet. Users will be aware of this grid. When moving or resizing app widgets, users will be shown a help grid like the one in Figure 8-8.

Figure 8-8: When moving an app widget on Android 4.0, the user is shown a shadow grid to help position the app widget.

Source: Android

DEFINING YOUR APP WIDGET'S MINIMUM SIZE

Take time to figure out what the best minimum size of your app widget is. The minimum width and height you set defines what size your app widget will default to when added to a home screen. Too small size make it unusable and too large will take too much room on the home screen. So be considerate and don't take more space than you actually need!

There is an easy formula to calculate the space you have per grid cell. Available size for your app widget is always $70 \times n - 30$ density independent pixels (dp), where n is the number of cells. The same formula applies to height and width, as the grid cells are square. For example, a 1×1 cell app widget is going to have 40dp × 40dp of available space. A 2×2 cell app widget will have 110dp × 110dp of available space, and so on.

Note that app widgets are resizable only in Android 3.1 and newer. In older versions, your app widget will be the minimum size and users can't change it.

AVAILABLE LAYOUTS AND COMPONENTS

You only have a limited set of layouts and components you can use to implement app widgets. Figure 8-9 gives you a good overview of what kind of app widgets are possible to build with the limited tools. The layouts are introduced in detail in Chapter 13 and the components are discussed in Chapter 11.

The available layouts are:

- FrameLayout
- GridLayout (only Android 4.1+)
- LinearLayout
- RelativeLayout

Dealing with Margins

The way margins are handled changed in Android 4.0. The operating system automatically adds a small margin to app widgets from apps that target the Android 4.0. You should not manually add any margins to your layouts. For older Android versions, you should include margins.

Due to the difference in the way margins are handled, you should provide two different layout files. You can use include tags to make sure that you don't duplicate the actual layout code.

I'll talk a lot about how to provide different layouts for different versions later in this book as well as using the include tags in layouts.

You can use following components:

- AnalogClock
- Button
- Chronometer
- ImageButton
- ImageView
- ProgressBar
- TextView
- GridView (only Android 3.0+)
- ListView (only Android 3.0+)
- StackView (only Android 3.0+)
- ViewFlipper (only Android 3.0+)
- ViewStub (only Android 4.1+)
- AdapterViewFlipper (only Android 3.0+)

Figure 8-9: Examples of very different looking widgets. The widgets are Books on Google Play, Calendar, Power control, and Bookmarks.

Source: Google Inc.

Tip: Google has made a template set available online that contains graphics you can utilize when building your app widget. You can download all the graphics from the Android developer website at: `http://developer.android.com/guide/ practices/ui_guidelines/widget_design.html#templates.`

RESIZABLE WIDGETS

The Android release for tablets 3.0 Honeycomb brought with it richer app widget functionality. As you already saw in the component list, the new version added new components to the mix.

The new version also allowed users to resize the widgets. In order to enable the resize feature, you simply have to add the `resizeMode` attribute to the XML configuration file. You can make the app widgets resizable only horizontally, only vertically, or both. Consider which ones make sense in your case. In some cases, making the app widget resizable doesn't make sense.

APP WIDGET PREVIEW

On Android 3.0 or newer, the user is presented with a preview of the app widget in the app widget list. Having a good-looking app widget preview is important. You want your app widget to look tempting and be noticed. Figure 8-10 shows how the app widget previews are shown to the users. You can also see how an app widget without a preview image is shown. If you don't provide a preview, the operating system will use your app icon. In Figure 8-10, the app widget in the bottom-left corner doesn't have a preview.

Figure 8-10: App widget preview view on Android 4.1.

Source: Android

To add an app widget preview picture, you add the `previewImage` attribute to your app widget configuration XML.

The preview image should be a representative picture of how the app widget will look once it is added to the home screen.

IMPLEMENTING AN APP WIDGET

To make everything more concrete, let's look at an example of the different components that must be created to include an app widget in your app.

To create an app widget, you need to provide your app configuration file, add the required broadcast receivers to your app's manifest file, create an app widget provider implementation, and create the actual layout of the app widget.

CONFIGURATION XML

The app widget configuration XML defines many of the features discussed in this chapter. It adds a preview image, sets the minimum width and height, and points to the initial layout file that is used to create the app widget user interface. You must place this file in the `res/xml/` project folder.

```xml
<?xml version="1.0" encoding="utf-8"?>
<appwidget-provider
        xmlns:android="http://schemas.android.com/apk/res/android"
    android:initialLayout="@layout/example_app_widget_layout"
    android:minHeight="70dp"
    android:minWidth="70dp"
    android:updatePeriodMillis="300000"
    android:previewImage="@drawable/example_preview"
    android:resizeMode="horizontal|vertical">
</appwidget-provider>
```

APP WIDGET LAYOUT

Your app widget's layout is handled the same as any other layout. You can only use user interface components and layouts that are allowed in app widgets. These layouts and components were listed earlier in this chapter.

```xml
<?xml version="1.0" encoding="utf-8"?>
<LinearLayout xmlns:android="http://schemas.android.com/apk/res/android"
    android:id="@+id/layout"
    android:layout_width="match_parent"
    android:layout_height="match_parent"
    android:background="@drawable/example_app_widget_shape" >

    <TextView
        android:id="@+id/update"
```

```
            style="@android:style/TextAppearance.Medium"
            android:layout_width="match_parent"
            android:layout_height="match_parent"
            android:layout_gravity="center"
            android:gravity="center_horizontal|center_vertical"
            android:layout_margin="4dip"
            android:text="Some Text" >
    </TextView>


</LinearLayout>
```

APP MANIFEST FILE

You must also add a broadcast receiver definition to your app's manifest file. The broadcast receiver needs to register to listen for android.appwidget.action.APPWIDGET_ UPDATE broadcasts.

```
<receiver android:name=".appwidget.ExampleAppWidgetProvider" >
    <intent-filter>
        <action android:name="android.appwidget.action.APPWIDGET_UPDATE" />
    </intent-filter>

    <meta-data
        android:name="android.appwidget.provider"
        android:resource="@xml/example_widget_info" />
</receiver>
```

APP WIDGET PROVIDER

The app widget provider is the implementation of your app widget's logic and functionality. This is the place where you must write code to fill in the actual data to your app widget's user interface.

```
public class ExampleAppWidgetProvider extends AppWidgetProvider {

    @Override
    public void onUpdate(Context context, AppWidgetManager appWidgetManager,
            int[] appWidgetIds) {

        // update widget here
        RemoteViews remoteViews = new RemoteViews(context.getPackageName(),
          R.layout.example_app_widget_layout);
        // Set the text
      remoteViews.setTextViewText(R.id.update,
        String.valueOf(System.currentTimeMillis()));
    }
}
```

SUMMARY

Adding an app widget is a good way to make your app more appealing to users. If your app has a great app widget that the users add to their home screen, they will see it every day. You can use app widgets to retain user interest and make your users to come back to your app.

App widgets aren't for every app, though. In fact, most apps don't benefit from having one. Consider carefully if an app widget brings any benefits to your users. If not, you're probably better off spending your efforts on something else.

The app widget functionality is very limited and they cannot be updated automatically more often than every 30 minutes. You can also only use a very limited set of user interface tools to build your app widget. For these reasons, be sure an app widget fits what you are trying to do and meets the user's expectations before you waste your time building one.

CHAPTER

NOTIFYING AND INFORMING USERS

SOMETIMES THE USER'S ATTENTION needs to be directed away from the task she's currently occupied with. Different situations need different notification methods. Few things demand user's attention immediately and most can be brought to the user's attention more subtlety.

This chapter covers notifications in a wider sense. It covers more than just the Android status bar notifications, which are the most common

association people make when talking about Android notifications. Android SDK provides developers with multiple ways to notify and inform users.

All notifications are interruptive by nature. Using the right kind of notification method in the right circumstance is important for creating a good user experience. This chapter explains when notifications should be used and which method is best in which situation.

ANDROID NOTIFICATION METHODS

Let's first take a look at what kind of notification methods Android offers. Each of the methods is suited for a different situation. Some of them are more interruptive than others and must therefore be used more carefully. On the other hand, the less interruptive notifications go unnoticed more easily and, therefore, aren't a great choice for important notifications.

The following sections cover these techniques in order from the least interruptive to the most interruptive.

INLINE/EMBEDDED NOTIFICATIONS

Inline or embedded notifications include information about tasks and events and are shown as part of the user interface. This kind of notification doesn't interrupt the users, but also goes unnoticed very easily. Evernote's notification messages, which appear at the bottom of its landing screen, are a good example of an embedded message. See Figure 9-1.

In general, use these kinds of notifications to indicate something that adds value to the user's experience but isn't something that users have to worry about or react to.

TOASTS

A *toast* is a simple text message that appears on-screen for a short time and then disappears automatically. Users cannot interact with toasts.

Toasts are rendered on top of the user interface, so they are likely to draw the user's attention. Therefore they are slightly more interruptive than inline notifications. Because the toasts get dismissed automatically, they are unlikely to irritate users if used moderately. They can also be easily missed by users who are distracted. Therefore toasts cannot be used to indicate anything that is important enough not to be missed. You would not want to use toasts to notify users about new emails, for example.

A very good use for toasts is to confirm operations and operation success. For example, the Gmail client shows a toast message when a message the user has composed is being sent (see Figure 9-2). If the user misses this message, it's not a big deal. The toast also does not prevent or delay the user from moving to a new task.

STATUS BAR NOTIFICATIONS

Whenever Android notifications are mentioned they generally refer to Android status bar notifications. Status bar notifications are subtle but informative. They also have a very low risk of being unnoticed by users. Also Android APIs provide developers very easy ways to implement them.

Figure 9-1: Evernote uses very subtle notifications on the bottom of the application's side navigation.

Source: Evernote Corporation

Figure 9-2: A toast message notifies the user about a task that is being performed and was triggered by user (in this case, the message is being sent).

Source: Android

By far the biggest problem plaguing Android applications related to status bar notifications is overuse. Consider the following criteria before creating a status bar notification. Each notification should fill all of these criteria.

- There is a single screen where the tapping the notification will naturally take the user, or tapping the notification directly terminates the ongoing task.
- The user can do something about the information and react to it.
- The user needs or wants that information. I mean the user! It is not enough for you to want the user to see it.

Tip: A good example of a status bar notification is a new email notification. Users are likely going to react to a new email or at least want to be informed about it. A bad status bar notification would be a notification about a background task, such as an email being sent successfully.

POP-UP DIALOG BOXES

There are very few situations when pop-up windows are justified. A pop-up always interrupts the user's task and thought process. They are likely to irritate users and make the app feel cumbersome.

Use a pop-up dialog box to alert users about something critical that simply cannot be ignored. A good example of a justified pop-up is the Android system pop-up telling the user that the device battery is nearly empty (see Figure 9-3).

Figure 9-3: The Android system battery low window is an example of justified pop-up usage.

Source: Android

WHEN TO NOTIFY USERS

Users don't need to know everything that's going on in the system. Never bother users if you don't absolutely have to. Unnecessary notifications will only irritate your users and make your app look bad.

The following sections take a look at few situations where a notification is needed and justified.

ONGOING BACKGROUND TASKS

When your app is doing something in the background that consumes a lot of resources or uses a network connection, you should let the users know that is going on. This doesn't apply to short network usages like checking if a server has updates or sending short burst of information over the network. This applies to downloading large data files or maintaining a continuous connection to a server, for example during an IP phone call.

Using status bar notifications in these cases is the right choice. If you can estimate how long the process will take, you should use a progress bar to give users a better understanding as to what is going on and how long they can expect the task to continue. The progress bar also gives the users an idea as to how fast the task is going. Google Play uses the on-screen progress indicator (see Figure 9-4) and the status bar notification (see Figure 9-5) when users are installing an app. The on-screen notification allows users to cancel the process. The status bar notification, if tapped, takes the users to the app installation page where they can cancel the process.

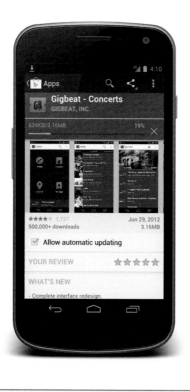

Figure 9-4: Google Play uses on-screen notifications when installing apps.

Source: Google Inc.

Figure 9-5: In addition to the on-screen progress bar, Google Play uses a status bar notification so users know that a background operation is running even if they leave the Google Play app.

Source: Google Inc.

It is very important that users feel like they are in control of everything that is happening on their phones. This is especially important with background tasks.

EVENTS

Updates can be sent to users via event notifications. These kinds of events might be a new email, an incoming message, a calendar event notification, and even a completed background task. These are by far the most common cases for using event notifications.

Figure 9-6 demonstrates three event notifications. Each one takes the user directly to the logical app and screen if tapped. The screenshot notification opens the Android gallery, allowing the user to view and share the image very easily. The notification opens the email app directly from the email, which is being previewed in the notification. The Google Play notification opens the newly installed app. Note that the Google Play notification actually opens a different app that has triggered the notification. Nothing prevents you from doing that if it makes sense.

Figure 9-6: Three event notifications using status bar notifications.

Source: Android

Tip: Do not use status bar notifications if the event is happening on the screen the user is currently viewing. Use user interface components, and embedded notifications to keep the information in context.

ERRORS

When an app encounters an error that it cannot correct automatically, it must usually be brought to the user's attention. Depending on how critical the error is and if it happens on a foreground or on a background task, the means of notification can be very different.

A good error notification should always do the following:

- Try to fix itself automatically without notifying the user. Only after you have tried this first should you show an error!
- Explain what happened, concisely and using laymen's terms. Avoid long explanations and technical terms.
- Provide the user a direct and simple way to react and fix the problem.
- Stay out of the way.
- Be displayed in the context where the error happened.

Errors in Foreground Tasks

When there's an error in the foreground task, the one the user is trying to perform, it usually stops the workflow. These errors also have the biggest probability to irritate the users. When users are already dealing with an error, you should make sure that the user interface that displays the error is as helpful as possible.

Consider an example of a common error-handling situation, an app login. Many apps require users to log in to the app system in order to fully benefit from the app. A user is normally provided a login screen with two text fields—a username and password.

If the user types in the wrong password or username, the app will fail to log the user in. There isn't much the app can do to automatically recover from the problem, so an error notification is needed.

What is the best notification method to use in this case? A status bar notification would not make sense as the error happens in the foreground task. You have to select among a pop-up window, a toast, and an inline notification. Compare the following three screenshots. Figure 9-7 shows an example of an app using a pop-up window; Figure 9-8 shows an example of a toast; and Figure 9-9 shows an example of using an inline message.

Figure 9-7: An app using a pop-up window to tell the user that the password is wrong.

Source: Evernote Corporation

Figure 9-8: An app that uses a toast to tell the user that the password is wrong.

Source: Twitter

A short analysis of the three options clearly points to the inline error notification. Its benefits are many. It is displayed right in the context, users cannot miss it, and it does not prevent users from continuing. The same approach applies to many problems. The pop-up will always prevent the user from trying again directly. The toast is too subtle and can be missed easily by the user, especially when you consider the hectic environments in which many people use their phones.

Make sure your errors stay out of the way, and don't prevent users from trying to solve the issue.

Figure 9-9: An example app that uses an inline message to tell the user that the password is wrong.

Errors in Background Tasks

When something goes wrong with an automated background task, you must use more subtle ways to notify the user. A failing background task rarely needs the user's attention right away. Figure 9-10 shows an example of an app using a subtle embedded notification to tell the user that a background task, syncing in this case, did not work due to a connection problem. A failure in the sync process does not prevent users from using the app, so there's no reason to make the notification more obtrusive. The same thing applies if your app is loading new information like emails, tweets, or news stories. Let the users continue to use the app without interrupting them.

Figure 9-10: Evernote uses an embedded notification to tell the user that background sync did not work.

Source: Evernote Corporation

Sometimes there is an error in a background task that the user started. This could be, for example, when installing an app to the device. Because the user started the task and the error is preventing the task from being completed, this error needs to be brought to the user's attention. Creating a status bar notification is the best option. Make sure that tapping the notification takes the user directly to the screen where the user can do something about it or at least see more information about the problem.

WHEN NOT TO NOTIFY USERS

As mentioned, users don't have to and don't want to know everything that is going on in their phone. Apps launch processes and check data on servers all the time. You can use an embedded notification in the form of an animated progress bar or something similar to tell the user that the current app is doing something. You should never use a status bar notification to simply point out that your app is checking for new messages or something similar.

Many apps download data in the background. Not all of the data, like social network messages, are directly aimed at the user. Think carefully when using notification in cases like that. Flooding users with notifications is probably going to annoy them and likely lead to a bad review and users uninstalling your app.

Note that giving a user an option to disable notifications is not an excuse to overuse them. Your default notifications settings must be good. You can give users options to add more notifications through the app settings, but pick a conservative default to begin with.

AVOIDING POP-UPS

There is a good reason why most desktop Internet browsers ship with pop-up blockers enabled by default. At some point the Internet was overwhelmed with unnecessary pop-up windows. Many users still associate pop-up windows with bad Internet websites. You don't want your app to be one of them!

Here are some things you should never use pop-up windows for:

- Ask users to rate your app. A much better alternative is to use embedded notifications to do this.
- Advertise anything.
- Ask users to subscribe to additional services or mailing lists.
- Notify users about a completion, progress, or failure of a task that is not in the foreground.

As a rule of thumb, never use pop-ups. Break this rule only when you're sure that the pop-up is the only possible way to notify your users. Only when the app is simply unable to continue without user input should a pop-up be used. You might think that having to press the OK button is just one tap and it should not matter, but it does. Figures 9-11 and 9-12 show two examples of apps handling the same error, a loss of network connection. The first app uses a pop-up, which forces users to stop and press the button. The second app simply replaces the content with the error message. The second app is much more fluent and pleasant to use.

You might be tempted to think that using pop-ups is okay if you time the pop-up trigger to open the pop-up between user tasks. Although on paper it appears as if user tasks have natural points where users seem idle and not concentrating on anything, in practice this is not usually true. Users are likely already occupied by the next task, and a pop-up will interrupt them.

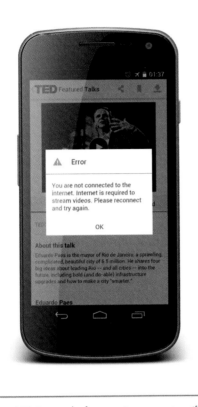

Figure 9-11: An example of an app using a pop-up to notify the user about a connection problem.

Source: TED Conferences

Figure 9-12: An example of an app that avoids using pop-ups by embedding the message about connection problems in the UI. This makes the user experience more fluent.

Source: TED Conferences

GETTING THE MOST FROM STATUS BAR NOTIFICATIONS

As mentioned, status bar notifications are very useful in many situations. The Android notification system is also very flexible and easy to use for both developers and users. This section looks into using the status bar notifications and related design guidelines. Using the status bar notifications correctly will make your app that much better.

The Android Design guidelines have a lot more information about status bar notifications at: `http://developer.android.com/design/patterns/notifications.html`. Note that in the design guidelines when they refer to notifications, they generally mean only status bar notifications.

NOTIFICATION CONTENT

A status bar notification is composed of multiple parts. Note that not all of these are available in older Android versions.

The status bar notification icon is the most important part of the notification. Once the operating system has rotated the text, users can see the icon only until they pull the notification bar down (see Figure 9-13, F).

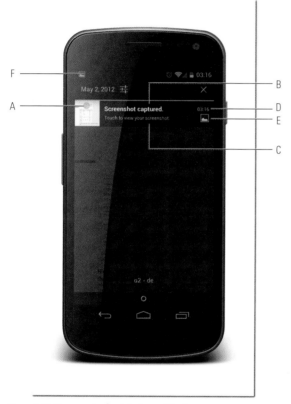

Figure 9-13: Components of a status bar notification.

Source: Android

Pulling down the notification bar expands the status bar and displays more information about the notifications. Table 9-1 describes the components outlined in Figure 9-13.

Table 9-1   Notification components shown in Figure 9-13.

Symbol	Description
A	Large icon or image. If this is not provided, the operating system will use the notification icon.
B	Notification title. This should be short but descriptive.
C	Notification text. This describes what the notification is about in more detail or tells users what actions they can take.
D	Notification timestamp. The time of the event.
E	Notification secondary icon. This is the same icon used on the status bar. If no large icon or image is provided, this area will be empty.
F	Status bar notification icon.

The notification bar icons are covered in more detail in Chapter 11 with rest of the platform icons.

STACKING NOTIFICATIONS

Events often occur multiple times before the user reacts to them. For example, maybe the user receives multiple emails, or maybe there are multiple instant messages. You have two options to handle situations like this. Either you create a new notification, or amend the one that is already visible. The right method depends on the situation. When the notifications are very similar in nature and come from the same source—for example multiple instant messages from the same person—stacking them into a single notification makes sense. But when the user receives emails from different accounts, it probably makes sense to create a separate notification for each account.

For stacked notifications, you can add a number that indicates the number of notifications pending next to the secondary notification icon.

BE TIMELY

Events happen at certain times. Remember to track the time correctly. The timestamp on your notification can tell the user a lot about the notification if it is correct. If you, for example, poll a server for new information every hour and notice new messages, you should use the time information in the messages to set the notification timestamp. The information as to when the message was received is more valuable to the users than when your app decided to poll the server.

In some cases notifications are meaningful only for a limited period of time. You should consider if your app's notifications are like that. If it is clear that a notification is no longer useful to your users, consider removing it automatically.

ONGOING TASKS

There is a special notification type for ongoing tasks like music playing, background downloads or other ongoing background tasks, and so on. If you set the ongoing flag on your notification, it cannot be removed from the status bar. Even when a user clears all notifications, all the ongoing notifications will remain.

For any ongoing notifications, make sure that you provide an easy way for users to terminate the operations. Also remember to handle all errors correctly. Few things are more annoying to users than ongoing notifications that are left behind due to an error in the process.

To cancel an ongoing notification, you can either open a page where the user can cancel it or you can cancel the task directly when the user taps the notification. In the later case, you must add text informing users about that. Add something like "tap to cancel download" as the notification text.

IMPLEMENTING STATUS BAR NOTIFICATIONS

To create a status bar notification, you use a `NotificationManager` class. You get an instance of the class from a context object with the following call.

```
(NotificationManager) context.getSystemService(Context.NOTIFICATION_SERVICE);
```

To create the notification itself, you create a new notification object and set the parameters and flags you need. Note in Android 3.0 or newer that you can use a helper class `Notification.Builder` to create the notification.

```
Notification notification = new Notification(icon, tickerText, when);

notification.setLatestEventInfo(context, title, text, pendingIntent);
notification.flags |= Notification.FLAG_AUTO_CANCEL;
notificationManager.notify(NOTIFICATION_ID, notification);
```

To make the example an ongoing notification, you simply add an ongoing flag to the notification, as the following line of code demonstrates.

```
notification.flags |= Notification.FLAG_ONGOING_EVENT
```

For the full specification, see the Android developer documentation at `http://developer.android.com/reference/android/app/Notification.html` and `http://developer.android.com/reference/android/app/Notification.Builder.html`.

What actually happens when a user taps the notification? Well, the notifications are integrated into the rest of the system using the Android intent system. When you create a notification, you give the operating system a pending intent that is triggered when the user taps your notification. As discussed in Chapter 6, the intent mechanism is very powerful and flexible. You can use what you've learned about intents when building your notifications.

The pending intent is given as a parameter to the notification (see the previous code snippet). To create the pending intent, you first create the intent you want to be triggered and wrap it into a `PendingIntent` object. You can use everything you've learned about intents here. All flags and so on are available to you.

```
Intent notificationIntent = new Intent(this.context,TargetActivityActivity.class);
notificationIntent.setFlags(Intent.FLAG_ACTIVITY_CLEAR_TOP);
PendingIntent pendingIntent = PendingIntent.getActivity(this.context,
    NOTIFICATION_ID, notificationIntent, 0);
```

Status Bar Notifications in Android 4.1 Jelly Bean

One of the best features of Android 4.1 Jelly Bean is its much improved notification system. The new notification system allows developers to build much richer notifications that can contain graphics and action buttons for users to perform actions lime posting a Google+ post directly from the notification. Figure 9-14 shows two examples of the new notifications on Android 4.1.

Figure 9-14: Two examples of the Android 4.1 notifications.

Source: Android

To create these new notifications, you can utilize a helper class called `Notification.Builder`. You can easily build notification with larger images, more text, as well as new inbox style notifications. You can find the full definition of all of the new notification types from the Android online documentation at `http://developer.android.com/reference/android/app/Notification.BigPictureStyle.html`, `http://developer.android.com/reference/android/app/Notification.BigTextStyle.html`, and `http://developer.android.com/reference/android/app/Notification.InboxStyle.html`.

The following example shows how to use the `Notification.Builder` helper class to build the second notification in the Figure 9-14:

```
Notification.Builder builder = new Notification.Builder(this)
        .setContentTitle("Inbox Style")
        .setContentText("This is a inbox Style notification")
        .setSmallIcon(R.drawable.ic_launcher)
        .addAction(android.R.drawable.ic_dialog_dialer, "first action",
                pendingIntentFirst)
        .addAction(android.R.drawable.ic_delete, "second action",
                pendingIntentSecond);

Notification notification = new Notification.InboxStyle(builder)
        .addLine("First message").addLine("Second message")
        .addLine("Thrid message").setSummaryText("+5 more messages")
        .build();
```

Scan the QR code with your Android phone to open the companion app and try out a functional example.

Notification Priority

Android 4.1 also added notification priorities. This is a welcome change as it allows developers to define how important each notification is. There are five notification priority levels. They are defined as constants in the `Notification` class (see `http://developer.android.com/reference/android/app/Notification.html`).

The notification priority affects the way the operating system shows each notification. Low-priority notifications might be shown only when a user opens the notification tray. High-priority notifications might be shown more often expanded.

> *Tip: When defining your app's notification priorities, be conservative. Use the lowest priority that is appropriate. That way your app will feel like it knows how to behave. Setting all notifications to the maximum priority will likely only annoy your users.*

Backward Compatibility of Notifications

The new notifications will not be back-ported to the older operating system versions. Notifications are such an integral part of the system that they cannot be changed without updating the whole system. This doesn't mean that you should not use the new notifications in your apps. You should! You just need to make sure that doing so won't break the compatibility with older Android versions.

Google has hinted that the new notification builder helper will be added to the support package, and developers can use it to build notifications. They are automatically adapted to the runtime Android version. At the time of this writing, Google has not yet made this addition. There are, however, community-maintained projects that have the same functionality. One of them is Jake Wharton's NotificationCompat2 project. You can find it from github at `https://github.com/JakeWharton/NotificationCompat2`.

SUMMARY

Informing users is a delicate task. Picking the wrong mechanism to inform them can lead to compromised usability. You must carefully consider which method you should use in each case. Your notifications should be as discrete as possible, but also noticeable. Different types of events require different methods. Correctly selecting among inline notifications, toasts, pop-ups, and status bar notifications is important.

The Android status bar notification system is a very powerful tool in your toolbox. Status bar notification can be used in many different cases. Be careful not to overuse these notifications, though. Overuse can annoy the users and your app can seem to behave arrogantly.

DESIGNING FOR HARDWARE BUTTONS, INPUT METHODS, AND SENSORS

THE WAYS USERS control their Android devices are many. Hundreds of different Android devices ship with different hardware configurations. Android devices in different categories are used in different ways. The way users use their Android smartphones and tablets is very different from the way they use their Android-powered TVs.

The differences don't stop there. Nearly all Android devices can connect into external devices that add more control and input mechanisms. Different keyboards, mice, trackpads, and other devices add even more variety to the controller selection of Android.

However, don't fret. Not every app needs to build support for every control mechanism out there. The typical app doesn't benefit from most of them. Many of them are also supported pretty much automatically and are transparent to the apps. It is, however, good to know about these devices and understand the opportunities they provide.

DESIGNING FOR THE TOUCH SCREEN

All Android phones and tablets have touch screens as their primary control mechanism. There are two different prominent touch screen technologies that are being used in devices right now—capacitive touch screens and resistive touch screens. The difference is in the technology but this also has implications for users.

Most of this book concentrates on the touch screen part of the user interface and how to work with the touch screen in the right way. This section covers the different types of touch screens technologies and explains how they affect the way users interact with their devices.

RESISTIVE TOUCH SCREENS

Resistive touch screens require users to physically press the screen to make it react. Resistive touch screen technology is older and cheaper than the capacitive one. These kinds of screens are generally going away and are seen only on cheaper and older devices. However, there is still a notable selection of very low-end Android tablets that are built with resistive screens.

From the user interface point of view, the resistive touch screen has two notable effects. For one, performing gestures can be more difficult. For example, performing a *bezel swipe* (a swipe gesture starting from outside the screen) is practically impossible, and relying on that gesture as the only way to navigate is inherently a bad idea.

Resistive touch screens also don't support any multi-touch features. Users with these devices must rely on single touch. It is good to remember that these older kind of devices are out there. Always build an alternative way to achieve what multi-touch gestures do.

CAPACITIVE TOUCH SCREENS

Capacitive touch screens are the newer generation technology and now the prominent one. Capacitive screens do not require any pressure to register touch events. The lightest contact is enough. This technology also allows for multi-touch gestures. Many newer capacitive touch screens recognize as many as 10 different touch points simultaneously. Although more than two finger gestures are rarely used or useful, some specialist apps might benefit from this enhanced touch-recognition technology.

THE FUTURE OF TOUCH SCREENS

As touch screens are becoming more prominent in user devices, more and more technology companies are investing in research in this field. You are likely going to see new innovation in the touch screen technology in the near future.

Two branches of screen technology research that have already popped up in concept forms are flexible displays and touch screens that don't require touching. Flexible displays are going to change the design of the phone hardware by releasing the phone manufacturers from the flat surface constraint. Companies will likely introduce devices with screens that change size and can be moved around while using.

Some manufacturers have prototyped touch screens that detect the user's finger before it touches the screen. This technology will bring a whole new interaction to touch screen devices, albeit one that people have been using for years on other devices—the mouse hover gesture. Suddenly users will be able to hover over a user interface control and get more information about it without having to click.

Both of these features are still some time away from the mass market, but they're coming. It is good to keep your eyes open and follow what new innovation the OEMs are bringing to the technology.

DESIGNING PHONE HARDWARE BUTTONS

Until recently all Android phones were required to have at least three hardware buttons. All phones shipped with Menu, Home, and Back buttons. Some phones also had a hardware Search button, but that was an optional choice left to the hardware manufacturers.

The requirement for hardware buttons was lifted when Android 3.0 Honeycomb was released. The hardware buttons became optional and were usually replaced by software buttons.

There are still millions of older devices in use and will be for many years. This is a legacy burden for designers and developers alike. Users with old devices must still be able to fully utilize their device capabilities.

THE MENU BUTTON IS DEAD

One of the hardware buttons, the Menu button, was a user interface design blunder. Although having a Menu button was sometimes convenient, there was no way for users to tell if an app had a Menu button or not without first trying it. It took some time for Google to fix this design problem, but they finally did so. Menus can now be considered deprecated and should not be used the same way anymore.

The menu system has been replaced by the Action Bar design pattern (the Action Bar design pattern is introduced in detail in Chapter 18). Although use of the old menu structure is discouraged it is still part of the operating system as a fall-back mechanism for apps that have not been updated to the new system. Figure 10-1 shows how the old menu looks on a newer device.

Figure 10-1: An app using the deprecated menu system. The three dots in the bottom bar indicate availability of the old menu to the users.

Source: Twitter

DESIGNING FOR THE ON-SCREEN KEYBOARD

The Android operating system ships with a powerful on-screen keyboard. Although the exact keyboard layout differs among Android versions, different manufacturer skins, and different device sizes, the principles are the same. A portion of the screen is dedicated to the on-screen keyboard when it is needed.

The on-screen keyboard is rendered by the software and, therefore, very flexible. Developers and designers can help users by utilizing the Android keyboard correctly. The following sections discuss a few of the most important keyboard features of the Android platform.

INPUT METHODS

You can define the way on-screen keyboard affects the user interface layout and whether or not the keyboard is visible automatically. These are called *soft input modes*. They are defined per activity by adding the `SoftInputMode` attribute to the activity's definition in the Android app manifest file.

```
<activity
    android:name=".keyboard.InputModeResizeActivity"
    android:windowSoftInputMode="adjustResize" >
</activity>
```

The most important parameters are `adjustResize` and `adjustPan`. If the former is set, the operating system will resize the activity's window to accommodate the on-screen keyboard, and the latter attribute will place the on-screen keyboard on top of the user interface and pan the user interface so that the active input field is visible. The following figures and code example demonstrate the difference. Let's first look at the layout code that follows. It is a simple layout that defines a `ScrollView` containing many `EditText` elements. Figure 10-2 shows how the layout is rendered before the on-screen keyboard is activated.

```xml
<?xml version="1.0" encoding="utf-8"?>
<LinearLayout xmlns:android="http://schemas.android.com/apk/res/android"
    android:layout_width="fill_parent"
    android:layout_height="fill_parent"
    android:orientation="vertical" >

    <ScrollView
        android:layout_width="fill_parent"
        android:layout_height="fill_parent"
        android:layout_weight="1"
        android:fillViewport="true" >

        <LinearLayout
            android:layout_width="fill_parent"
            android:layout_height="fill_parent"
            android:orientation="vertical" >

            <EditText
                android:layout_width="fill_parent"
                android:layout_height="wrap_content"
                android:text="" />

// … many more EditText elements here …

            <EditText
```

```
                android:layout_width="fill_parent"
                android:layout_height="wrap_content"
                android:text="" />
        </LinearLayout>
    </ScrollView>

    <Button
        android:layout_width="fill_parent"
        android:layout_height="wrap_content"
        android:text="example button" />

</LinearLayout>
```

Figure 10-2: The example layout before the on-screen keyboard is activated.

Now, let's look at two activities that use the exact same layout but have a different input mode definition. In Figure 10-3 the activity uses the `adjustResize` mode. When a text field is activated and the keyboard appears, the operating system changes the layout size and then draws the layout again. Therefore, in this example, the example button remains visible.

In Figure 10-4, the activity uses the `adjustPan` mode. In this case, the example button will not be visible. In fact, users cannot focus the button without closing the on-screen keyboard first.

It is advisable to always use the `adjustResize` mode if there is no good reason not to. You can control the resulting user interface much better by placing `ScrollViews` wisely in the right places and making the interface scalable.

INPUT TYPE

Scan these QR codes with your Android phone to open the companion app and try out a functional example.

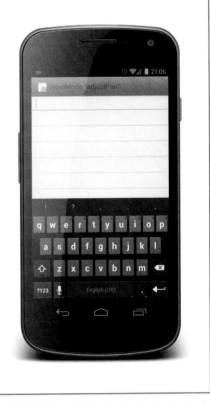

Figure 10-3: Activity rendered using the adjustResize input mode.

Figure 10-4: Activity rendered using the adjustPan input mode.

An input type is a definition a developer can assign to a text field to instruct the operating system as to what kind of information the user is expected to type into it. The operating system uses that information to show the user a best possible keyboard layout configuration. Making sure that all of your text fields have the correct type definition is probably the most effortless way to improve your app's user experience. For example, when typing an email address, users are going to need the @ sign. By setting the input type to the correct text field (`textEmailAddress`), you force the operating system to show the users an @ sign (see Figure 10-5). Another good example of how you can make your user's life easier is to enable the number pad for typing numbers (see Figure 10-6). If you have a field that accepts only numbers, you will not only help users type the numbers more easily but also help avoid confusion about accepted values.

Figure 10-5: A selected text field with the input type set to an email address makes it easier for users to access special characters that are likely to be needed when typing an email address.

Figure 10-6: A number pad is much easier for typing a number field than using the default keyboard.

There are more than 20 input types. You should refer to the Android documentation for the full list at http://developer.android.com/reference/android/R.styleable. html#TextView_inputType.

Here are the most important input types:

- text—Just plain old text
- textCapCharacters—Capitalization of all characters
- textAutoCorrect—Auto-correction of text being input
- textAutoComplete—This field will be doing its own auto-completion
- textMultiLine—Multiple lines of text in the field
- textNoSuggestions—Should not show any dictionary-based word suggestions
- textUri—Text that will be used as a URI
- textEmailAddress—Text that will be used as an email address
- textShortMessage—Text that is the content of a short message
- textPersonName—Text that is the name of a person
- textPassword—Text that is a password
- number—A numeric only field
- phone—Text for entering a phone number
- datetime—Text for entering a date and time
- date—Text for entering a date
- time—Text for entering a time

(Portions of this page are reproduced from work created and shared by the Android Open Source Project and used according to terms described in the Creative Commons 2.5 Attribution License.)

A single text field can have more than one input type assigned to it. Not all combinations make sense, but for example a multi-line no-auto-correct field might be useful in some context.

ACTION BUTTON AND IME OPTIONS

Scan the QR code with your Android phone to open the companion app and try out a functional example.

An action button is a button on the on-screen keyboard that changes based on context to perform different actions. By default, any single-line text field will have an action button that's called Next if there is a logically following field on-screen. Tapping the Next button focuses the following field. If the operating system cannot find a suitable field to follow, the action button is labeled with Done instead. Tapping that button will simply close the on-screen keyboard.

Developers can override the action button label by selecting from a predefined list of supported options for each text field and then setting the imeOptions attribute. The most important available options are the following:

- normal—There are no special semantics associated with this editor.
- actionUnspecified—There is no specific action associated with this editor; let the editor come up with its own if it can.
- actionNone—This editor has no action associated with it.
- actionGo—The action key performs a go operation to take the user to the target of the text they typed.
- actionSearch (see Figure 10-7)—The action key performs a search operation, taking the users to the results of searching for the text they have typed.
- actionSend (see Figure 10-8)—The action key performs a send operation, delivering the text to its target.
- actionNext—The action key performs a next operation, taking the user to the next field that will accept text.
- actionDone—The action key performs a done operation, closing the soft input method.
- actionPrevious—The action key performs a previous operation, taking the user to the previous field that will accept text.

(Portions of this list are reproduced from work created and shared by the Android Open Source Project and used according to terms described in the Creative Commons 2.5 Attribution License.)

The actions can be detected from code by setting an onEditorActionListener to the corresponding text field.

The same attribute also controls parts of how the on-screen keyboard is used in the user interface. By default when a text field is focused in landscape mode, the app user interface is replaced with full-screen text-editing mode (see Figure 10-9). This functionality can be overridden by setting the imeOptions attribute to flagNoFullscreen (see Figure 10-10). These flags can be combined with other imeOption attributes by using the pipe symbol (|) to separate multiple values in a single attribute like in the following example.

```
android:imeOptions="actionSend|flagNoFullscreen"
```

Figure 10-7: A text field with the imeOption actionSearch set.

Figure 10-8: A text field with the imeOption actionSend set.

Figure 10-9: A text field in the default full-screen edit mode.

Figure 10-10: A text field in landscape edit mode when the flagNoFullscreen flag is set.

 Scan the QR code with your Android phone to open the companion app and try out a functional example.

THIRD-PARTY KEYBOARDS

Not all Android phones have the same keyboard. Device manufacturers often replace the default keyboard with their own custom keyboards, and users might replace them with downloadable apps. This means that while defining the keyboard configurations is always a good idea, you cannot trust every device to function the same way. Some keyboards might provide different configurations with the same type.

DESIGNING FOR HARDWARE KEYBOARDS

Some Android devices ship with hardware keyboards. Probably the best known examples of this are the very first Android device, G1, and the original Droid. Both of them shipped with a slide-out hardware keyboard.

The Android operating system is fully capable of handling hardware keyboard events automatically, but they present few design implications. The first one is an important one: Never disable landscape mode in your app! Most of the hardware keyboards are meant to be used in landscape mode. If you force your app to be in portrait mode, all the users with these keyboards are going to be annoyed with your app.

The second implication to design is that you cannot depend on your app's user interface window to shrink when the user enters input mode, because if they are using a hardware keyboard, it won't take any space on-screen.

DESIGNING FOR D-PADS AND TRACKBALLS

Fewer and fewer phones seem to be shipping with trackballs or D-pad controls, but some phones still do and some large-volume older phones are still in heavy use.

D-pads (and trackballs) are used to change focus between user interface components. Although the feature is not critical to use, it sometimes is convenient and some users have learned to depend on them. You should aim to support D-pad navigation in your app.

You often don't need to go to any additional effort to support D-pads in your apps. The Android operating system is pretty good at figuring out which component should be the next one to receive focus.

> Tip: D-pads are the main navigation method of Android TV users. If you want your app to be capable of running on a TV, it must support directional navigation as its main navigation method.

In some cases the default logic fails. In these cases, you can easily override the default functionality by manually defining which user interface component should be focused next in each direction. You do this simply by adding the nextFocusDown/Up/Left/Right attribute to any user interface component definition. In the following example, these two FrameLayouts are part of a larger grid. Both of them have focus order definitions to ensure correct focus order.

```
<FrameLayout
        android:id="@+id/grid_1_selected"
        android:focusable="true"
        android:nextFocusDown="@+id/grid_5_selected"
        android:nextFocusRight="@+id/grid_2_selected"
        android:clickable="true"/>


<FrameLayout
        android:id="@id/grid_2_selected"
        android:focusable="true"
        android:nextFocusDown="@+id/grid_6_selected"
        android:nextFocusLeft="@id/grid_1_selected"
        android:nextFocusRight="@+id/grid_3_selected"
        android:clickable="true"/>
```

DESIGNING FOR THE STYLUS

A *stylus* is a pen that's used with a touch screen device. Styli were popular with older resistive touch screen devices due to their pressure points, but the capacitive touch screen revolution has made them all but disappear. It seems more recently that thy might be making a comeback. Samsung, HTC, and Asus have been incorporating styli into their phones and tablets, and many third-party manufacturers sell them as accessories that are compatible with all capacitive devices. Unlike the previous generation styli, this new generation is based on capacitive technology and act more as secondary input devices.

A stylus enables users to interact with the device much more precisely. Accessories like the stylus will enable new possibilities to app developers. Activities that previously weren't feasible, such as drawing, become possible. Although the Android operating system has APIs to support many stylus interactions, the manufacturers have released their own extended SDKs to add to the functionality.

> Tip: Using a stylus will naturally limit the devices the apps can run on, but sometimes it might be a compromise worth making.

DESIGNING FOR VOICE CONTROL

Voice control is widely integrated into the Android operating system. Users can switch to voice input on any app by enabling voice input from the Android keyboard (see Figure 10-11). Using this feature on devices running Android versions older than 4.1 requires a fast data connection, because the voice analysis is done on Google's servers. Starting from Android 4.1 voice typing is available also offline.

In addition to the voice typing, users can control their phone with voice commands. After opening the voice command prompt, users can give predefined voice commands to the phone. For example, the command "navigate to London" will open a navigation app and set the destination to London (see Figure 10-12).

The quality of voice recognition and of the voice commands depends heavily on the Android operating system version. Later versions have greatly improved the voice interface. For example, on an Android 4.0 phone users can see continuous feedback of the text they are speaking near real time. In older phones, users have to speak a full sentence and then wait for the results to appear.

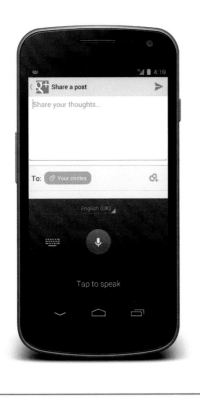

Figure 10-11: Android voice typing is always available to users without developers having to do anything.

Source: Android

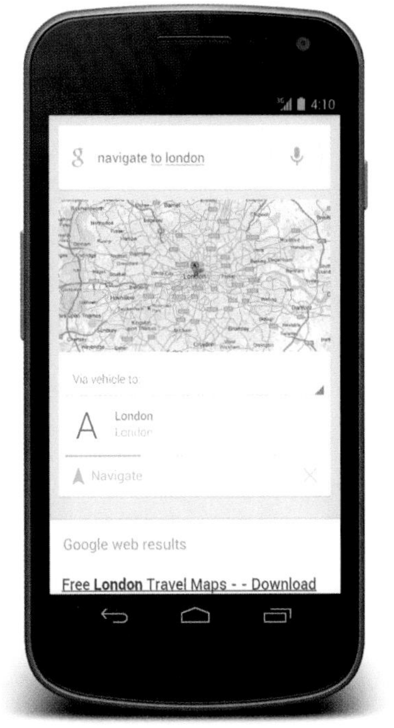

Figure 10-12: You can direct your phone to complete certain tasks simply by speaking the task into the phone.

Source: Android

DESIGNING FOR EXTERNAL KEYBOARDS, MICE, AND TOUCHPADS

Android has great support for external Bluetooth and USB devices, starting with version 3.0. External Bluetooth touch pads like the Apple's Magic Trackpad are fully supported, including its multi-touch gestures. When the operating system detects multiple touch points, it displays multiple cursors on the screen. Figure 10-13 shows an example of five cursors on-screen at once.

Figure 10-13: An Android tablet controlled by an external touch pad. Five cursors are shown on-screen, corresponding to a five-finger touch.

Source: Android

DESIGNING FOR CONNECTED SMART ACCESSORIES

With the popularity of Android devices increasing, the number of connected accessories has been growing fast. They range from big-name manufacturers like Motorola and Sony to small startups. Many of these smart accessories are like wristwatches with a display. They usually connect to an Android device via Bluetooth and allow users to control and extend the device's functionality. Most common features are controlling music playback, showing caller IDs, and displaying exercise-related information.

DESIGNING FOR SENSORS

The Android operating system has very good support for a wide range of sensors. Sensors can be very different in nature and their possible uses vary a lot. Categories of supported sensors are motion sensors, position sensors, and environmental sensors.

- Motion sensors measure device movements like acceleration and rotation.
- Environmental sensors measure conditions outside the device. These kinds of sensors can be, for example, light sensors and thermometers.
- Position sensors measure the physical location of the device. Sensors in this category can be, for example, magnetometers and orientation sensors.

DESIGNING FOR A SECOND SCREEN

Sometimes a phone or tablet controls other devices or extends the functionality of other devices. A common example of this is when users use their smartphones or tablets together with a connected TV device. An Android device is a natural companion device, especially for a Google TV. Scenarios and opportunities for apps like this are going to be limitless once the connected TV market picks up the speed. You can already find many great remote control apps like the Able Remote for Google TV, shown in Figure 10-14.

Figure 10-14: The Able Remote is a smartphone app that allows users to control their Google TV device.

Source: Able Remote app

SUMMARY

The diversity of Android devices manifests itself in the hundreds of different control mechanisms in both hardware and software. When building your app, you cannot rely on the devices you have to be the norm. Remember that some devices are used in different ways.

The software controls on Android are flexible and if you use them correctly, they can be very helpful to your users. When building an app, think about the ways your user will be filling in forms and using the buttons. Remember to design natural ways for data types and keyboard action buttons to make data entry as effortless as possible.

Also think about the opportunities that the large accessory ecosystem brings. Maybe your app would benefit from adding better stylus support or a connection to an external smartwatch?

With the diversity and growth of the Android ecosystem, the opportunity for designers and developers to create something novel and useful is growing by leaps and bounds.

DESIGNING PLATFORM USER INTERFACE COMPONENTS

THE ANDROID PLATFORM provides a large variety of user interface widgets, typography options, icons, and animations. Writing your own components is very seldom necessary. The platform components are flexible and easily customizable by changing parameters.

This chapter introduces the bulk of the default components for building Android user interfaces. User interface layouts are covered in Chapter 13.

USING USER INTERFACE WIDGETS

User interface widgets form the core of the Android user interface. They are the buttons, text fields, and images that your users interact with. User interface widgets are not to be confused with app widgets, which were covered in Chapter 8.

The following sections give you a brief overview of the user interface widgets that are available out of the box.

 Scan the QR code with your Android phone to open the companion app and try out a functional example.

TEXT WIDGETS

Text widgets are the simplest components on your app's user interface. You can use the `TextView` component to show text and the `EditText` component to display an editable field. Figure 11-1 shows examples of the default Android text components.

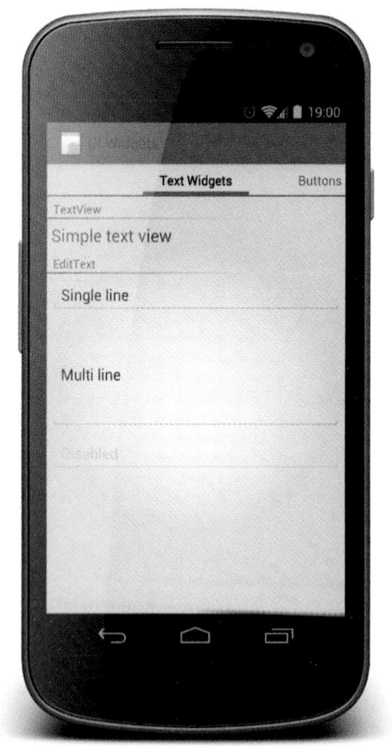

Figure 11-1: Example text components.

Text View

A `TextView` component displays texts on-screen. By default, a `TextView` component does not register taps or gain focus, but you can override both settings by adding corresponding attributes to your layout definitions.

Changing the text appearance is possible. You can learn more about customizing the text appearance in the typography section of this chapter.

Text Field (Edit Text)

`EditText` is the basic text field input component. Users can use it to type in text or numbers. `EditText` components by default show only a single line, but you can make it appear as a multi-line text field by adding the `lines` attribute. It is important to define the correct input type for every `EditText` component in order to make it easier for users to type the data. Input types are covered in Chapter 10.

BUTTONS

Buttons are the basic action components of any user interface. Users know how to interact with buttons. Android buttons have all the states and visuals to represent them out of the box. The default button visually represents both focused and pressed states.

For any button you can define drawables to any direction of the button label. (A *drawable* is a graphical element defined in XML or as a bitmap—more about drawables in Chapter 14.) You can, for example, simply add icons to your buttons by setting the `drawableLeft` attribute like so:

```
android:drawableLeft="@drawable/drawable_example"
```

See Figure 11-2 for examples of this and other buttons.

Image Buttons

The image button is an extension of the default button. It allows you to use an image as a button. You can even combine images to create custom buttons.

TOGGLE COMPONENTS

Toggle components like checkboxes and radio buttons are familiar components from other platforms. Android adds a few new components to that list. See Figure 11-3 for examples.

Figure 11-2: Examples of Android and image buttons.

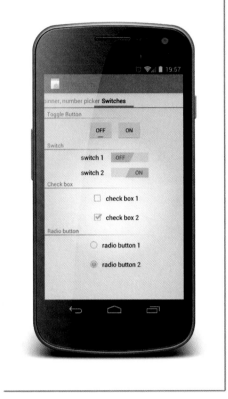

Figure 11-3: Examples of Android's toggle components.

Toggle Button

The toggle button is exactly as the name implies; it's a button that can be on or off.

Switch

A switch is functionally very similar to the toggle button but differs visually. It is designed to fit visually with lists of preferences and settings, but can be used elsewhere. The switch component was added to Android in version 4.0 so it cannot be used on devices running older versions of the operating system. If you plan to support older versions, which you should in most cases, you need to define different layout files for older versions. A toggle button or a checkbox is a good substitute for a switch.

Checkbox

The checkbox is this same familiar component that users have seen on other platforms. It functions on Android as you would expect. The label of the checkbox is defined in the same component definition by adding the text attribute. The label is automatically part of the area that changes the checkbox's selected state.

Radio Button and Radio Group

Radio buttons function very similarly to checkboxes. You can group radio buttons by surrounding them with a `RadioGroup` element in your layout definition. Only one radio button in a group can be selected at a time.

SELECTION COMPONENTS

If you have a list of options that the users must select from, it is better to present the users with the options than make them type the options into a text field. Android has few different components you can use depending on your needs. See Figure 11-4 for some examples.

Figure 11-4: Examples of Android selection components.

Dropdown Spinner

A dropdown component is called a *spinner* on the Android platform. It has two operating modes. There is a dropdown mode where the options appear below the menu (or above if there's no room below), and there is pop-up mode where the options appear in a pop-up window for the users to select from.

Number Picker

A number picker can be used to select a number from a predefined range. This component was added in Android version 3.0 and is not available in the older versions.

A number picker component supports multiple gestures. Users can drag the number up and down and even fling to rapidly move between a large selection of choices (fling can be disabled using an attribute). Another way to use this component is to tap the small up and down arrows to move the selection one by one.

Note that the number picker is implemented as a scrolling container. It cannot be placed inside another scrollable container.

DATE AND TIME WIDGETS

Android offers you a set of components that allow you to easily handle dates and times.

Calendar View

The calendar view shows the traditional calendar grid representation. Users can scroll through months by swiping up or down. Figure 11-5 displays the default calendar view. Calendar view is available only on Android 3.0 or newer.

Date Picker

The date picker presents users with a calendar view and controls to pick a date. The date selector and calendar view controls are both interactive and the component is automatically kept in sync. The date selector is based on number pickers. Figure 11-6 shows an example of how the date picker looks out of the box.

Time Picker

The time picker is a combination of number pickers that are formatted in a time format. Figure 11-6 shows the time picker.

Figure 11-5: Android calendar view.

Figure 11-6: Android date picker and time picker.

PROGRESS BARS

Progress bars are used to indicate ongoing processes. The Android framework provides components with multiple styles to do this.

Progress bars have also been adapted to functionally that's very similar—although from the user's point of view they might seem like very different tasks. Figure 11-7 shows examples of different progress bars and progress bar adaptations.

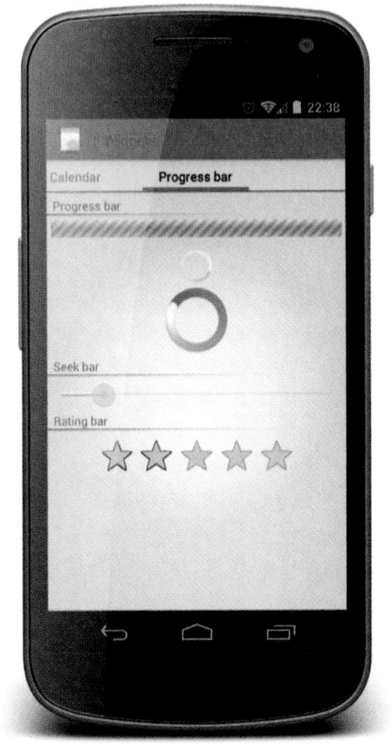

Figure 11-7: Progress bar, seek bar, and rating bar.

Progress Bar

There are two main styles for displaying running background processes using the default Android progress bar. You can use the horizontal bar, which is often used to display running tasks that are finite and have an estimated task duration. The second style is the round spinning animation. It usually indicates that, while the background task is running, it is not possible to know when it is going to be finished.

To change the progress bar appearance, you can use styles provided by the platform. For example, setting the progress bar element attribute as follows shows the progress bar as a horizontal bar instead of using the spinning animation:

```
style="@android:style/Widget.ProgressBar.Horizontal"
```

If you chose the horizontal progress bar presentation you can an endless animation or use it as a finite progress indicator. Setting the attribute `android:indeterminate="true"` will cause the progress bar to animate endlessly. Setting it to false means you must bind the progress bar to the ongoing process in your code.

Seek Bar

The seek bar is an adaptation of the progress bar that lets the users select the value by dragging the thumb icon. The seek bar is used in the standard media controller to display the video position.

Rating Bar

A rating bar has a very specific purpose. The users can select how many stars are activated by dragging or tapping the stars.

MEDIA WIDGETS

Android allows you to build media-rich apps easily. There are many components that help you on the way and provide you with rich functionality out of the box.

Image View

Image view is a component for displaying images on-screen. There are few tricks for getting your images right when using the `ImageView` component.

If you are using graphics you include in your app remember to provide images for each supported screen density. Android's automatic scaling algorithm sometimes does good work scaling images but most graphics look much better when you scale them manually. Screen density is covered in Chapter 12.

When you use an `ImageView` to display images that you load dynamically it is not always possible to provide different assets for different densities. It is also sometimes difficult to know the image size beforehand. To maintain control of your layout, you can make your `ImageView` a fixed size and tell the operating system how scaling should be handled.

To define how the image should be handled you can set the `scaleType` attribute of the `ImageView`. Table 11-1 shows the different `scaleType` options.

Table 11-1   ImageView ScaleType Options as Defined in the Android Documentation

ScaleType Value	Scaling Method
CENTER	Center the image in the view, but perform no scaling.
CENTER_CROP	Scale the image uniformly (maintain the image's aspect ratio) so that both dimensions (width and height) of the image will be equal to or larger than the corresponding dimension of the view (minus padding).
CENTER_INSIDE	Scale the image uniformly (maintain the image's aspect ratio) so that both dimensions (width and height) of the image will be equal to or less than the corresponding dimension of the view (minus padding).
FIT_CENTER	Compute a scale that will maintain the original aspect ratio, but will also ensure that original fits entirely inside target. At least one axis (X or Y) will fit exactly. The result is centered inside target.
FIT_END	Compute a scale that will maintain the original aspect ratio, but will also ensure that original fits entirely inside target. At least one axis (X or Y) will fit exactly. END aligns the result to the right and bottom edges of target.
FIT_START	Compute a scale that will maintain the original aspect ratio, but will also ensure that original fits entirely inside target. At least one axis (X or Y) will fit exactly. START aligns the result to the left and top edges of target.
FIT_XY	Scale in X and Y independently, so that original matches target exactly. This may change the aspect ratio of the original.

(Source: `http://developer.android.com/reference/android/widget/ImageView.ScaleType.html`)

Note that the image view can also have a background image. This allows you to create, for example, shadow effects on your images.

Zoom Controls

The zoom controls are two buttons (zoom in and zoom out). They can be used to add the standard controls for zooming in any app. It is always good to remember that not all devices support multi-touch gestures and pinch-to-zoom is not always available. Figure 11-8 shows an example of how zoom controls look in an app.

You need to manually connect the zoom controls into the zooming logic in your code.

Video View

`VideoView` makes it very easy to play video content in your app. You can use `VideoView` to play local videos and stream remote content. To learn how to use and set up the video view see the Android documentation at `http://developer.android.com/reference/android/widget/VideoView.html`.

Figure 11-8: This app uses zoom controls to let users zoom in and out without using pinch-to-zoom.

Media Controller

In combination with the `VideoView` you can use media controller to add standard video controls to the user interface. The media controller provides Play/Pause, Fast Forward, and Rewind buttons as well as a seekbar for jumping to any part of the video. It also shows the elapsed time and total time of the video being played (see Figure 11-9).

Figure 11-9: An example of a video view with the standard media controller.

Source: Android

SLIDING DRAWER

The sliding drawer component allows you to create a drawer that the user can make visible by dragging from a handle. This component can be very useful for secondary screen actions.

There is no default drawer handle graphics, so you must define it manually. You can use any view as the handle, for example `ImageView`, which makes the sliding drawer visually very flexible.

The sliding drawer component should be placed as an overlay to the layout you use. The best way to achieve it is to use it inside a `FrameLayout` on the same level as its sibling view. That way you will achieve the correct drawer effect, and it will slide on top of the other components at the view. In Figures 11-10 (sliding drawer closed) and 11-11 (sliding drawer opened), you can see an example of this component in practice.

Figure 11-10: Sliding drawer closed.

Figure 11-11: Sliding drawer open.

LISTS

Lists are one of the most useful components of the Android platforms. They are very flexible and provide tons of functionality out of the box. As a tradeoff they are fairly complicated to program correctly. List is what is called an adapter view. It means that you must provide a special class that handles assigning list items to the list.

List Performance

Lists can be critical components when it comes to performance. Users can scroll through a large number of list items in a short time. You need to be considerate of the complexity of each list item if your lists are long. Although Android can handle reasonably complex lists, you can run into the risk of your application's user interface not being fluent on some older generation devices.

> Tip: Building the list adapters is outside of this book's scope. There are good resources for getting a deeper understanding of how to build memory-effective lists—check out Professional Android Application Development by Reto Meier for one. Probably the best online reference is a set of tutorials written by Mark Allison on his website at `http://blog.stylingandroid.com/archives/605`.

List Items

You have free hands in defining the layouts and user interface widgets you use to build the list items. A list item is simply a layout. You can use any non-scrolling components in it. You should keep in mind the way that users use lists. If you plan to add any clickable components inside your list items you need to make sure that the components don't conflict with the row selection.

It is very common for list items to have a checkbox on the left side and often a secondary selection component on the right side while still allowing users easily select the items. When adding clickable items to a list item only add them to the far left or far right. You also should extend the item hit area, making it larger than it is by default. This is due to the fact that the list item is clickable. There are no safety margins between the additional clickable components on your list item and the list item itself. Figure 11-12 shows a diagram explaining how list items should be laid out.

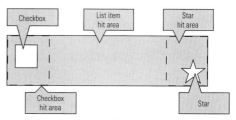

Figure 11-12: List items should have a maximum of two clickable components. These components should be placed only at the ends of the list item and the hit areas should be extended to prevent users from making accidental list row selections.

Gallery List

A gallery is a list that is scrolled horizontally while the selected item stays in the middle position. A gallery component is implemented the same way as a list. It is also an adapter view and you can define the items in it freely. The name "gallery" is, therefore, a bit misleading. You can use the gallery to create many styles of horizontally scrolling lists.

The gallery component has some default behaviors that are not present in the vertical list component. The selected item stays horizontally centered and there is a snapping effect when users drag the selection and let go.

CUSTOMIZING USER INTERFACE WIDGETS

The Android default components offer a lot of possibilities to customize their look and feel. You can easily modify the colors directly or by using the selector mechanism. You can also extend these components by subclassing them in code; this is a way to add completely new functionality.

COLORS

Android has multiple ways to define colors. You can set colors in your layout files as well as in code. In the layout file you can set any color value by defining a hexadecimal color code. The color code can also contain alpha (transparency) value, but it doesn't have to.

The following syntaxes are allowed in the layout definitions. A = alpha, R = red, G = green, and B = blue.

- #AARRGGBB
- #RRGGBB
- ARGB
- #RGB

To define colors that are easier to maintain and reuse, you can define colors as resources. Add a file, for example `colors.xml`, in your `res/values/` project folder. In that file you can add color resources like in the following example code.

```xml
<?xml version="1.0" encoding="utf-8"?>
<resources>
 <color name="background_color">#FFFFF0</color>
</resources>
```

By doing this you can refer to these colors whenever you need to define a color in your layout or code. Using color files has two great benefits:

- You can easily change your colors uniformly by changing the code in one place only.
- You can also easily change the whole theme of your app if you're creating multiple versions by simply replacing the color file in a build script or overriding it in a project where you use the original project as a library project.

SELECTORS

A selector is a great concept that can help you with any components that have different states, such as a button's down and focused states.

A selector is a XML file added in the `res/drawable` project folder. It defines a set of items that have state parameters and tells the operating system which of the items should be used and when. You can put anything inside the item element that you can use to draw from XML. I'll talk about drawing from XML more in Chapter 14.

The following example is probably the simplest selector possible. If you put this example code into your project's `res/drawable/example_selector.xml` file, you can use it as a background for almost any component by setting the background attribute to point to it like this `android:background="@drawable/example_selector"`.

If the component you're using with it has a pressed state (such as a button), the operating system will take care of changing the button color whenever the user presses and releases the button.

```
<selector xmlns:android="http://schemas.android.com/apk/res/android">
    <item android:state_pressed="true">
        <color android:color="#FFFF0000" />
    </item>
    <item>
        <color android:color="#55FF0000" />
    </item>
</selector>
```

If you want to add custom visuals to any component that has different visual states, you should always use selectors. The state parameters can be combined to create complex conditional statements. You can for example specify a background when a button is focused and pressed.

The available state parameters are as follows:

- `state_pressed`—True if this item should be used when the object is pressed
- `state_focused`—True if this item should be used when the object is focused
- `state_selected`—True if this item should be used when the object is selected
- `state_checkable`—True if this item should be used when the object is checkable
- `state_checked`—True if this item should be used when the object is checked
- `state_enabled`—True if this item should be used when the object is enabled
- `state_window_focused`—True if this item should be used when the application window has focus

See the Android documentation for the full specification at `http://developer.android.com/guide/topics/resources/color-list-resource.html`.

> *Tip: These states can be complex, so it's wise to create them so that multiple states are applicable at once. The operating system uses a very simple resolution method. It always picks the first state that matches the current state. For this reason, you can always add a last item without any state attributes as the default.*

Selectors are particularly powerful tools in combination with 9-patch images. I'll introduce the 9-patch images in Chapter 14.

ADJUSTING THE TYPOGRAPHY

Using text wisely is important to draw attention to the right places and to help you users get the information they need. Android has very powerful and flexible tools for altering the look of your text.

 Scan the QR code with your Android phone to open the companion app and try out a functional example.

FONTS

Android default font is something that at least for now any device manufacturers have not replaced in their devices. Android devices with version 4.0 or newer have the newer font, called Roboto, as their default font, and older devices still use the older Droid font.

Roboto

The Roboto font was redesigned to make fonts look good on the new high-resolution screens that are becoming more common. The Roboto font is the default font in Android 4.0 and newer operating system versions. If you don't change the font, your app will use this font.

You can download the font as well as a specimen book from `http://developer.android.com/design/style/typography.html`.

Droid

Droid was the default font for devices all the way up to Android 3.2.

Adding Your Own Fonts

You don't have to stick with the default fonts. You can also include fonts with your app and use them. To install any fonts in your app, simply copy the font file to your app's `assets/fonts` folder. You can then create a new typeface and set it to any text component. See the following example code for how to do that.

Creating Your Own Class

If everything else fails you can always override any functionality of any component by creating your own class. You should pick the component that is closest to what you need, and create a subclass that overrides only the necessary methods. This way you keep most of the tested and designed code of the framework and add your own functionality. Only in very extreme cases should you create subclasses to the `View` class.

```
Typeface tf = Typeface.createFromAsset(getAssets(),"fonts/Gamaliel.otf");
TextView customFontTextView = (TextView) findViewById(R.id.CustomFontExampleText);
customFontTextView.setTypeface(tf);
```

Most custom fonts work in Android apps without any problems. Figure 11-13 shows some examples of a few fonts.

TYPEFACE

You can change your font's typeface for any text component simply by setting the `android:typeface` attribute of the component. You can select sans, serif, and monospace. Figure 11-14 shows some examples of the different typefaces with the Roboto font.

Figure 11-13: Example fonts rendered in text components.

Figure 11-14: Example typefaces with Roboto font.

TEXT STYLE

Text style can be used to highlight text components. You can set text styles to bold, italic, normal, or bold and italic. Figure 11-15 shows some different text styles. Text styles can be changed by setting the `textStyle` attribute to the text component. For example, `android:textStyle="bold"`.

Figure 11-15: Examples of the available text styles.

TEXT SIZE

Text size can be changed by setting the `textSize` attribute. To make sure that your app scales correctly and fits with the rest of the platform, make sure that you use scalability features and default sizes correctly when possible.

Text Size and Scalability

Normally text sizes are defined in pixel size. As with everything else size-related on Android you must take screen densities into account. That is why text size should always be defined in scale-independent pixels (sp). One scale-independent pixel corresponds to one pixel on a 160dpi screen. Using scale-independent pixels ensures that when your user interface is scaled to other screen densities, your text size stays in correct proportions.

Default Text Sizes

You can use any size you want in your app. There are few preset values that are used elsewhere in the operating system. It's best to use those values if you don't have a good reason not to. It will make your app look and feel more a part of the platform. Table 11-2 lists the recommended default text sizes from the Android design guidelines.

Table 11-2   Recommended Text Sizes

Size Label	Font Size in Scale-Independent Pixels (sp)
Micro	12sp
Small	14sp
Medium	16sp
Large	18sp

Accessibility

When designing the text portions of your app you should also keep in mind the accessibility factor. Some people prefer or need to have larger text to see the text properly. In Android settings users can choose to have larger text. If you have defined your app's text sizes in scale-independent pixels, that setting will automatically scale all your app's fonts to a larger size. You can see how this shows in practice in Figures 11-16 and 11-17. Both figures show the same activity and the same layout. In Figure 11-16 the accessibility setting is off and in Figure 11-17 the accessibility large font setting is enabled.

TEXT COLOR AND SHADOW

Naturally, you can also change the text colors. As with other color definitions, text color can also be set to translucent by changing the color alpha channel.

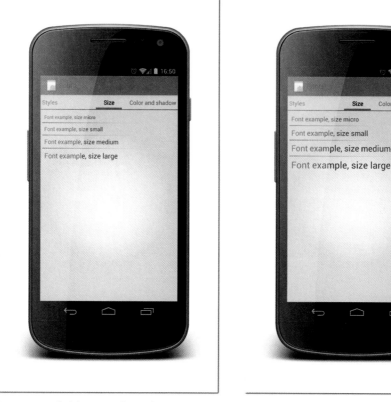

Figure 11-16: Default font sizes with normal settings.

Figure 11-17: Default font sizes with large fonts setting enabled.

The operating system also defines a few default colors that are used throughout the default apps. These colors can be a good starting point for your design unless you can spend time to define your own colors. The default colors are defined for primary text color and secondary text color for both dark and light theme. To set the default colors of your text, refer to the Android attributes by setting your text color to for example `@android:color/ primary_text_light`.

> *Tip: You can also set a shadow to your text. Avoid overusing this feature, though. Adding shadows can make your user interface look corny. Android user interfaces are generally flat in style, and shadows don't fit the picture.*

See Figure 11-18 for examples of different text color settings, including examples of the default colors and shadow.

Figure 11-18: Example color settings, including a shadow setting.

FORMATTING FROM HTML

Sometimes you want to emphasize only a few words inside one text component or add other more complex formatting that can be applied only to parts of the content instead of all the text in one text field. In cases like this you can use HTML styling to get the effect you want. It is possible to load HTML markup inside a text component; the operating system will format it correctly. It is worth noting that you cannot use everything that is defined in the HTML specification but the supported subset is often enough. Note that you can also make links in your text component clickable and make them open in a browser.

To load HTML content into a text component, you need to invoke HTML helper in code. See the following code example for how to do that.

```
TextView textView = (TextView) findViewById(R.id.text_from_html);
textView.setText(Html.fromHtml
  ("Example <b>HTML</b> text with a <a href=\"#\">link</a>"));
```

CREATING APP-WIDE TEXT STYLES

Setting text styles separately to each text component doesn't make sense in the long run. Fortunately, Android offers you a way to define styles that you can then assign to any component. The benefit of doing this is that your text styles are unified across the whole application. You can also easily change them later and can benefit from the Android's runtime asset selection mechanism by placing your style files into language/screen size/screen density specific folder.

To define your own style, you need to add a XML file to your app project's res/values/ folder. In that file you can define style elements that you can then refer to with the name you define. In the style element's child elements you can define any of the text component's attributes. These will be applied to each element you add this style.

```
<style name="ExampleStyleText" parent="@android:style/TextAppearance.Medium">
  <item name="android:textSize">20sp</item>
  <item name="android:textStyle">bold</item>
  <item name="android:textColor">#CC0000FF</item>
</style>
```

To add this style to a text component you simply refer to it in the style attribute like this:

```
style="@style/ExampleStyleText"
```

> Tip: Note that when defining styles you should define a parent from the styles provided by the platform. That way you ensure that all the attributes you don't define are correct and consistent with rest of the content.

USING ICONS

Icons are abstract images that represent functions, display status, and guide users. Icons can be used on many user interface components and they can often replace text and save screen real estate.

Getting icons right requires careful planning and design. An icon must be representative and easily understood. Icons whose meaning is not immediately clear to users are going to make the app user interface difficult to use. Users should be able to just glance at the icon and understand the meaning of it. On touch screen devices, users cannot hover the cursor over an icon to invoke a tooltip that defines it like they can on desktop environments.

Each platform also has established icons for many actions. Android is no exception. Study carefully how other apps use icons, and avoid bringing icons over from other platforms. Always follow the platform icon guidelines.

Tip: Special attention must be paid to icons that perform actions that cannot be undone, such as permanent deletion or send actions. Make sure that your users won't confuse these icons with other functionality.

DEALING WITH SCREEN DENSITIES

Icons are extremely vulnerable to automatic scaling algorithms. Many icons are very small, and even slight automated scaling is likely to distort them and make them look bad. The Android framework allows you to draw icons separately for each available screen density to prevent automated scaling. You should always provide icons for each supported screen density and not rely on automated scaling.

More about screen densities and how to actually provide assets for different densities in Chapter 12.

ICON TYPES

Different icons have different roles and should be treated differently. It is important that icons that belong to same group have the same look and feel. They must look like they belong together. This is why Google has provided exact guidelines for each of these icon groups.

A free online tool, Android Asset Studio, can be used to generate many of the icons from text and clipart. Although not all of the generated icons are good enough for production, this tool is a great way to get placeholder graphics to your app. The tool can be found at `http://android-ui-utils.googlecode.com/hg/asset-studio/dist/index.html`.

Launcher Icons

The launcher icon is the only icon that is visible to users outside your app. It is also used in multiple places (in launcher and in multi-tasking menu). Following launcher icon guidelines is doubly important. You don't want your app to stand out in a bad way.

It is also good to remember that for many users your launcher icon is one of the very first contact places to your app. A high-quality launcher icon helps users get a better first impression of your app.

The design of the launcher icon is difficult also in the sense that you have no control of the background in which the icon is going to be displayed. Users might be using anything as their home screen background. You must make sure that your icon will look good on any background. Using one-color icons is generally a bad idea for this reason. What if the user happens to have exactly that color home screen?

Here are few tips for designing good launcher icons:

- Not all launcher icons are square. Use transparency correctly to create a unique shape.
- The icon should reflect your brand.
- Avoid having text on your icon. Text doesn't scale well, and your app's name is always visible next to your icon anyway.
- Use 3D effects and gradients carefully. Android style is often flat.
- Too many small details will make the icon look blurry.
- The icon must work on all backgrounds.
- Use launcher lighting: top-lit.
- Don't make your icon too heavy or too light. Try to match the average weight of other icons.
- Provide an icon for all screen densities that your app supports.

Study the icons used by other apps. In Figure 11-19 you can see a selection of Android app launcher icons for Android default apps and apps by Google.

Figure 11-19: A selection of Android app launcher icons for Android default apps and apps by Google.

Source: Google Inc.

Menu Icons

Android menu is a deprecated concept and should be avoided. The menu has been replaced by Action Bar overflow menu (I talk about Action Bar in Chapter 18).

If you still decide to use the menu, following the guidelines is very important. It is very likely that your icons will be displayed next to icons that are provided by the platform. Having icons with different styles would be a disaster.

For more about menu icon design and strict guidelines, see the Android documentation at `http://developer.android.com/guide/practices/ui_guidelines/icon_design_menu.html`.

Action Bar Icons

Action Bar is a user interface pattern that has been around in Android for a while, but was added as part of the core platform in Android 3.0 Honeycomb. I talk more about Action Bar in Chapter 18.

Icons on the Action Bar represent the most important function on any given screen. Although it is possible to include text with the action, it is very rarely used as it takes too much room. The Action Bar icons must be clear to the users so they have the confidence to use them as intended.

Action Bar icons are grayscale, flat, and appear face on. The icons must not have a background and use transparent background instead. To ensure consistency between apps, Google has specified the exact palette for Action Bar icons. Depending on the theme you are using as the basis of your app theming (Holo dark or Holo light), you should make sure that your Action Bar icons follow the guidelines.

For Holo dark theme the Action Bar icons should use fill color `#ffffff`, 80% opacity. For the Holo light theme, use fill color `#333333`, 60% opacity.

Status Bar Icons

Status bar icons are used to represent events that the user is being notified about. Although the status bar notification itself can contain text, users often only see the icon. The icon must be descriptive and users must be able to recognize its meaning.

It is also important that users understand which app is triggering the notification, as notifications from all apps are shown exactly the same way in the status bar. If your app has only one event that it uses status bar notifications for, the best icon to use is often an abstract version of your app icon.

In short, status bar notification icons are grayscale icons. The size of the icons is relatively small, so the simpler the better. Using text in the icons usually doesn't work.

Status bar notification icon guidelines are very different on different Android versions. Older than 2.2 Android versions require icons to have a background, whereas 2.3 and newer don't. Android 3.0 versions added secondary icons to the notifications. Supporting all Android versions is going to take a lot of work. You need to provide multiple versions of your notification icons that match each version of the guidelines and multiple screen density versions of each.

See the full status bar icon guidelines online, including color palettes and size requirements, at `http://developer.android.com/guide/practices/ui_guidelines/icon_design_status_bar.html`.

Tab Icons

On a tabbed interface, the text on the tabs is sometimes replaced by icons. Tab icons are also grayscale images with transparent backgrounds. Tab icons are a bit larger than Action Bar icons or status bar icons.

Tab icons aren't generally as critical as Action Bar icons. If the user taps a wrong icon (tab), it's easy to simply press another one. Changing tabs never causes irreversible damage. Users can therefore easily determine what an icon means by simply tapping it without risk.

Tab icon guidelines were changed after Android 1.6. Market share of 1.6 and older Android versions is now so small that they can safely be ignored. You can find the full guidelines at `http://developer.android.com/guide/practices/ui_guidelines/icon_design_tab.html`.

Dialog Icons

Dialog boxes should generally be avoided, as discussed in Chapter 9. There are some situations where they are the only way to get the user's attention. An Android dialog box can have an icon, but it doesn't have to have one. As a general guideline, an icon is a good idea when a dialog box is required.

Make sure that the icon reflects the situation's severity correctly. If you use a pop-up dialog box to tell user that something is really wrong, using an exclamation mark icon is appropriate.

List View Icons

List icons are used in lists to identify individual list items. In custom list items these icons aren't strictly defined. There are, however, guidelines for standard list icons like the ones in the Android settings app. The guidelines are often broken down by device manufacturers, rendering them somewhat useless.

PLATFORM ICONS

The Android platform has tons of ready icons and graphics. All of these assets are distributed under the Apache 2.0 Open Source license. This means that they are all available for you to be used in your apps regardless of whether you are working on a commercial or non-commercial project.

Direct Reference Use vs. Making Copies to Your App

Some of the icons are available using Android's internal reference structure, but many of them are not public, which means that you cannot use them directly.

Google has recommended that developers not use the icons in the framework using the direct reference. A better way to use them is to copy them into your app. The reason they've made this recommendation is that many Android device manufacturers replace many of the icons with their own. The icons are also different between different platform versions.

Copying the assets to your project has drawbacks. You need to support users on multiple different devices, and if you pick one icon for sharing and sending, those icons will be used on all devices regardless of the Android version or manufacturer skin.

The decision you should make is whether to use all of your icons in one context directly from the platform or copy all of them into your app. The worst possible solution is to mix these two options. In that case your app will always look wrong—part of the icons are derived from the runtime environment, and part of them from your app. So pick one option and follow it throughout your app.

Accessing the Platform Graphics

Once you have the Android SDK installed, you can easily access all included graphical components. You can browse icons of different Android versions and different screen densities. To find icons of, for example, Android 4.0.3 (API level 15) and extra high-density screens, go to the folder `<your Android SDK installation>/platforms/android-15/data/res/drawable-xhdpi`.

ICON PACKS

To help developers and designers Google has provided a downloadable icon pack containing multiple icons that can be used for many purposes. These can be especially useful for implementing Action Bar actions, but you might find use for them elsewhere, too. The icons in the icon pack come in multiple screen density versions as well as Photoshop files. You can download the Google's icon pack from `http://developer.android.com/design/downloads/`.

There are also many more places where you can find icons for your app. Some of them are free, and some of them are not. A quick Internet search before starting to implement your own icons can save you a lot of your time.

USING ANIMATIONS AND TRANSITIONS

Animations can make your app look and feel polished. Correctly used animations can also be used to help your users understand how your application works.

Overusing animations can cause negative effects. The human eye is automatically drawn toward any motion. Animations can, therefore, be very distracting. The screen should always be fully static when the users are reading something, for example.

Animations should always serve a purpose. If, for example, your app's layout changes, using animation to highlight the layout change might make sense. This might make it easier for the users to follow where individual components move.

Transitions between screens should always enforce the user's sense of location within the app. If a button takes your users deeper into the app, the transition should indicate that. When the user presses Back, the same animation should play backward, thus reinforcing user's understanding of the app navigation.

ACTIVITY TRANSITIONS

Whenever a new activity starts, the operating system plays a subtle animation by default. Although the animation can vary between devices of different manufacturers and Android versions, it is always carefully selected to make the navigation feel natural. Whenever users press the Back button, the same animation is played backward.

You can override activity transitions. In most cases it is not necessary and often it's even a bad idea. Users are familiar with the default transition animation. The default transitions enforce users' understanding when they dive deeper into the app. They usually know that they can use the Back button to navigate back.

No Transitions

Sometimes playing animations between activities doesn't make sense. Maybe you want two activities to feel like one to the users. In this case, you can prevent the transition animation altogether by setting the intent flag `Intent.FLAG_ACTIVITY_NO_ANIMATION` to the triggered intent.

Overriding Activity Transitions

If you have a good reason to override the transition animation, you can do so when you trigger the intent to start the next activity. Immediately after you call startActivity you must call the `overridePendingTransition()` method from the `activity` class. See the following example code:

```
startActivity(new Intent(ExampleActivity.this, AnotherActivity.class));
overridePendingTransition(R.anim.custom_animation_in, R.anim.custom_animation_out);
```

The `overridePendingTransition` method takes two parameters. The first parameter is the ID of the animation that is played for the incoming activity and the second parameter is the ID of the outgoing activity animation. You can set either of these parameters to 0 so as not to play animation. Both parameters refer to animation defined in XML. See the next section for information about how to do that.

The Android platform provides a couple of defined animations. You call them using the `android.R.anim` class. For example, you can use `android.R.anim.slide_in_left` to have an animation slide in from the left side of the screen. Other options are `slide_out_right`, `fade_out`, and `fade_in`.

TWEEN ANIMATIONS

The Android view animations can be used to animate a view and its content, for example, by moving, rotating, or zooming. Each animation can consist of a single animation or can be a set of animations that are played together. The animations are usually defined in the XML files but can also be built-in code.

The following example code illustrates a very simple tween animation. This animation scales the view of the X and Y values. Tween animation files must be placed in the `res/anim/` project folder.

```xml
<?xml version="1.0" encoding="utf-8"?>
<set xmlns:android="http://schemas.android.com/apk/res/android"
    android:fillAfter="true"
    android:shareInterpolator="false" >

    <scale
        android:duration="700"
        android:fromXScale="1.0"
        android:fromYScale="1.0"
        android:interpolator="@android:anim/accelerate_decelerate_interpolator"
        android:pivotX="50%"
        android:pivotY="50%"
        android:toXScale="2.4"
        android:toYScale="0.6" />

</set>
```

Tween animations allow you to animate view scale, alpha position, rotation, or location (translate). For the full XML definition, see the Android documentation at `http://developer.android.com/guide/topics/resources/animation-resource.html#Tween`.

Scan the QR code with your Android phone to open the companion app and try out a functional example.

Problems with Tween Animations

Tween animations are applied to the view elements only superficially. This means that the position of a view element does not actually change in the app's user interface. Although you can force the animation not to reset once it is complete (using `android:fillAfter= "true"`), doing so will cause problems if any of the animated components are interactive. For example, a button whose location is animated will not respond to user interactions properly. The touch events are still recognized in the old location.

Tween animations have their place, but they are mostly being replaced by the newer API, property animations. I talk about property animations later in this chapter.

FRAME ANIMATIONS

Frame animation is the simplest kind of animation. A frame animation is simply a sequence of images displayed one after another in a set order. Frame animations are drawable resources and can be used anywhere drawable resources are allowed. You can set a frame animation as a background image, for example.

The following example code shows a simple frame animation definition that defines a three-image sequence that is played in a loop until it is stopped. This file must be placed in the `res/drawable/` project folder.

```xml
<?xml version="1.0" encoding="utf-8"?>
<animation-list xmlns:android="http://schemas.android.com/apk/res/android"
    android:oneshot="false">
    <item android:drawable="@drawable/animation_a" android:duration="200" />
    <item android:drawable="@drawable/animation_b" android:duration="200" />
    <item android:drawable="@drawable/animation_c" android:duration="200" />
</animation-list>
```

It is not enough to just place the frame animation as, for example, a background of a component. It must be started from code. It's a very simple command. See the following code for an example.

```java
ImageView animatedImage = (ImageView) findViewById(R.id.animated_image);
animatedImage.setBackgroundResource(R.drawable.example_frame_animation);
AnimationDrawable exampleAnimation = (AnimationDrawable) animatedImage.
  getBackground();
exampleAnimation.start();
```

Scan the QR code with your Android phone to open the companion app and try out a functional example.

PROPERTY ANIMATIONS

A property animation is a new animation framework introduced in Android 3.0 Honeycomb. The property animation framework is superior to the old tween animations, as it can be used to animate any view properties as well as any other object properties. The framework also has very flexible definitions of each animation set.

Property animations differ from tween animations fundamentally as property animations apply the animation properties to the user interface components. This means that the same problems with hit areas do not exist with property animations. If you, for example, move a part of the user interface that has the buttons in it, the buttons correctly reach to your touch events the way users expect. This is true even when the buttons are pressed during the animation or after it's complete. The animated properties are not reset at the end.

Scan the QR code with your Android phone to open the companion app and try out a functional example.

Property Animations to Older Devices

Still at the time of this writing, older android versions like Android 2.3 Gingerbread are so prominent that supporting them is wise. Fortunately there is a community-maintained project lead by Jake Wharton that has back-ported most of the new framework's functionality to older devices. The library is Open Source and free to be used in any project. You can find and download it from the project's website at `http://nineoldandroids.com/`.

Creating Property Animations

Property animations can be simple value animations that calculate values from start to beginning, object animations that change an object property value, or animation sets that combine these features.

Object animations are created by defining objects that tell the system which property should be animated. These objects are called *object animators* and are implemented by the `Object Animator` class. You can set animators easily with a simple call like this:

```
ObjectAnimator.ofFloat(exampleView, "rotationY", 0, 180)
```

This call creates an animator object that can be run alone or be grouped together with other animator objects to create more complex animations.

To start an animation, simply make this call:

```
<your animator object or animator set>.setDuration(3000).start();
```

Keyframes

Not all animations should run at a constant speed. You can define keyframes in your animations to make them irregular. Note that easing effects are not implemented with keyframes but using interpolators. I'll explain use of interpolators later in this chapter.

With keyframes you can, for example, make a component move across the screen, stay in place for a while, and then continue moving again in a single animation.

For more about using keyframes, see the Android developer documentation at `http://developer.android.com/guide/topics/graphics/prop-animation.html#keyframes`.

Layout Animations

Scan the QR code with your Android phone to open the companion app and try out a functional example.

You can use property animations to automatically trigger when components are added or removed from view or when component layout changes. The layout animations are defined the same way as any other property animation.

The platform also offers default layout animations that don't require any code. You can enable the default layout animations by setting `android:animateLayoutChanges="true"` on any layout in your app. Any layout that has `animateLayoutChanges` set to true will automatically call the default layout animations whenever the content of the view is changed.

ANIMATION INTERPOLATORS

Both tweening animations and property animations can use interpolators to tweak animation timing to make the animations feel and look better. A straightforward animation where values are adjusted at a constant rate from the animation start to the end does not look right. No objects in the real world behave like that, and that is why our brains automatically make us dislike animations like that. An interpolator can, for example, make the animation first accelerate and then decelerate at the end. That mimics the way objects move in the real world.

The Android platform provides multiple interpolators for you. The platform interpolators are going to be enough for most cases, but it is also possible to create your own. Figures 11-20 through 11-28 show all the interpolators that are part of the Android platform.

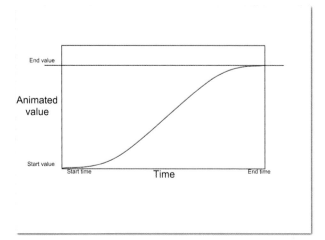

Figure 11-20: AccelerateDecelerateInterpolator. Animation speed is slower at the end and at the start of the animation.

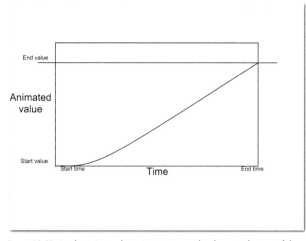

Figure 11-21: AccelerateInterpolator. Animation speed is slower at the start of the animation.

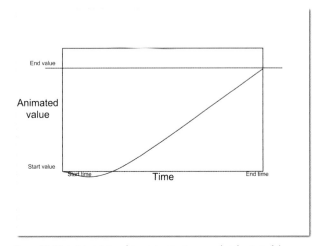

Figure 11-22: AnticipateInterpolator. Animation is reversed at the start of the animation.

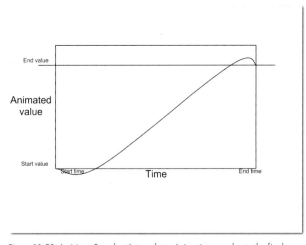

Figure 11-23: AnticipateOvershootInterpolator. Animation overshoots the final value at the end of the animation and the playing is reversed at the beginning.

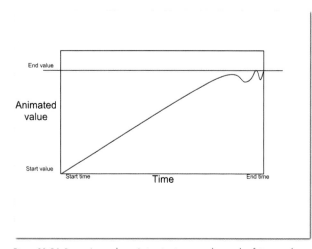

Figure 11-24: BounceInterpolator. Animation is reversed a couple of times at the end of the animation to create a bounce-like effect.

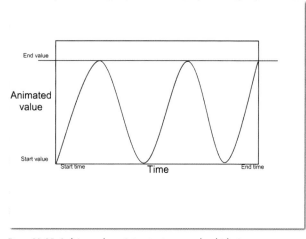

Figure 11-25: CycleInterpolator. Animation is repeated multiple times.

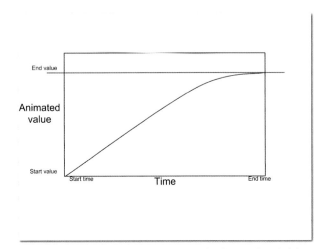

Figure 11-26: DecelerateInterpolator. Animation speed is slower at the end of the animation.

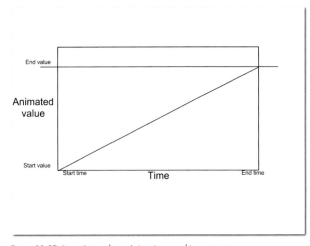

Figure 11-27: LinearInterpolator. Animation speed is constant.

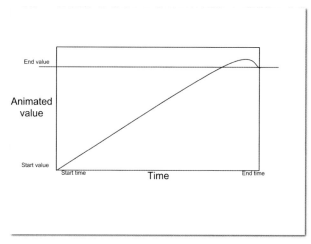

Figure 11-28: OvershootInterpolator. Animation overshoots the final value at the end of the animation.

SUMMARY

The Android platform offers a rich toolset for building user interfaces. User interface components are flexible and customizable. Most apps can be built using ready components, and you typically need to tweak only some of the parameters.

The platform typography options let you tweak the look of any of your text components almost limitlessly. You need to remember to implement the text components using scalable measures like scale-independent pixels, and be prepared for users who use the large text accessibility option.

Animations can add polish and smoothness to your app if used correctly. By avoiding overuse and keeping in mind the purpose of each animation, you can utilize different animation frameworks to create almost any effect you want.

PART

SCALABLE ANDROID DESIGN

CHAPTER

MANAGING ANDROID RESOURCES

ANDROID DEVICES COME in many different forms and sizes. You've read in several places in this book that the Android SDK provides developers with great tools for building software that scales nicely to all devices. Now it is time to take a look at those tools.

This chapter talks about the Android resource management framework. It allows developers and designers to provide multiple alternative resources for an app and let the operating system use the correct ones for each device. After the resource manager overview, this chapter dives into the individual device properties, or qualifiers, that you can use.

USING ANDROID RESOURCES

The Android operating system allows you to add multiple alternative resources to your app. The operating system picks the correct resource during runtime based on the runtime environment. This way, you can provide correct density graphics, the right kind of layouts for larger screens, correct language translations, and even alternative attributes for non-touch devices.

There are multiple types of resources that can be used in any Android app. The Resource Manager manages them, and the same rules apply to them. They need to be placed into the correct resource folder in your app project structure under the `res/` folder:

- Animation definitions. (`res/anim/` and `res/animator/`)
- Color state list definitions. (`res/color/`)
- Drawables. These can be bitmaps or XML drawable definitions. More about these in Chapter 14. (`res/drawable/`)
- Layout definitions. (`res/layout/`)
- Menu definitions. (`res/menu/`)
- Simple value definitions. These can be strings, colors, and integers. `res/values/`
- XML files. (`res/xml/`)
- Raw data. (`res/raw/`)

Don't let the `res/xml` folder fool you into thinking that it is the only place for XML files. In fact, most of Android resource files are XML.

CONFIGURATION QUALIFIERS

The operating system cannot automatically determine which alternative resource is for which device type. You must tell the system which resources you want to be used in which kind of environment.

The Android platform has a set of predefined qualifiers that you can provide as extensions to your resource folder names. Based on these qualifiers the operating system determines which resources should be used on a particular device. The qualifiers are added to the end of the resource folder name, separated by dash (-). For example, `res/drawable-hdpi/` is the drawable folder that should be used when the app is running on a device that has a high-density screen (screen density is explained later in this chapter).

> *Tip: You don't always have to provide all resources in all of the folders. In many cases you'll have a large set of resources that don't need any qualifiers, in which case you can leave them in the default folder and only add folders with qualifiers to the resources that need to have alternatives.*

The operating system uses smart resolution when it tries to determine which resource should be used. A simplified way of thinking about how the operating system looks for the best match is to think about it as a game of elimination. The operating system eliminates all folders with qualifiers that do not match the current system configuration. Often, that is not enough, as multiple folders might remain after the elimination process (for example, `res/values-en` and `res/values/`). The second step in the resolution is to look for qualifiers that match the current configuration. If a matching qualifier is found, the operating system then eliminates all folders that do not have the qualifier.

Most of the time you can simply trust the operating system to find the best match. Complex cases are pretty rare. If you ever find yourself confused as to why wrong resources are being used, you can find the exact algorithm the operating system uses described in detail in the Android documentation. You can read it at `http://developer.android.com/guide/topics/resources/providing-resources.html#BestMatch`.

The available qualifiers are covered in the following sections in this chapter.

COMBINING QUALIFIERS

In many occasions using the right resources requires using more specific definitions than just a single qualifier. The Android platform allows you to combine the qualifiers in any way you like. Some of the combinations don't make sense but some are very important. For example, graphics sometimes contain text. In that case the graphical asset must be localized as well as provided for multiple densities. You could have the folders `res/drawable-en-hdpi/` and `res/drawable-en-mdpi/`, as well as `res/drawable-de-hdpi/` and `res/drawable-de-mdpi/`.

LIBRARY PROJECTS AND OVERRIDING RESOURCES

Library projects are a very important part of the Android project structure and organization. When you're using library projects, the main project resources always override resources with the same name and same qualifiers as the library project. This can be a very powerful technique to use for creating different apps from the same source or from Android library projects that provide components.

API LEVEL REQUIREMENTS

Some qualifiers have been added in later phases of the Android platform development. Fortunately, the Android platform runtime is smart about them. It simply ignores folders with qualifiers it doesn't understand. Using newer qualifiers won't cause problems on older devices as long as you also provide resources in folders with qualifiers that the runtime Android version understands.

DESIGNING FOR SCREEN DENSITY

Screen density is probably the most important and most used qualifier in any Android project. Without understanding how to handle screen densities correctly, it is nearly impossible to create apps that look good on all devices.

WHAT DOES SCREEN DENSITY MEAN IN PRACTICE?

If you have a dual monitor setup for your computer, for example a laptop and an external display, you probably have two separate density displays. Consider the following example. Your laptop has a 15-inch full HD display (1920×1080 resolution), and your external connected display is a larger 30-inch display with the same full HD resolution. If you drag a window from your laptop's display to your external display, its physical size grows. The window still has exactly the same pixels, but each pixel is larger. If you want to prevent this from happening you need to lower the resolution of your laptop display until the pixels on that screen are physically the same size as on the larger external display. Once you get the resolutions right the windows will stay the same physical size when you drag them between your displays. So these two displays have different display densities.

Consider another example. Let's say that you have two smartphones, A and B, that both have 4-inch screens. Phone A has a 320×240 pixel resolution, and phone B has a 640×480 pixel resolution. An image using the same number of pixels on these two devices will be a very different physical size on each. See Figure 12-1 for an abstract example of this.

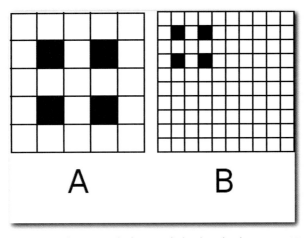

Figure 12-1: An abstract example of a picture displayed on a low-density screen (A) and a high-density screen (B).

WHY IS SCREEN DENSITY IMPORTANT?

Why does this matter so much that I've dedicated multiple pages to it in this book? On a desktop screen, density isn't a big deal, and you very rarely care about the physical size of the user interface on your computer displays. Physical size of user interface components matter much more on touch screen devices. Users interact with them with their fingers. User interface components that are the correct size on a 320×240 pixel 4-inch screen would be unusable on a 640×480 pixel 4-inch screen. Buttons would be too small to tap, and user interface components would be too close to each other. Users would not be able distinguish between their touch areas, causing them continuously tap the wrong components.

To fix this problem you must make sure that everything in the user interface is defined in a way so they end up being the same physical size no matter what screen density is. In case of images it requires the images either to be scaled automatically or for you to provide separate assets for different screen densities. Figure 12-2 shows an example of separate assets being displayed on the lower-density screen (A) and the higher-density screen (B). These two images will end up looking the same size for users due to the screen density difference.

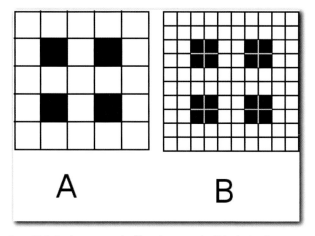

Figure 12-2: An abstract example of how the images should be displayed on two different density screens.

SCREEN DENSITY IN ANDROID TERMS

Dots per inch (DPI) is the metric used to describe screen density. The term is derived from its former use from print media and printers describing the same thing in that media. You might see pixels per inch (PPI) used sometimes. It is the same thing.

It is not feasible to support all possible screen densities separately. That is why the Android SDK groups them in categories with fixed range of densities. In practice it means that on devices that have close to each other's screen density but not exactly the same your user interface will be a slightly different size. The categories have been selected in a way that these variations are minimal and don't cause problems for user. Android documentation calls these groups *generalized densities*.

There are four screen density groups that can be used on Android devices plus one extra for TVs with 720p resolution (TVs are a different matter in this density case). Table 12-1 shows the Android supported density categories and corresponding resource qualifiers. Each device will fall into one of these categories. The manufacturer decides which generalized density a device has, but you can trust that any device is grouped appropriately. There have been exceptions in the past, most notably the first Galaxy Tab, but the exceptions are rare, and there really is no need to prepare for them.

Table 12-1   Android Screen Density Qualifiers

Name	Qualifier	Corresponding Density	Example Device
Low density	ldpi	120 dpi	HTC Wildfire
Medium density	mdpi	160 dpi	HTC Legend
High density	hdpi	240 dpi	Nexus One
TV density	tvdpi	213 dpi	A 720p TV
Extra high density	xhdpi	320 dpi	Galaxy Nexus
Non-scaled images	nodpi	-	-

AUTOMATIC GRAPHICS SCALING VS. SEPARATE ASSETS

If you don't provide separate graphical assets for different screen densities the operating system performs an automatic scaling operation. The operating system uses the asset that is the closest fit to the target density.

In some cases the automatic scaling is good enough, but more often than not the result of the automatic scaling is not good enough. In the best case the scaled picture is blurry, and in the worst case it can be distorted badly.

On the other hand, producing assets takes time. It is always a matter of a compromise. You need to make the decision on case-by-case basis. Larger images often scale down nicely but upwards badly. Small icons rarely scale well in either direction.

RES/DRAWABLE/ FOLDER IS FOR XML ONLY

Always place your graphical assets into folders with the density qualifier. Never leave any GIFs, PNGs, or JPGs in the res/drawable/ folder. Although graphical assets from that folder do technically work, it can cause confusion. XML drawables on the other hand are density independent and should be in the default folder. You'll learn more about XML drawables in Chapter 14.

PREVENTING SCALING

Although it's rare, you might sometimes need to provide assets that are not going to be scaled on any density screens. You can use the special density qualifier nodpi. If a graphical asset is found only from this folder, the operating system will draw it on the screen without performing any density scaling.

SCREEN DENSITIES THAT MATTER

There are devices out there with every kind of the screen density type, but the distribution is not even. As with picking the Android version to support, you should base your decision as to which screen densities to support on the device distribution. The optimum solution is, of course, to support all of them but that is not always possible.

Google publishes up-to-date data about the current screen density and size distribution on the Android developer website at `http://developer.android.com/resources/dash-board/screens.html`. It's worth taking a look at this chart when making your decision.

At the time of this writing, about 3 percent of Android devices have LDPI screens. By far, the massive majority of devices have MDPI or HDPI screens and only few have XHDPI screens. My advice is to always provide assets for HDPI and MDPI. LDPI can probably be safely ignored as it's not being used as much in new devices. XHDPI, on the other hand, should not be ignored, even though it has a relatively small market share. Most new flagship phones are going to ship with gorgeous XHDPI screens. These devices are also perfect ways to demo your app.

DENSITY INDEPENDENT PIXELS, DP

Although this topic isn't directly related to the Android Resource Manager, it is such an important part of creating content that's independent of screen density that it cannot be ignored here.

When creating layouts and defining component sizes you often need to give the operating system a desired size for the component. Although you can give a pixel size for a button, for example, doing that would lead to the same problem described previously. The button would be the wrong size on every density device other than the one you designed it for.

The Android SDK has a solution to this. You can define any size in density-independent pixels (dp or dip). In fact, you should always use dp definitions! Breaking this rule will break your app on a large amount of devices.

Density-independent pixel definitions are automatically handled by the operating system, which converts them to correct pixel sizes during the app runtime, depending on the pixel density of the device the app is running on. You can think of dp as an abstract pixel. If you design and define your whole user interface using dps, all your components will be the same physical size on all devices. You don't have to do anything else. The operating system takes care the rest.

The concept of density independent pixels can be difficult concept to get your head around at first. The easiest way to think about density independent pixels is to think of them as pixels on a medium density screen. In fact, the definition goes like this 1dp = 1px on MDPI screen. Table 12-2 shows some dp to px conversions.

Table 12-2   Example of a 100dp to Pixel Conversion

Screen Density	100dps in Pixels
ldpi	75.00px
mdpi	100.00px
hdpi	150.00px
xhdpi	200.00px

You rarely need to think about these conversions with user interface components, but you need to know them when creating graphical assets. An icon that is 50×50px on a MDPI screen must be 75×75px on an HDPI screen, and so on. The between each screen density is 1.5. The fraction can make conversion difficult. One-pixel lines, for example, can cause trouble. You can't make anything 1.5 pixels in size.

DPs from Code

When writing your app's layout XML files you can always use the dp size definitions. But what if you need to set a component size in the code? All Android API size definition methods expect to get pixel size as the parameter.

Unfortunately, you need to do the conversion yourself. The following code example does the conversion. It asks the operating system for the current screen density multiplier and applies it. Note the added 0.5 on the last line ensures that any conversion never ends to value 0. According to Romain Guy (an Android engineer working at Google), this is also how the operating system performs the conversion:

```
// you must have a context object
DisplayMetrics metrics = context.getResources().getDisplayMetrics();
float dp = 20f; //this is the dp size you want to have
int pixels =
   (int) (metrics.density * dp + 0.5f); // this results to correct pixel size
```

Density Independent Text Size

Text and typography were discussed in Chapter 11. In that chapter, I instructed you to use the sp (scale-independent pixels) size definitions for text. This corresponds to the dp definitions for other sizes.

DESIGNING FOR SCREEN SIZE AND FORM

Screen size is another relevant issue when it comes to building Android apps. Android devices ship with screens as small as three inches all the way up to 13-inch tables. Most likely you are going to use screen size related qualifiers to provide different layouts for tablets and phones. I'll talk much more about that in Chapter 15.

GENERALIZED SIZE

Just as screen densities are grouped into generalized density categories, screen sizes have four size categories that can be used as qualifiers to provide alternative resources. Table 12-3 includes more detail about these four qualifiers.

Table 12-3   Android Generalized Screen Size Qualifiers

Qualifier	Appropriate Screen Size
small	320×426dp units
normal	320×470dp
large	480×640dp
xlarge	720×960dp

These qualifiers are good enough for most phone screens, but when it comes to tablets these categories might be too vague. An xlarge screen is about seven inches or larger. Note that the xlarge qualifier was added in Android API level 9.

The resource system will never use resources from a folder with a qualifier that defines a larger size than the runtime environment has. If you don't provide resources in a suitable folder it will cause a runtime crash.

FINE GRAINED SCREEN SIZE

The first Android versions didn't really take tablets into account but that changed with the release of Android 3.2 Honeycomb. The Honeycomb release added new qualifiers that can be used to support more fine-grained screen sizes. These three new qualifiers allow you to define an exact density independent pixel size for your resource folders.

As the qualifiers can contain any value, knowing which one to use isn't as simple as with generalized size qualifiers. In the case of these three qualifiers, the system always uses the one that's closest to the device configuration without exceeding it.

Smallest Width

The Smallest Width qualifier allows you to define resources based on the device's screen size. This qualifier replaces the old categorized screen sizes. The Smallest Width qualifier is the smallest width of the device available to your app. This width is not dependent on the device orientation and also takes into account any additional space used by operating system components.

The syntax for defining this qualifier is as follows:

```
sw<N>dp
```

As an example, `res/layout-sw720dp/` is used for a 10-inch MDPI 720x1280 tablet.

Available Width and Height

Unlike the smallest width available width and height are affected by the device orientation. These values refer to the currently available value. The syntax is w<N>dp for available width and h<N>dp for available height.

ASPECT RATIO

You might never use this one, but it can be quite useful in some cases. The two available qualifiers are long and notlong. These qualifiers are not dependent on the screen orientation.

The long screen form factor is slightly different from notlong. For example, the Nexus One is a notlong screen with 480×800 resolution, whereas the Motorola Droid with the 480×854 resolution is a long device. It has 54 more pixels on its long edge. The difference isn't much and can often be ignored. Long screens include WQVGA, WVGA, FWVGA, and not-long screens include as QVGA, HVGA, and VGA.

SCREEN ORIENTATION

Screen orientation is simple and powerful. You can define different layouts when the device is on portrait mode and when it is in landscape mode. The qualifier values are port and land.

DESIGNING FOR LANGUAGE AND REGION

The language and region qualifier is very useful when you have multiple languages on your app. All you need to do is to provide the language files in the right resource folders and the operating system takes care of the rest.

The syntax for the language and region qualifier is <language code>-r<region code>. The language code is a two-letter ISO 639-1 language code and the region code is two-letter ISO 3166-1-alpha-2 region code. The region code is optional and cannot be given alone. The qualifier is not case-sensitive.

You can also use mobile country code and mobile network code as a resource qualifier. The syntax for this is mcc<code>-mnc<code>. The first code is the mobile country code, and the second one is the mobile network code. The mobile country code can also be used alone.

DESIGNING FOR DEVICE CONTROLS

The platform has many qualifiers defining availability of control mechanisms. You might provide different functionality for devices with a stylus and for devices with a D-pad. Take a look at Table 12-4 for a list of these qualifiers and their corresponding explanations.

Table 12-4   Device Control Resource Qualifiers

Qualifier	Explanation
notouch	Device does not have a touch screen.
stylus	Device has a resistive touch screen.
finger	Device has a touch screen.
nokeys	Device doesn't have a hardware keyboard.
qwerty	Device has a hardware QWERTY keyboard. This category includes other QWERTY-like keyboards regardless of the actual layout like the German QWERTZ keyboard as well.
12key	Device has a hardware 12-key keyboard.
navexposed	Navigation keys are currently exposed.
navhidden	Navigation keys are currently hidden.
nonav	Device doesn't have separate navigation keys.
dpad	Device has a D-pad.
trackball	Device has a trackball.
wheel	Device has a directional wheel.

In the case of the keyboards, these qualifiers are not dependent on whether the keyboard is currently being used.

DESIGNING FOR PLATFORM VERSIONS

You can also provide different resources for devices running different operating system versions. This can be very useful when you want to utilize some components that aren't available on older platforms but still support the older devices. You can, for example, provide alternative layouts using the latest user interface components.

The qualifier syntax is -v<minimum API level>. Read more about API levels from the Android documentation at http://developer.android.com/guide/appendix/api-levels.html.

DESIGNING FOR DEVICE MODES

Far fewer qualifiers are available to you if you plan to support device modes like docks or night mode. These were added in Android API level 8 and are not available on older devices.

For night mode, you can use the qualifiers night and notnight. These can change while your app is running.

You can also use two dock mode qualifiers—car and desk—to provide separate resources when the device is docked.

SUMMARY

As you can see, Android is designed to run on a wide range of devices. The Resource Manager combined with the flexible layouts (introduce in the next chapter) are powerful tools that allow you to build apps that support all or most Android devices. By using these tools, you can turn the infamous Android fragmentation from a problem into a platform feature.

You need to choose where you invest your time, though. Providing different graphics for different screen densities is very important, but you probably won't want to support all of them from the get-go.

CHAPTER

ANDROID APP LAYOUTS

ANDROID LAYOUTS ARE the best tools in your toolkit for creating scalable applications. Because the Android platform was designed to support multiple device sizes and forms, it has a great set of layouts that you can utilize out of the box to support the widest possible selection of devices.

ANDROID LAYOUT STRATEGY

You should never define your Android user interfaces by setting absolute pixel positions to your components like you might do on other platforms. A user interface with an absolutely defined layout would look right on only one device. Instead of the absolute layout strategy Android user interfaces are built by defining how components relate to each other. In this sense designing layouts for Android is much closer to web design than to iOS design.

To make a layout scalable you must tell the operating system how the layout is to be scaled. Not all areas in the user interface should be resized. Android's layouts let you define fixed areas and resizable areas. When used properly, these two types of areas will make your user interface scalable but maintain certain constraints for good results when scaling.

FIXED AREAS

A *fixed area* is a part of the user interface that cannot be resized. A typical example of this kind of area is a user interface icon. Icons are often a fixed size, and resizing them makes them look distorted.

Sometimes a fixed area is only fixed in one direction and resizable in the other. For example, a button bar often has a fixed height but is resizable horizontally to fill the whole screen.

RESIZABLE AREAS

Resizable areas are the opposite of fixed areas. They can be resized to fill in a space in the user interface. Even resizable areas have their limitations. They often have a minimum size that is required to show all the content and sometimes also a maximum size as well. When it comes to these constraints, you can start to utilize responsive design principles to avoid too small or too large resizable areas. You'll read much more responsive design in Chapter 15.

Resizable areas often utilize scrollable containers to make sure that the content will be fully accessible, even on very small devices.

COMBINING FIXED AND RESIZABLE AREAS

Making your user interface scalable requires you to utilize both fixed and resizable areas correctly. There is one simple rule you can use to check if your design is on the right track. If all the components on your user interface are fixed in one dimension (height or width), your interface is not scalable, and the operating system will not be able to adjust your interface to multiple screen sizes.

> *Tip: This is a good point to create a screen design for your app. Think about the resizable sections and the fixed sections, and make sure that your screen design has enough places for resizing.*

Consider the example shown in Figure 13-1. The example screen design has three composite components—the top Action Bar, a list, and a bottom button bar. In this fairly typical Android screen design, the top Action Bar and the bottom button bar are a fixed height. The list component in the middle is resizable. I'm certain that you've seen layouts like this in many apps you've used. No matter what the screen size, this layout always works and displays the data correctly. On a smaller screen the list area will simply be smaller and fewer list items will be displayed at a time.

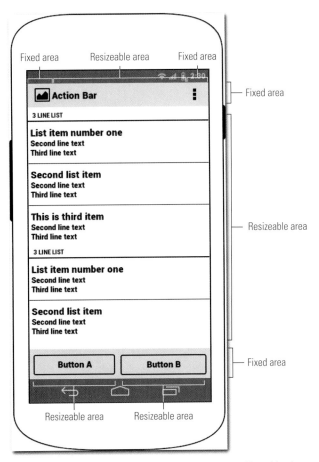

Figure 13-1: A simple example screen design demonstrating resizable and fixed areas.

LAYOUTS IN LAYOUTS

Android layouts can be composed from other layouts. In fact, layouts inside layouts are very common. Take another look at Figure 13-1 but this time in the horizontal dimension. For example, the Action Bar is a resizable component, but it contains two fixed areas. In this case the left app icon and the right menu item are fixed, leaving the middle title part to be resizable. The bottom bar on the other hand contains only two user interface components, and they are designed to fill in the area together. They are both resizable.

LAYOUTS FROM XML AND CODE

The most common way you will define layouts is to use Android's resource system discussed in Chapter 12. Most applications can define all layouts in the Android XML files placed in the `res/layout/` folder or any of the related layout folders with a qualifier.

Most of the examples in this chapter are explained using XML layouts. For any and all layouts or layout structures you can also always use code to create the corresponding layout objects and their attributes. Using XML will save you a lot of time as well as make the project structure easier to maintain and better organized. Layout XML files can also benefit from the Android resource management system as well as be built by using various graphical development tools like the Android Eclipse plug-in's visual user interface builder.

LAYOUT MANAGERS

Now that you have established a basis for your Android layout strategy, you're ready to take a look at the actual layouts the Android platform provides for developers. These layouts, when used correctly, allows developers to implement almost any screen design.

RELATIVE LAYOUT

Relative layout is by far the most powerful layout manager on Android. Whether you are an Android developer or designer, you should take some time to learn how this layout works in detail. Relative layout is the cornerstone of any Android app design. If designers understand its flexibilities and limitations, they can more easily specify user interfaces that the developers can implement the way they wanted. It is scalable and massively flexible. With that flexibility inevitably comes some complexity.

 Scan the QR code with your Android phone to open the companion app and try out a functional example.

As the name suggests, relative layout is based on the idea of defining component locations based on their relation to other components. You can think about a relative layout as a set of anchor points to which you can anchor your user interface components. Each added user interface component becomes an anchor point once it's added to the layout.

First, take a look at the anchor points available to you related to the parent component (the layout). Whenever you add a user interface component to the relative layout, you can set any of these anchor points. These points define where the component will be placed. Table 13-1 lists all of these anchor points. These values are all set to true or false as they are only related to the parent component.

Table 13-1   Relative Layout Anchor Points Related to the Layout Itself

Anchor Point Name	Explanation	XML Parameter
Parent bottom	Aligns the child's bottom edge with the parent's bottom edge.	`android:layout_alignParentBottom`
Parent left	Aligns the child's left edge with the parent's left edge.	`android:layout_alignParentLeft`
Parent right	Aligns the child's right edge with the parent's right edge.	`android:layout_alignParentRight`
Parent top	Aligns the child's top edge with the parent's top edge.	`android:layout_alignParentTop`
Center horizontally	Centers the child horizontally with respect to the bounds of the parent.	`android:layout_centerHorizontal`
Center vertically	Centers the child vertically with respect to the bounds of the parent.	`android:layout_centerVertical`
Center	Centers the child with respect to the bounds of the parent.	`android:layout_centerInParent`

Take a look at the example in Figure 13-2. The large rectangle represents the relative layout, which might or might not be the whole user interface of an app screen. There are three components that are placed in the layout. Component A has a parent top and parent left layout attributes set. Component B has a center layout attribute set, and component C has a center horizontally and parent bottom layout attributes set.

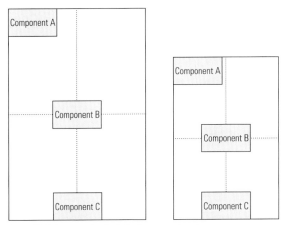

Figure 13-2: An example of relative layout used to place user interface components related to the parent.

Setting component locations based on their parent is very helpful, but that alone is not enough. Relative layout also allows you to set component location relative to the other components in the same layout. Table 13-2 describes the anchor points you can use to place components relative to their sibling components. Each of these attributes requires you to define another component as the anchor point.

Table 13-2   Relative Layout Anchor Points Related to Sibling Components

Anchor Point Name	Explanation	XML Parameter
Above	Aligns bottom edge with another child's top edge.	android:layout_above
Below	Aligns top edge with another child's bottom edge.	android:layout_below
Left of	Aligns right edge with another child's left edge.	android:layout_toLeftOf
Right of	Aligns left edge with another child's right edge.	android:layout_toRightOf
Align baseline	Aligns baseline with another child's baseline.	android:layout_alignBaseline
Align bottom	Aligns bottom edge with another child's bottom edge.	android:layout_alignBottom
Align left	Aligns left edge with another child's left edge.	android:layout_alignLeft
Align right	Aligns right edge with another child's right edge.	android:layout_alignRight
Align top	Aligns top edge with another child's top edge.	android:layout_alignTop

Let's look at another example in Figure 13-3. In this example, component B is the same as in the previous example. It is placed in the center of the layout. Component D combines the bottom layout attribute and the center horizontally layout attribute. It is laid out below component B. Component E is set to be laid out below the component D as well as set to align right of the component D. Now, no matter what the layout size in total is these components always stick together.

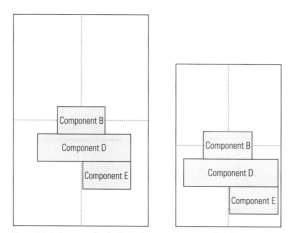

Figure 13-3: An example of relative layout components placed relative to each other.

The following source code shows you how the components from Figures 13-2 and 13-3 can be defined in Android layout XML. Figure 13-4 shows the resulting user interface.

```xml
<?xml version="1.0" encoding="utf-8"?>
<RelativeLayout xmlns:android="http://schemas.android.com/apk/res/android"
    android:layout_width="fill_parent"
    android:layout_height="fill_parent"
    android:orientation="vertical" >

    <Button
        android:layout_width="wrap_content"
        android:layout_height="wrap_content"
        android:layout_alignParentLeft="true"
        android:layout_alignParentTop="true"
        android:text="button a" />

    <Button
        android:id="@+id/button_b"
        android:layout_width="wrap_content"
        android:layout_height="wrap_content"
        android:layout_centerInParent="true"
        android:text="button b" />

    <Button
        android:layout_width="wrap_content"
        android:layout_height="wrap_content"
        android:layout_alignParentBottom="true"
        android:layout_centerHorizontal="true"
        android:text="button c" />

    <Button
        android:id="@+id/button_d"
        android:layout_width="150dp"
        android:layout_height="wrap_content"
        android:layout_below="@id/button_b"
        android:layout_centerHorizontal="true"
        android:text="button d" />

    <Button
        android:layout_width="wrap_content"
        android:layout_height="wrap_content"
        android:layout_alignRight="@id/button_d"
        android:layout_below="@id/button_d"
        android:text="button e" />

</RelativeLayout>
```

Figure 13-4: Screenshot of the user interface produced from the relative layout example code.

LINEAR LAYOUT

Linear layout is a much more simple than the relative layout manager. In a linear layout all components are placed one below the other, or side-by-side. It is worth noting that unlike some similar layouts on other platforms, linear layout does not support automatic flow of elements. It always places the elements in exactly one row or exactly one line.

You can set the direction of a linear layout by setting the `android:orientation` attribute value to `horizontal` or `vertical`.

You can also add a layout `weight` attribute to any child components you place inside a linear layout. This attribute defines how much extra spacing is added to the child component. By default, the child components are not stretched and their `weight` values are 0. Any value higher than 0 will make the child component use more of the available space related to its siblings.

The following code example and Figure 13-5 demonstrate the linear layout and layout weight in practice. Note that button A takes only the vertical space it needs, whereas the other two buttons are stretched to fill the space of the parent layout. Button B is twice the size of button C as it has double the layout weight.

Figure 13-5: Screenshot of the user interface produced from the linear layout example code.

Note that the values of the `weight` attribute do not have to be between 0 and 1. Values 5 and 10 have exactly the same effect as 0.5 and 1. It is also worth noting that components that have the same weight are not necessarily the same size in the resulting screen. The `weight` attribute affects only the division of the empty extra space between the components.

```xml
<?xml version="1.0" encoding="utf-8"?>
<LinearLayout xmlns:android="http://schemas.android.com/apk/res/android"
    android:layout_width="fill_parent"
    android:layout_height="fill_parent"
    android:orientation="vertical" >

    <Button
        android:layout_width="fill_parent"
        android:layout_height="wrap_content"
        android:text="button a" />

    <Button
        android:layout_width="fill_parent"
        android:layout_height="wrap_content"
```

```
        android:layout_weight="1"
        android:text="button b" />


    <Button
        android:layout_width="fill_parent"
        android:layout_height="wrap_content"
        android:text="button c"
        android:layout_weight="0.5"/>
</LinearLayout>
```

 Scan the QR code with your Android phone to open the companion app and try out a functional example.

FRAME LAYOUT

Frame layout is the simplest layout of all, but it can still be very useful. A frame layout is simply a container for elements. Usually a frame layout contains only one child element, but in some cases you might want to add more elements to it. The only control you have over where the child element is placed is using the layout gravity setting, which is explained in the next section. Otherwise, all the components you add to a frame layout are placed on top of each other. The *z-order,* or the order in which the components are drawn, is defined by the order you add components to the layout. Components added early are drawn first and components added later are drawn on top of them. In the following code, the button labeled button b will be drawn on top of the button labeled button a, covering it.

```
<?xml version="1.0" encoding="utf-8"?>
<FrameLayout xmlns:android="http://schemas.android.com/apk/res/android"
    android:layout_width="fill_parent"
    android:layout_height="fill_parent" >

    <Button
        android:layout_width="wrap_content"
        android:layout_height="wrap_content"
        android:text="button a" />

    <Button
        android:layout_width="wrap_content"
        android:layout_height="wrap_content"
        android:text="button b" />

</FrameLayout>
```

A common use for frame layouts is when a component is shown only temporary, such as when showing a loading indicator. You might place your main user interface layout and the loading indicator as a child of the same frame layout. This makes sure that the loading indicator is in the center of your user interface. Once the process is finished, you simply set the loading indicator visibility to gone and you're done.

Layout Gravity

Layout gravity defines where in the parent layout the child components are placed. Not all layouts support layout gravity and it is more important on a frame layout than on other layouts. For any component, you can set an `android:layout_gravity` attribute, which tells the layout where the component should be placed related to the layout.

The following example code and Figure 13-6 show how the `frame` layout and `gravity` attribute works.

```xml
<?xml version="1.0" encoding="utf-8"?>
<FrameLayout xmlns:android="http://schemas.android.com/apk/res/android"
    android:layout_width="fill_parent"
    android:layout_height="fill_parent" >

    <Button
        android:layout_width="wrap_content"
        android:layout_height="wrap_content"
        android:layout_gravity="top|right"
        android:text="button a" />

    <Button
        android:layout_width="wrap_content"
        android:layout_height="wrap_content"
        android:layout_gravity="center"
        android:text="button b" />

    <Button
        android:layout_width="wrap_content"
        android:layout_height="wrap_content"
        android:layout_gravity="bottom|center_horizontal"
        android:text="button c" />

</FrameLayout>
```

Scan the QR code with your Android phone to open the companion app and try out a functional example.

Figure 13-6: Screenshot of the user interface produced from the frame layout example code.

GRID LAYOUT AND TABLE LAYOUT

Grid layout is a very flexible but rarely useful layout. As its name suggests, it's a layout you can use to create grids of user interface items. The layout has a wide variety of attributes you can use to specify how the child components are laid out. For the full set of available options, see the Android documentation at `http://developer.android.com/reference/android/widget/GridLayout.html`.

Note that the grid layout is available only with API level 13 (Android 4.0) or newer.

The following example code creates a very simple grid layout. Figure 13-7 shows how it looks on a phone.

```xml
<?xml version="1.0" encoding="utf-8"?>
<GridLayout xmlns:android="http://schemas.android.com/apk/res/android"
    android:layout_width="wrap_content"
    android:layout_height="wrap_content"
    android:columnCount="2" >
```

```
<TextView
    android:layout_margin="5dp"
    android:background="#AA222222"
    android:padding="10dp"
    android:text="col1 row1" />

<TextView
    android:layout_margin="5dp"
    android:background="#AA222222"
    android:padding="10dp"
    android:text="col2 row1" />

<TextView
    android:layout_columnSpan="2"
    android:layout_gravity="fill_horizontal"
    android:layout_margin="5dp"
    android:background="#AA222222"
    android:padding="10dp"
    android:text="col1,2 row2" />

</GridLayout>
```

Figure 13-7: Screenshot of the user interface produced from the grid layout example code.

Table layout is somewhat similar to the newer grid layout but it is available from the API level 1. The table layout has some problems, though. It is nowhere near as flexible as the grid layout. Table layout has a very limited set of uses and most of them can be handled better by a relative layout.

 Scan the QR code with your Android phone to open the companion app and try out a functional example.

TABS

Tabbed user interfaces are very powerful and useful concepts. You'll learn more about tabbed user interfaces in Chapter 19.

DEFINING A LAYOUT SIZE

Every Android user interface component must have both width and height set. Not providing these attributes will cause a runtime crash. In an XML layout definition, these values are provided by adding the `android:layout_width` and `android:layout_height` attributes to all user interface components, including the all layouts.

In order to define the component's size you can give any of the following values to the attributes.

- `wrap_content`—Setting a component width or height to `wrap_content` makes the component use only as much space as it needs. The actual size of the component depends on its child component sizes.
- `match_parent` (formerly `fill_parent`)—The dimension of the component will fill all available space. The `match_parent` value was previously called `fill_parent`. The name change was made in Android API level 8. The values are synonyms; there is no difference.
- Dimension value in density independent pixels—Recall that the concept of density independent pixels was explained in Chapter 12. Never use pixels to define any size; always use density independent pixels instead.

SCROLLING

Scrolling containers or scroll views are familiar tools from other platforms and have been around for a long time. A scrollable container allows you to have larger user interface structures than the screen can hold. Users can then scroll the viewport (the area that is visible) to see the entire area.

Scroll views work a bit differently on touch screen devices than they do on computers that are operated with a mouse. On a mouse-controlled system, the viewport moves by moving scroll bar controls up and down and left and right. On a touch-based device, users move the viewport by dragging it.

The difference in interaction methods causes some problems on touch devices that are not present on other devices. On touch devices it is not possible to have two scrollable components inside each other if both of the components can be scrolled in same direction (horizontal or vertical). This limitation also extends limiting use of any swipe gestures inside scroll views that have same direction as the scroll view.

SCROLL VIEW

Android `ScrollView` is the component providing scrolling functionality. It has fairly limited functionality but it is sufficient for the large majority of cases.

A scroll view can have only one child component, usually a layout. It also supports only vertical scrolling.

An important attribute to know for scroll views is `android:fillViewport`. Setting this attribute to true will cause the scroll view's child component to expand to fill the view port in case it is smaller than the available space. This is usually the functionality that users expect. Setting the child component height to `fill_parent` alone is not enough.

Z AXIS, LAYOUT ORDER

Sometimes it is necessary to place components on top of each other. In that case it is important to define the component z-order correctly. The *z-order* is the order that components are drawn. Components that are drawn later appear to be on top of the ones drawn before.

In Android layouts, the z-order is defined simply by the component definition order on the layout file or the order the components are added to a layout from code. Any components that are added to the layout earlier (on top of a layout file) are drawn first.

PADDING AND MARGIN

Getting the component spacing right makes your user interface look much nicer. Android provides you two sets of controls to influence the component spacing on any user interface.

Margin defines how much empty space should be left outside the component. Components should almost always have set margins. Placing components too close to each other will make your user interface look too busy. More importantly, because Android user interfaces are touch interfaces, leaving margins between different controls helps users press their intended target. Margins between two touch controls should be at least 2mm, which in Android is about 13-15dp.

Padding on the other hand defines how much space should be left inside the component border but outside the component content. Figure 13-8 shows a helpful illustration of padding and margin.

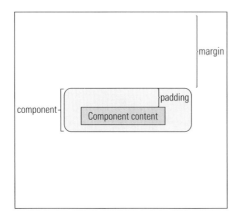

Figure 13-8: An abstract illustration of padding and margin related to a user interface component.

 Scan the QR code with your Android phone to open the companion app and try out a functional example.

IMPORT AND MERGE LAYOUT FILES

It is always good to avoid copying any code; this will make maintaining and debugging the code easier. Due to the folder structure and the resource qualifier use, you might end up in situations where you need the same code either partially or fully in multiple places. You might also have some reusable layouts you want to use as part of multiple different screens.

Fortunately, there's a good way to reuse the same code in multiple places. You can use the `include` element to import a layout file to another file. You simply give the element a parameter that tells the system which file you want to include. See the following example:

```
<?xml version="1.0" encoding="utf-8"?>
<FrameLayout xmlns:android="http://schemas.android.com/apk/res/android"
    android:layout_width="fill_parent"
    android:layout_height="fill_parent" >

    <include layout="@layout/merge_example"/>
</FrameLayout>
```

Using `include` might lead to a situations where unnecessary layouts are created. For example, in the previous code example, if the included layout has another root layout the frame layout element is unnecessary. This is where the `merge` element enters the picture.

You can use the `merge` element as the root element of any of your layout XML files. When a layout like the following example code is induced in another layout, the system simply ignores the `merge` element and adds its child elements to the layout.

```xml
<?xml version="1.0" encoding="utf-8"?>
<merge xmlns:android="http://schemas.android.com/apk/res/android" >

    <Button
        android:layout_width="wrap_content"
        android:layout_height="wrap_content"
        android:layout_gravity="top|right"
        android:text="A button from merged layout" />

</merge>
```

 Scan the QR code with your Android phone to open the companion app and try out a functional example.

CUSTOM LAYOUTS

As with any other user interface component you can also create your own layouts. Although this is very seldom needed, it can sometimes be a lifesaver. All layouts derive from the `ViewGroup` class and any custom layout class must do the same. Often the best way to reach your goals is to utilize one of the ready layout classes and then slightly modify its functionality instead of fully creating a new layout class from scratch.

ANDROID DEVELOPMENT TOOLS USER INTERFACE BUILDER

The Android Eclipse plug-in—Android Development Tools (ADT)—provides a graphical user interface builder that you can use to compose your user interface definitions by dragging and dropping components. The Eclipse plug-in is under active development by the Google's Android tools team, and it is likely that by the time you are reading this, the user interface builder will have multiple improvements. Therefore, this section doesn't fully explore all of its features. Instead, I encourage you to look into the tools and experiment with them.

Even when the graphical tools get better, it is always good to make sure that the generated XML code is exactly the way you meant it to be. The graphical tools can be used to create user interfaces faster than manually writing them. You can save a lot of time—while prototyping for example—by leveraging the graphical tools. The graphical user interface builder can be very helpful for learning the more complex layouts like the relative layout. Figure 13-9 shows an example screenshot of the tool helping users understand how the selected component will be anchored in a relative layout.

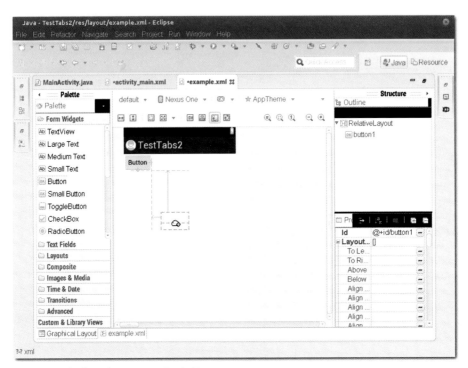

Figure 13-9: Android ADT plug-in user interface builder.

Source: Android SDK

DEBUGGING LAYOUTS

It is sometime very difficult to understand the complex dynamic layout structures that are generated in the app runtime. These dynamic layouts are very difficult to debug when something goes wrong, such as when a view that should be visible isn't. The Android SDK provides you with one more, great tool for debugging your views—the Hierarchy Viewer. You can find this tool in your Android SDK's installation folder under the `tools` folder.

The Hierarchy Viewer connects to a runtime process and creates a graphical presentation of the layout tree. You can then inspect individual elements to better understand what's going on. You can, for example, see elements that have zero width or zero height in the tree, and, therefore, do not show up. This tool can be a lifesaver. I encourage you to explore it. Figure 13-10 shows an example screenshot of this tool in action. Note that the Hierarchy Viewer can be used only with the Android emulator or with developer devices. It cannot load the layout hierarchy from non-developer devices.

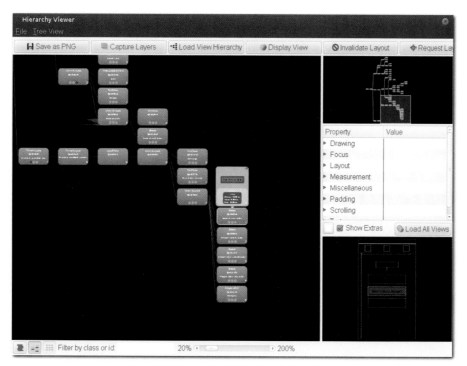

Figure 13-10: The Android Hierarchy Viewer shows detailed information of the runtime layout.

Source: Android SDK

SUMMARY

Android layout managers are very powerful tools that you can use to create flexible and scalable user interfaces. Take time to learn the layouts to understand where they are best utilized and to know their limitations. The best and most flexible of all Android layout is the relative layout. Make sure you have mastered it. If you are a designer, the relative layout will be the key to drawing user interface specifications that your developers can easily implement.

SCALABLE GRAPHICS

GRAPHICAL COMPONENTS ARE the most difficult ones to scale correctly of all of the different screen sizes and densities that Android devices have. There are many types of graphics that cannot be stretched or resized without destroying the look. Anything with gradients, diagonal lines, or text will look weird when stretched or scaled even a little bit.

Take a look at the example background in Figure 14-1. Having diagonal lines combined with a circular gradient would be a nightmare scenario

if you could only use bitmap graphics. How would you create that bitmap? The aspect ratio must be the same because even a small distortion will make the circular form seem wrong. Scaling the image will not work either, because the spacing between the lines would then be wrong. You could provide one very large bitmap that would fit to the largest display. However, in addition to this looking bad on the smaller screens, the large bitmap would cause performance problems in your app due to its larger memory consumption.

Figure 14-1: The round gradient with its diagonal lines is an example of a graphic situation that would be impossible to provide as a single file in a scalable manner.

Fortunately, there are a lot of useful tools and techniques that allow you to create complex graphics that are scalable. This chapter explains how and when to use them.

NINE-PATCHING

Nine-patching is probably the most powerful tool that the Android platform provides when it comes to handling scalable graphical assets.

The idea of nine-patching is not new or unique to Android. It has been in use in web graphics for some time. The theory of nine-patch images is very simple. An image, for example a button background, is divided into nine images. Each of the corners is a separate image, the bits between these corner images are separate images, and then the part that is left in the middle is an image (see Figure 14-2). As a result of this splitting, the image can be scaled without ruining its rounded corners and borders. When content is placed in a nine-patch image, the corners remain their original sizes, but the parts between them and the center part are scaled to accommodate the content.

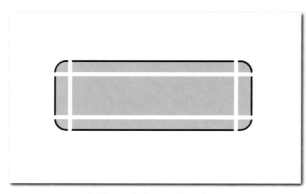

Figure 14-2: An example of button background divided into a nine-patch image.

NINE-PATCH STRUCTURE IN ANDROID

Although nothing prevents you from building nine-patch images the same way they are used in the web, it can be done much more simply. Android provides with you a shortcut that can save a lot of time and effort as well as making the nine-patching on Android more flexible than the original idea.

 Scan the QR code with your Android phone to open the companion app and try out a functional example.

On Android nine-patch images are defined by adding a one-pixel border to the full image. On that one-pixel border, you can define where the image is going to be stretched and where the content will be placed by placing black pixels in the border. The operating system automatically strips the one-pixel border out of the resulting graphics and uses the information to correctly scale the image and place the content. The top and right parts of the border define which parts of the image are stretched and the bottom, and right parts of the border define where the content is placed (the padding).

Nine-patch images must have a special identifier in their filename for the Android operating system to recognize them as such. All nine-patch images must be named `<imagename>.9.png`.

The following example will make it easier for you to understand how nine-patching works in practice. Figure 14-3 shows a Polaroid-style picture border. Say that you want to use that as a border for your images but the images vary in sizes. The image contains text. Having text is always problematic when scaling, as different aspect ratios will always make the text look bad. Scaling text is also not very desirable; the result is likely to be pixilated.

Figure 14-3: An example background image imitating a Polaroid-style picture border.

Let's see how the example image can be used in a scalable way by utilizing the Android nine-patching. For this image to work, it's important that the background is stretched from places where it will not cause the text to be distorted as well as to keep the borders the correct size.

Figure 14-4 shows how this example is defined to be scalable. To keep the text from stretching, I've set two pixels on both sides of the text to be the scaling pixels on the top border. Now, I've only added one pixel to be scaled because the background is a constant color. If you have color patterns or other effects, you need to carefully consider how the stretching is going to be done. Note that I also added exactly one pixel on both sides of the text so the image is scaled in the same proportions on both sides and the text stays in the middle.

For height I've added only one pixel to be scaled. In this case it doesn't matter much where this pixel is placed as long as it is above the bottom-white part and below the top-white part. Note that the stretching area does not have to be only one pixel. It can be any size you like.

Content placement of the padding definition is very simple. The content image is placed in the gray area. Figure 14-5 shows a few examples of different size content images placed as content for this nine-patch example.

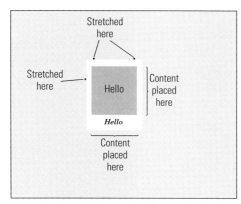

Figure 14-4: Example of nine-patch definition.

Figure 14-5: Resulting rendering of the example image border when nine-patching is utilized correctly.

Tip: When using nine-patch images, it's important to understand that the operating system never scales nine-patch images smaller than the original size. This means that you should aim to optimize your graphics to be as small as possible to accommodate all possible content. Making the images small also makes your app smaller and conserves runtime memory.

Figure 14-6 shows how the Polaroid-style example can be optimized. Using this image will yield exactly same results as the image in Figure 14-5.

Figure 14-6: Rendering of the example image border when nine-patching is utilized correctly.

USING NINE-PATCH IMAGES IN CODE

Nine-patch images are most useful when used as background images. Using them is very simple, as the content placement is included in the image itself.

The following code example demonstrates the use of nine-patch images as an `ImageView` background (you can use it on any other component background too). The reference to `@drawable/example_nine_patch` points to `example_nine_patch.9.png`. Note that you don't use the `.9` in the drawable reference.

```
<ImageView
    android:layout_width="wrap_content"
    android:layout_height="wrap_content"
    android:background="@drawable/example_nine_patch"
    android:src="@drawable/example_content_high"
    android:layout_margin="10dp"/>
```

NINE-PATCH TOOL IN SDK

The easiest way to build nine-patch files is to use a free utility tool called Draw 9-patch, which is provided with the Android SDK (see Figure 14-7). You'll find this tool in your Android SDK installation folder under the `tools` subfolder.

This tool allows you to take your original image and define the one-pixel borders easily. Any image you upload to the tool will have the border automatically added unless the image is already in the nine-patch format.

The tool also provides a handy preview of your image in different sizes so you can see immediately how it will be scaled. To see how the content will be placed when the nine-patch image is used as a background, you enable the Show Content checkbox. A content overlay will be drawn on the preview images.

NINE-PATCH IMAGES FROM DRAWING TOOLS

The Draw 9-patch tool isn't the most flexible tool in the world. Designers who are already familiar with the everyday tools will likely prefer to use them instead. Using Photoshop or any other similar tool is possible and easy too. You just manually add the one-pixel border. The border must be fully transparent other than where the control pixels are. The control pixels must be full black without any transparency. It's good idea to open the nine-patch images on the Draw 9-patch tool to check that everything works as intended. Using the wrong pixels on the border will cause a runtime crash when the image is used.

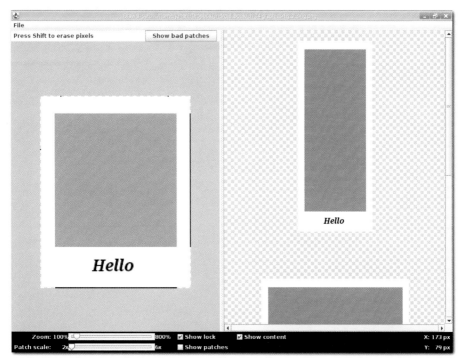

Figure 14-7: Android SDK's Draw 9-patch tool.

Source: Android SDK

DRAWABLE XML

Recall that the start of this chapter mentioned gradients and other graphics that are impossible to scale even when using the nine-patch method. Fortunately, the Android platform is not out of tricks yet. The platform supports creating simple graphical forms using XML-based definitions. You can create simple shapes, colors, gradients, and even bitmap effects by simply defining XML files. These XML files are placed in your project's resources folder in the `drawables` folder. They can be used in the same way as any other drawables and can also benefit from Android's excellent Resource Manager.

SHAPES

You can draw simple shapes by defining them in XML. The shapes available to you are rectangle, oval, line, and ring. My opinion is that these shapes are not very helpful alone but can be used in combination with other drawables to create visual effects very efficiently. Figure 14-8 shows some examples of rectangle and oval drawables.

Scan the QR code with your Android phone to open the companion app and try out a functional example.

Figure 14-8: Examples of rectangle and oval drawables from the XML definitions.

The way you define these drawables is to use a shape element and its `android:shape` attribute to describe which shape you want drawn. You can then add child elements to the shape element to change its properties. See the following code example. It is the top shape in Figure 14-8—the rectangle. The rectangle also has a gradient (more about gradients shortly) defined as the fill color, with rounded corners and a stroke color.

```xml
<?xml version="1.0" encoding="utf-8"?>
<shape xmlns:android="http://schemas.android.com/apk/res/android"
    android:shape="rectangle" >

    <gradient
        android:endColor="#66FF0000"
        android:startColor="#FF00FF00"
        android:type="sweep" />

    <corners android:radius="5dp" />

    <stroke
        android:width="3dp"
```

```
        android:color="#FF0000FF" />

</shape>
```

The following source code shows a different example. This code defines the other shape from Figure 14-8—the oval. The oval also has a fill color defined, this time it's a solid color and a stroke color.

```xml
<?xml version="1.0" encoding="utf-8"?>
<shape xmlns:android="http://schemas.android.com/apk/res/android"
    android:shape="oval" >

    <solid android:color="#44FF0000" />

    <stroke
        android:width="3dp"
        android:color="#FF00FFFF" />

</shape>
```

As you see these shapes are fairly simple but also very flexible. It is worth keeping these in mind when creating your graphical design. Using a shape instead of a bitmap will be much more memory efficient as well as more scalable.

PADDING

You can add padding to your shape's drawables by adding a padding element. However, you might not need to define the padding here, because you can define it in the layout XML. In some cases the padding element can be very useful. It can be especially important when defining layered drawables. You learn more about composite layered drawables later in this chapter.

GRADIENTS

Gradients are nearly impossible to implement in a scalable way when you have a bitmaps whose size is not well defined. Fortunately you can create gradients as fill colors for any shape. These gradients can then be used as backgrounds on your components or as part of a layered composite drawable. You'll learn about these composites shortly.

Android provides three gradient types for you:

- Linear—Gradient is drawn in one direction.
- Radial—Gradient starts from a single point and expands out in a radial manner.
- Sweep—Gradient direction follows a circular line.

The first two are very useful, and many designers use them in their designs. The sweep is much more rare, but at least there's the option if you ever run into a situation where it is needed.

For any gradient you need to define a start and end color. You can also define an optional third middle color. Other attributes vary between the gradient styles. For a linear gradient you can define an angle that tells the system which way the linear gradient is drawn. For the radial gradient, you need to define the radius and optionally set offset coordinates for the gradient's center.

 Scan the QR code with your Android phone to open the companion app and try out a functional example.

COLOR

A color drawable fills the available space with the selected color. This simple drawable can help make composite drawables easily customizable and maintainable. Note that (as in any other drawable) here too you can use the color resources to set the color. The following code example shows how simple it is to define a color drawable.

```xml
<?xml version="1.0" encoding="utf-8"?>
<color xmlns:android="http://schemas.android.com/apk/res/android"
    android:color="#FFFF0000" >
</color>
```

BITMAPS

You can also have a drawable XML for a bitmap. There is one very important use for this—tiling. If you want to have a background of an unspecified size component or have your app's background use a graphical pattern, this is pretty much the only option you have to implement it so it can scale and not suck massive amounts of memory.

The Android platform supports three tiling modes. Two of them are very useful. You can change the tiling mode by setting the `android:tileMode` attribute in the `bitmap` element to one of the following values (note that the default is no tiling):

- Repeat—Repeats the bitmap in both directions.
- Mirror—Repeats the shader's image horizontally and vertically, alternating mirror images so that adjacent images always seam.
- Clamp—Replicates the edge color.

Repeat is the simple mode where the available space is filled with the bitmap by repeating it as it is. Mirror does the same thing, but alternates with mirrored and normal bitmap for every other row. Clamp is a special mode that isn't tiling as such. It forces the bitmap's border color to be used to fill in the remaining space. Figure 14-9 shows examples of the repeat and mirror modes.

The following example code demonstrates the use of the tile mode in a bitmap XML element. The bitmap used is a simple single triangle. The same bitmap is used with both examples.

```
<bitmap xmlns:android="http://schemas.android.com/apk/res/android"
    android:dither="true"
    android:src="@drawable/example_triangle"
    android:tileMode="repeat" />
```

Figure 14-9: Examples of tiling bitmaps using repeat (above) and mirror (below) mode.

 Scan the QR code with your Android phone to open the companion app and try out a functional example.

COMPOSITE DRAWABLES WITH LAYERS

Android also allows you to create drawables by combining multiple drawables into one layer. This method can be very handy especially when combining bitmaps with simple shapes or colors. You might, for example, have some kind of chrome effect that is created as a nine-patch image and used in combination of a dynamic choice of color. You can create a simple composite drawable with a color layer combined with the bitmap.

For layered drawable you need to use the layer-list element. The layer-list can be placed into a drawable XML and used the same way any other drawable can. In the layer-list you define any number of child item elements. Each item can either refer to another drawable or can contain any of the drawable definitions described previously.

Take a look at the following example code and the resulting drawable shown in the Figure 14-10. In this example code you can see how the items can even be nine-patch images as well as any other drawables. Note that in case of a nine-patch image, the system automatically applies the padding values from the nine-patch. Padding values from other drawables are also automatically applied. The system considers elements that are defined later as child elements of the earlier defined elements.

Figure 14-10: An example layer-list drawable used to draw multiple layers.

```xml
<?xml version="1.0" encoding="utf-8"?>
<layer-list xmlns:android="http://schemas.android.com/apk/res/android" >

    <item>
        <nine-patch android:src="@drawable/example_nine_patch" />
    </item>
    <item android:drawable="@drawable/example_circular_gradient"/>
    <item>
        <color android:color="#3300FF00" />
    </item>
    <item android:drawable="@drawable/tiled_background"/>

</layer-list>
```

 Scan the QR code with your Android phone to open the companion app and try out a functional example.

SCALE AND ROTATE

You can also scale and rotate drawables using the drawable definitions. Scale and rotate elements allow you to apply scaling or rotation to any drawable.

See the following source code and Figure 14-11 for an example of rotation applied to the layered drawable created in the previous section.

```xml
<?xml version="1.0" encoding="utf-8"?>
<rotate xmlns:android="http://schemas.android.com/apk/res/android"
    android:drawable="@drawable/example_layer_drawable"
    android:fromDegrees="45"
    android:pivotX="50%"
    android:pivotY="50%" />
```

 Scan the QR code with your Android phone to open the companion app and try out a functional example.

Reminder About Selectors

Selectors are an important part of the drawable options. They allow you to define different drawables based on the user interface component state. The operating system then automatically handles the process of changing the graphics. Selectors were covered in Chapter 11 and so aren't repeated here.

Figure 14-11: An example layer-list drawable used to draw multiple layers.

DRAWING FROM CODE

Of course, using XML definitions to create graphics isn't always detailed enough. The Android platform also provides great tools for creating visual presentations of components in the Android code. On the code level, you can change almost everything but it is also noticeably more complex and requires more effort. My recommendation is to carefully research the available components and their functionality before implementing your own.

To draw your own graphics, you need to create your own class that inherits from the `View` class or one of its descendants. I encourage you to find the class that most closely resembles the functionality you need and make that your class's *superclass*. That way, you will likely need to customize only part of the class and can use the bulk of it as is. If, for example, you want to change the way some buttons work or look, you should start with the `Button` class and replace the functionality only when you must.

To define how your new component is going to be drawn, you must override the `onDraw(Canvas)` method. Depending on the situation you might not want to call . If you want to maintain the original component's visuals and simply add to it, you should call the `super` method. If you want to fully override the component's visuals, you can ignore it.

When you're writing code for the `onDraw` method pay extra attention to your code's performance. It is possible that this code will be called very often and all unnecessary object creation should be avoided here. It's likely that keeping objects that are needed on each drawing pass in memory will be better for performance.

DRAWING ON CANVAS

The tool for drawing is the canvas object you receive as a parameter to the `onDraw` method. The canvas class provides multiple helpful methods for you to draw different forms and bitmaps. A few of them are listed here, but for a full list of available methods and the full documentation, see the class documentation on Android developers website at `http://developer.android.com/reference/android/graphics/Canvas.html`.

- `drawArc`—Draws the specified arc, which will be scaled to fit inside the specified oval.
- `drawBitmap`—Draws a bitmap.
- `drawCircle`—Draws the specified circle using the specified paint.
- `drawColor`—Fills the entire canvas's bitmap (restricted to the current clip) with the specified color.
- `drawLines`—Draws a series of lines.
- `drawRect`—Draws the specified `Rect` using the specified paint.
- `drawText`—Draws the text using the specified paint.

PAINT OBJECT

The `paint` object is often a required parameter for drawing on the canvas. The `paint` object acts as the style definition for the object that is being drawn. It stores values like the colors, stroke style, transparency, and font style. Not all of these attributes apply to all shapes.

Plan the paints you use and create them outside the `onDraw` method if possible. Creating a `paint` object in the `onDraw` method will accumulate unnecessary garbage objects.

SHAPE-DRAWING EXAMPLE

Let's look at an example of dynamically drawing a shape on-screen. In the following source code you see a custom view. The only method that has been overridden is `onDraw`. The `onDraw` method draws a simple semi-transparent square. The location of the square is dynamic and decided by the coordinate variables. The coordinate variables on the other hand are controlled by the on touch listener. Note the `invalidate()` call at the touch event handler. That call causes the view to be redrawn whenever a user is moving his finger on the screen and the square follows that motion. Figure 14-12 shows the code rendered on a phone.

Note also the `paint` object created in the constructor. Because it is used on every draw iteration, recreating it every time would cause unnecessary garbage.

```
package com.androiduipatterns.smashingandroidui.examples.graphics;

import android.content.Context;
import android.graphics.Canvas;
import android.graphics.Paint;
import android.util.AttributeSet;
import android.view.MotionEvent;
import android.view.View;

public class ExampleCustomView extends View {

    private Paint paint;

    private int x = 0;
    private int y = 0;

    private int width = 200;
    private int height = 200;

    public ExampleCustomView(Context context, AttributeSet attrs) {
        super(context, attrs);

        // this Paint object is needed every time onDraw is called
        // therefore I create it here and keep it.
        paint = new Paint();
        paint.setColor(0x44FF0000);

        // To demonstrate dynamic drawing I've added a touch listener
        // that allows user to drag the drawn rectangle on screen:
        this.setOnTouchListener(new OnTouchListener() {
            int x_start = 0;
            int y_start = 0;

            int x_drag_start = 0;
            int y_drag_start = 0;

            @Override
            public boolean onTouch(View v, MotionEvent event) {
```

```
            if (event.getAction() == MotionEvent.ACTION_DOWN) {
                x_drag_start = (int) event.getX();
                y_drag_start = (int) event.getY();
                x_start = x;
                y_start = y;
            } else if (event.getAction() == MotionEvent.ACTION_MOVE) {
                int delta_x = (int) event.getX() - x_drag_start;
                int delta_y = (int) event.getY() - y_drag_start;
                x = x_start + delta_x;
                y = y_start + delta_y;

                //calling invalidate causes the component to draw itself
                invalidate();
            }

            return true;
        }
    });

}


/**
 * Draws a rectangle on screen where the user has dragged it.
 */
@Override
protected void onDraw(Canvas canvas) {
    canvas.drawRect(x, y, x + width, y + height, paint);
}
}
```

This component is placed into a layout by simply using the class's fully qualified name. See the following example code:

```
<com.androiduipatterns.smashingandroidui.examples.graphics.ExampleCustomView
    android:layout_width="fill_parent"
    android:layout_height="fill_parent"
    android:layout_margin="10dp" />
```

Scan the QR code with your Android phone to open the companion app and try out a functional example.

Figure 14-12: Example of how the code looks when rendered.
Users can drag the square to move it on the screen.

SUMMARY

With the various graphical drawing tools of the Android platform you can create infinitively scalable complex graphics like gradients and tiling backgrounds. Using these methods can save time and make your app work faster and more table. Although it is not necessary to memorize these techniques, it is a good idea to be aware of which drawing tools are out there.

BEYOND SCALABLE – RESPONSIVE DESIGN

UNTIL THIS POINT, the book has covered scalable Android user interfaces in the context of small variation of screen sizes. By utilizing layouts and other resources correctly, your app will scale nicely to phones with large 4.5-inch screens as well as to 3.5-inch screens. But what do you do when you want to go beyond these constraints?

A design approach called *responsive design* has become popular in web design when facing this same problem. Websites nowadays have to work on smartphones, tablets, laptops, desktops, and even on connected TVs. Simply stretching the layout from smaller screens to larger screens isn't enough anymore. The idea is to dynamically change the order of components that are visible by rearranging the page structure. This usually means reducing the number of visible columns.

This chapter introduces you to responsive design on the Android.

MORE ANDROID DEVICES THAN JUST PHONES

Let's look at the reasoning why more heavyweight methods are needed than just the layout managers. Android is a platform of diversity. As you read in the introductory chapters, there are hundreds of different devices out there. Many of them have much larger screens than the average smartphone device. The large screens require developers and designers to change their design approach. The smartphone design simply stretched to a larger screen doesn't utilize the screen effectively and makes for a subpar user experience. Take a look at Figures 15-1 and 15-2.

Figure 15-1: Twitter's tweet list on a 10.1-inch tablet screen.
Source: Twitter

These two screenshots from the official Android Twitter client illustrate very vividly why using scalable layouts is not enough (I'm hoping that by the time you're reading this Twitter has already released a better version of their client). A lot of screen space is wasted, and the layout does not look good. But it's much more than just looking bad and not using all the screen space. In both screens, part of the information loses its context. In Figure 15-1, the tweet time is moved very far from the tweet text and in Figure 15-2, the retweet and favorite numbers are on the opposite side of the screen from their labels.

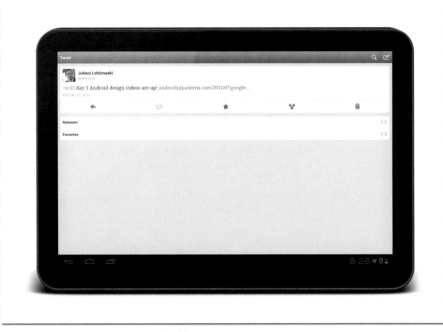

Figure 15-2: Twitter's tweet view on a 10.1-inch tablet screen.

Source: Twitter

ANDROID TABLETS

Android tablet is a fuzzy term. Tablets have as much or more variation than smartphones. In some cases it's not easy to tell if a device is a tablet or not. Is the Samsung Galaxy Note with its 5.3-inch display a tablet? Will the same interface that works on a 7-inch display work on a 13-inch tablet? And what if the tablet has a full size external keyboard? Should you also consider Android netbooks?

Fortunately, there's no real technical difference between an Android smartphone and an Android tablet, other than the screen size. Therefore, you can use the same techniques to make changes to the user interfaces on larger tablet devices.

GOOGLE TV

Android also runs on TVs. Although there is an official Google TV, it is not the only way to run Android apps on TVs. There are multiple devices that can be connected to large TV screens. The official Google TV is a separate version of Android that runs the same apps and provides the same APIs. The Google TVs have different controls and some added APIs. They, of course, don't have touch screens, which are the dominant control mechanism on the smartphones.

It should be pretty clear that the same user interface won't work on a TV screen controlled by a D-pad or touchpad that works on a smartphone or a tablet. But I think that the biggest difference with TVs, compared to the smartphone and tablet, are the different user goals. User goals are the foundation and requirements for an interface. TV apps must be different than just an adapted user interface. I strongly advise you to carefully evaluate your app's user goals and determine how they align with TV experience before jumping into adapting your app to the TV.

Also worth noting is that a TV is usually a shared device, unlike smartphones and tablets. Users are unlikely to log in to TV devices with their personal accounts. That is also why Google has not provided versions of Gmail or Google+ apps for Google TV. These kinds of apps work much better on personal devices than on TVs.

UNDERSTANDING RESPONSIVE DESIGN

Responsive design has its roots in web design. The web has always lacked strict size guidelines, and websites have to support many different resolutions. It's no surprise that designing for the Android platform requires a similar mindset and similar tools.

The starting point for designing Android apps is different than when designing websites. Websites must work perfectly on all computer screens, so that's where the interface design usually starts.

Let's look at an abstract example of a generic website design (see Figure 15-3). In this example the website has a three-column layout. The column A is the navigation, column B is the main content, and column C is additional or secondary content. All the columns resize nicely when the available space changes.

If the available space becomes much smaller—the user resizes the browser window or maybe opens the page on a tablet—the content might not fit within the screen anymore. Each of the scalable sections has a

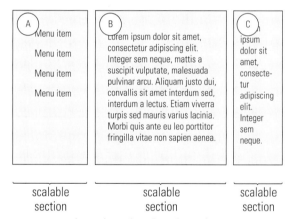

Figure 15-3: An abstract three-column design for a website.

natural minimum size at which they look good and are functional. When all of the sections reach that minimum size, you need a more drastic layout change.

Figure 15-4 shows how the layout could be rearranged. In this case the secondary content (C) moves below the main content (B), freeing more space for the main content and navigation (A).

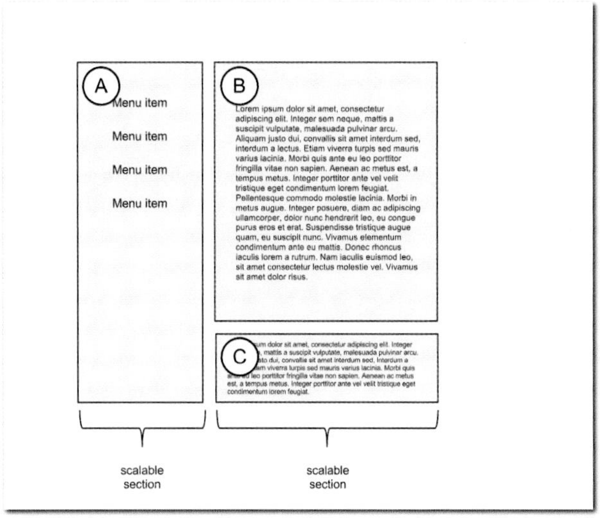

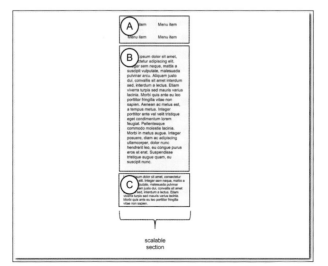

Figure 15-4: An example how the web design could be rearranged for a tablet device.

If the same website is viewed on an even smaller screen—a smartphone screen—the user interface must be rearranged again. Figure 15-5 shows an example of the same interface adapted to a smartphone screen. Note that the navigation section (A) is also rearranged internally due to the different shape of the container. This brings you into an important point of responsive design. Not only do the large component containers (A, B, C) rearrange, but each of them adapt internally as well.

Figure 15-5: An example how the web design could be rearranged for a smartphone.

Tip: An important feature of responsive design is that the components that are rearranged are not reimplemented for every different position they can have. Doing that would be way too costly in the development phase. The key to responsive design is to keep using the same components you already have built to support all the different layouts you have.

HOW TO APPROACH RESPONSIVE ANDROID DESIGN

After that short overview of the theory of responsive design, this section returns to Android apps and covers how the same techniques can be utilized there. As android apps are built using a very similar design approach, the same responsive design approach works very well on the Android platform.

That said, the technology used to implement responsive design on the Android platform is different from the web. The Android user interface APIs are much more flexible than their web counterparts, which means you can build even better and more flexible apps on the Android than you can on the web.

This section introduces the thought process and approach to responsive design for Android. This chapter covers the overview, and Chapter 16 covers the technical implementations of this approach. The technologies you'll use include the following:

- Android resource managers
- Android layout managers
- Fragments (A technical term for a reusable section of user interface. Fragments are explained in detail in Chapter 16.)
- Automatically adapting user interface components

Starting from a Phone

Responsive design on the web typically begins with the largest screen and then is modified to fit on smaller screens. On Android it is very likely that process will start from the other end. You are likely to start with an app that works on a smartphone and need to adapt it to a tablet. Even if you don't have an app yet, it's more likely that you'll start from the phone design, as the smartphone market is currently so much larger than the tablet market. (It makes sense to target the largest target group first.)

If you created an information architecture diagram during your design, you should get it out and look at it again. If you didn't draw one, now is the time to do it! This diagram will help you to visualize the relationships of each screen in your app.

A Simple Example

Consider this simple example—a list of items with an item detail screen and new item screen. For example, Gmail is a complicated version of this same structure. Figure 15-6 shows the information architecture diagram of this simple example app.

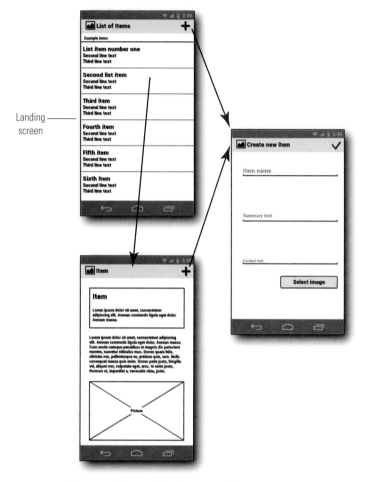

Figure 15-6: Information architecture of the abstract example app.

The structure of the information in this app is clear. The item list screen is a parent screen of the item details screen. The new items screen doesn't have a place in the hierarchy. It is more like a utility screen that can be invoked from multiple places.

First consider what you can do with the item list screen (see Figure 15-7) and the item details screen (see Figure 15-8). It should be apparent that simply stretching these screens won't be good enough. You need to rearrange the layout.

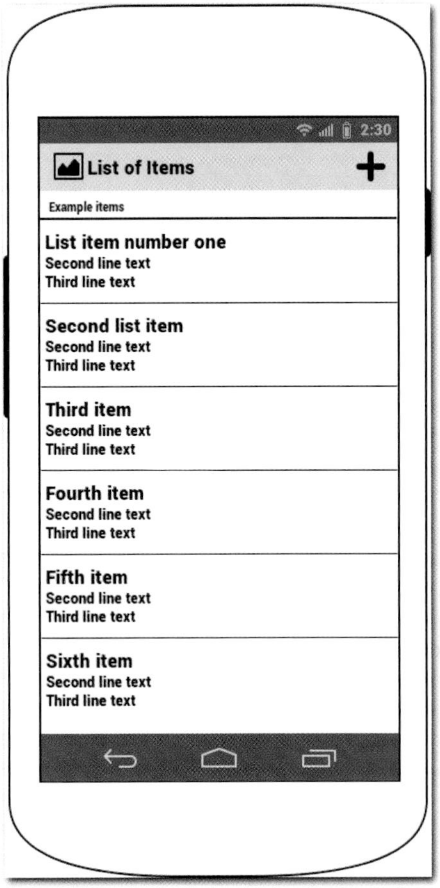

Figure 15-7: Item list screen on a phone.

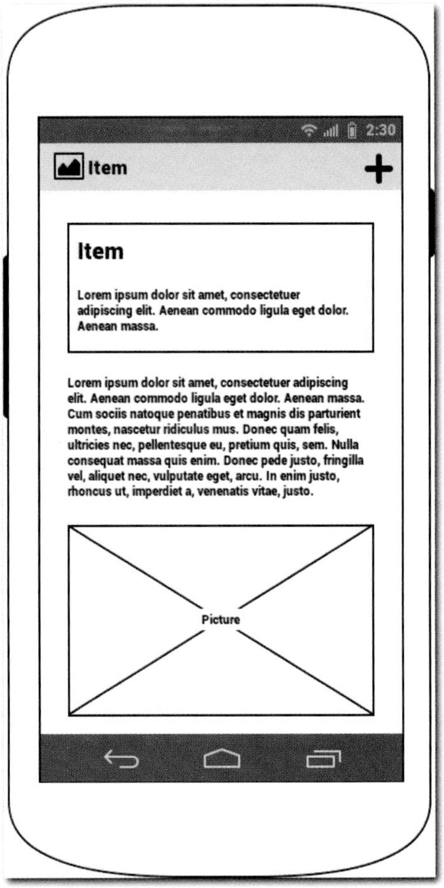

Figure 15-8: Item details screen on a phone.

On the Android, not all the content that is subject to the rearrange will always be on the same screen. You could bring the two item related screens into one large screen. Figure 15-9 shows an example of this approach. In this example I have placed the item list to the left and item details to the right. The screen functionality of these components is the same. When the user taps on any of the items on the list, the right side of the screen will update that item.

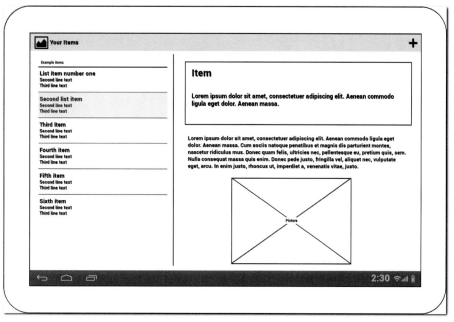

Figure 15-9: Item list and item details screen unified into one screen on a tablet.

But what about the Create New Item screen (see Figure 15-10)? Because this screen is not part of the screen hierarchy in an obvious way and combining it with any of the information in the other screens would probably not make it any better, you can keep it separate. In this example (see Figure 15-11), I'm using an overlay for the Create New Item screen on the tablet. That will help keep the width of the component smaller, thus making it look better. I've also added a text component on the left side of the form. This can include some help text of similar content.

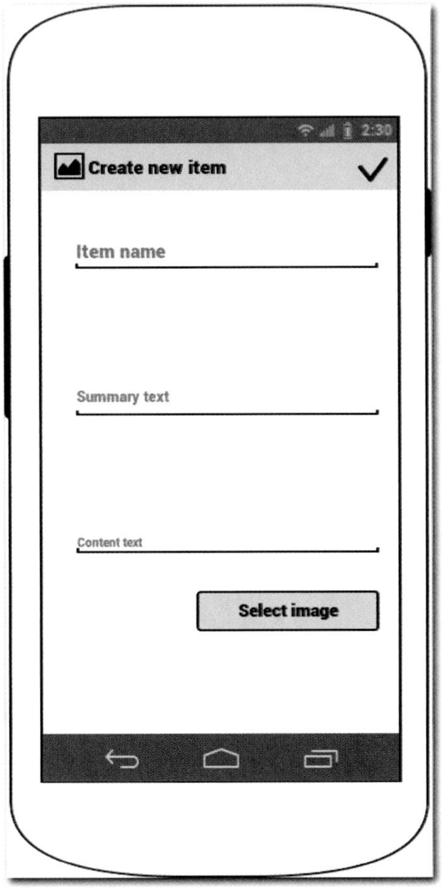

Figure 15-10: Create New Item screen on a phone.

This example shows a very general approach to responsive design on the Android platform. In practice, each app has its nuances. The rest of this chapter introduces techniques you can use to expand your toolkit in this field.

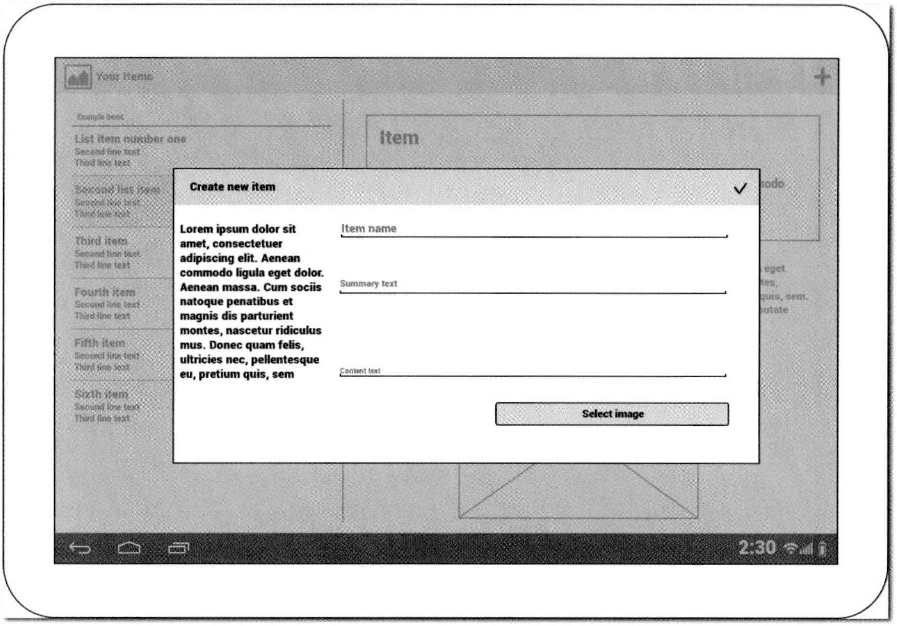

Figure 15-11: Create New Item screen on a tablet.

A Real Example

This section takes a look at a real example. This app is one of my favorites on the Android. It implements responsive design between phones and tablets nicely. You can see the app in the Figure 15-12. The structure of the app is very similar to the previous example.

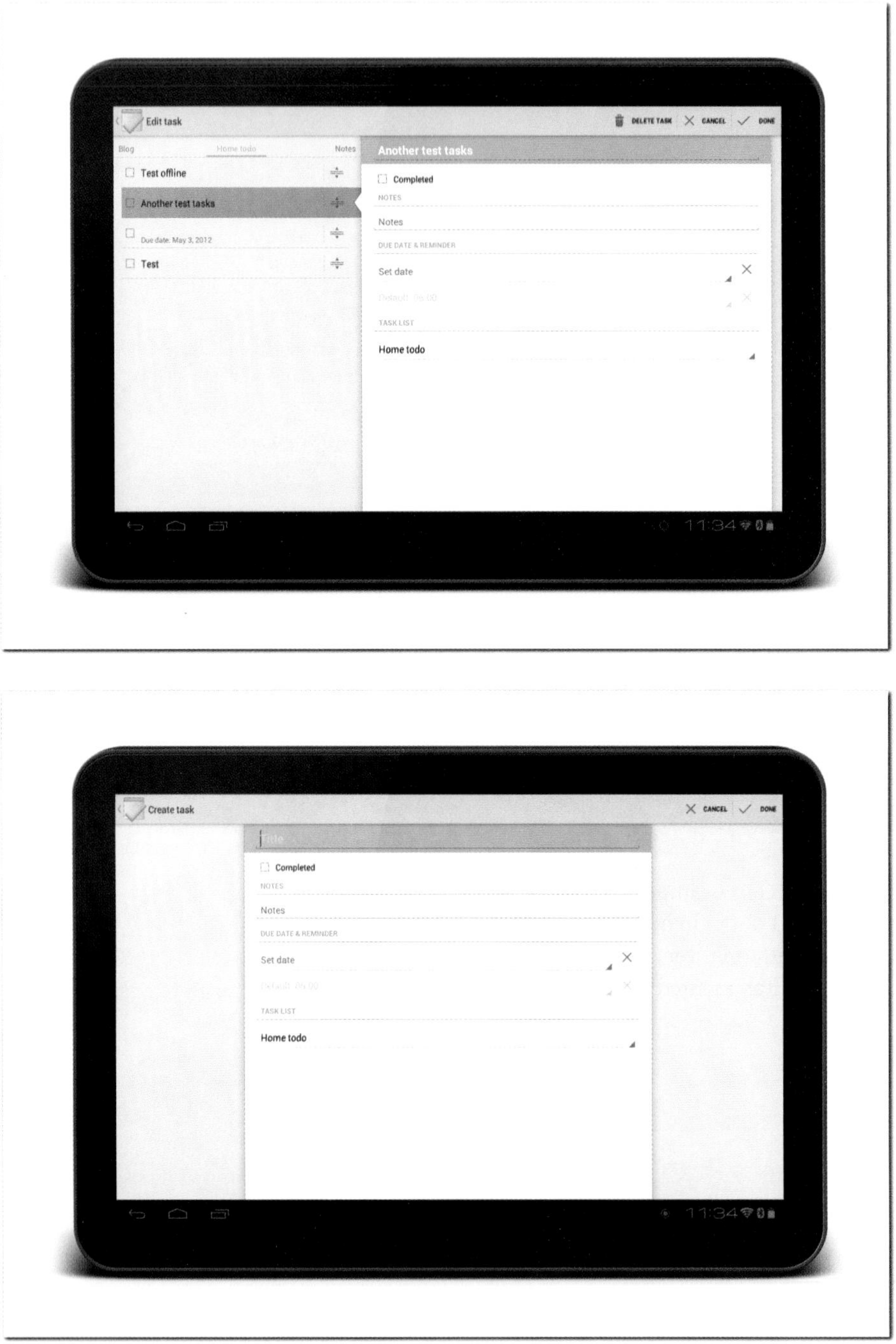

Figure 15-12: The Tasks app works great on phones and tablets.

Source: Tasks app

DON'T BUILD A TABLET APP: DESIGN FOR TABLETS

The goal of this process should not be to build a separate tablet version of your app. Your tablet app and phone app should be the same in Google Play or in any other store.

Think about your app as one app with different user interface configurations.

REUSABLE COMPONENTS (FRAGMENTS)

When designing your app, your goal is to define user interface sections, technically called *fragments*, that you can use and combine with any layout configuration to create the optimal user experience for each. In the previous examples, these sections or fragments were the list view, details view, and create new item view. All of these fragments can be implemented once and wrapped into different parent layouts to create different user interfaces to tablets and to phones without having to duplicate any of the functionality.

The Google Play Android app is an excellent example of the clever reuse of fragments in phone and tablet layout even when the layout is very different. The fragments in the Google Play app are relatively small, but they also are independent and, therefore, very easily redistributed in the user interface. Figures 15-13 and 15-14 show the similarities in the app's item screen on the phone and tablet platforms, even though the layout as a whole is very different. For example, the components marked 1 and 2 in both figures are the same, with only very small tweaks that can be implemented easily. I encourage you to carefully study the Google Play app to see this reuse of components throughout the app.

Figure 15-13: Google Play app's item screen on a phone.

Source: Google

Figure 15-14: Google Play app's item screen on a tablet.

Source: Google

Chapter 16 explains creating fragments and using them in activities and layouts in detail.

FINDING MINIMUM AND MAXIMUM SIZE

Although practicality might sometimes dictate that you design simply, you should keep flexibility in mind. There's no reason why the tablet user interface should not be used on devices that are technically phones if it is more suitable to them than the phone interface.

The key to flexibility is to find the minimum and maximum sizes of your user interfaces and the user interface fragments. For example, in the two-column layout I talked about previously, there is a certain point when the screen gets larger at which you can't use only one list screen. On the other hand, having two columns becomes impossible at some point when the screen gets too small. I encourage you to study your interface on different screen sizes. Create the layout points based on your observations instead of simply making a phone and a tablet user interface.

Tip: You don't have to create devices for all screen sizes. You can easily set up multiple emulators using the Android SDK.

COST-BENEFIT EVALUATION

Creating responsive user interfaces takes more effort than building a single user interface for one device group. This is true especially when the app was initially designed and built to run only on smartphones. As with everything you should always carefully evaluate whether your time is best spent doing this or something else.

The cost of responsive user interface can be minimized with careful planning. Reusing user interface components and fragments efficiently can save a lot of time. Even if you don't plan to support larger screens in the initial launch of your app, I recommend that you take time to plan and design for such possibilities from the start. Implement your interface for phone screens using the fragment APIs, and plan for reusable components. This will save you a lot of time later and won't make the initial implementation any slower.

COMMON WAYS TO CREATE RESPONSIVE USER INTERFACES

This section looks at some common ways you can adapt user interfaces from smaller to larger screens. You'll often need to combine these solutions in order to create great results.

SCREENS TO COLUMNS

As you already saw in the previous example, you can combine multiple small screens into one larger one (see Figure 15-15). This requires that the screens that you want to combine relate to each other.

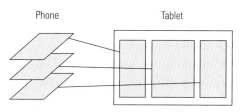

Figure 15-15: Overview of a screen-to-columns design.

I like to call this approach *responsive design in 3D* due to the added dimension of rearranging the activity stack to a flattened hierarchy.

FLOATING SCREENS

Utility screens (such as a Settings screen) often don't have a fixed place in the screen hierarchy and can be accessed from multiple screens directly, hence the term *floating screen*. Incorporating screens like this to a larger screen can be difficult. Often, they need to be shown alone without any helpful context, so the columns-to-screens design does not work.

Stretching the screen to a larger display isn't a great option, because doing so often makes the screen look bad and sometimes even difficult to use.

In this situation, consider laying these types of floating screens on top of other screens (see Figure 15-16). Doing so allows you to limit the layout width so that the screen looks and functions correctly. This overlay technique also helps the users understand that the screen is not part of the navigation structure but is instead a side step to get a short task done.

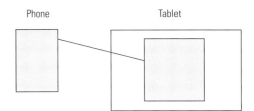

Figure 15-16: Screen to floating screen solution.

OPTIONAL CONTENT

What do you do if all the relevant information is shown on-screen, but you have leftover whitespace? Note that empty space isn't necessarily a bad thing, but it's still worth evaluating whether you have any content you can place there. Sometimes you might want to show content on a larger screen that isn't part of your phone design or is hidden in a menu (see Figure 15-17). Help info or advertisements are good examples of optional information you might consider including.

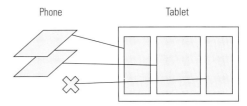

Figure 15-17: Optional content shown only on screens that have room for it.

ADJUSTING COMPONENTS ONE FOR ONE

Responsive design on the web often involves a one-to-one adjustment of all the existing components. The same technique can be used on the Android platform in many cases. You can rearrange all the components from your phone's user interface to the tablet layout so that the user can access the same information easily. Usually this means that you adjust the user interface fragments that are laid out vertically on the phone to a wider layout on the tablet (see Figure 15-18).

Replacing Components

Not all components work on a larger screen as desired. Sometimes you simply must create another component for the larger screen to utilize the increased screen real estate. A good example of a component that doesn't work that well on a large screen is the list view. Lists can, of course, be made to work on larger screens by making them much smaller, but sometimes that is not possible or desirable. In those situations you might consider replacing the list with a grid view (see Figure 15-19). A grid view utilizes the available horizontal space better because it fills in components horizontally.

Automatically Adapting Components

Some of the components provided by the Android APIs automatically adapt to larger screen sizes. One good example of this is the Action Bar. It automatically resizes when shown on a tablet screen.

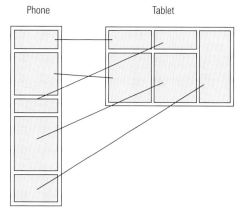

Figure 15-18: Abstract example from the phone to the tablet.

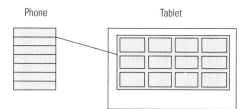

Figure 15-19: An abstract example of replacing a list component with a grid view when moving from a phone to a tablet.

Tabbed user interfaces also adapt automatically when more screen real estate is available by moving into Action Bar. You can see more about tabbed user interfaces in Chapter 19.

SUMMARY

Don't create a separate tablet version of your phone app. Instead, make your app's user interface responsive. There is no one Android tablet but a continuum of devices with various screen sizes. Supporting all of their screen sizes requires you to provide a continuum of scalable user interface configurations. Following responsive design principles will help you reach a good solution.

IMPLEMENTING RESPONSIVE USER INTERFACES

THE PREVIOUS CHAPTER introduced the theory behind using responsive design to support multiple screen sizes. This chapter dives into the technical side of the same concept. You'll learn all about fragments, including how to use them to create responsive user interfaces. After introducing the concept of fragments, the chapter goes through a full example of a responsive layout and also talks about migrating existing apps.

INTRODUCTION TO FRAGMENTS

Fragments are the key to implementing responsive user interfaces on Android. A *fragment* is an independent user interface section that can be added to a layout. Probably the best way to think about fragments is to think of them as sub-activities. Fragments are always controlled by an activity and their lifecycle is bound to the activity's lifecycle unless you manually change this aspect.

You implement fragments in a very similar way that you create activities. You create the implementing class and set a layout to draw the fragment's user interface. Fragments aren't required to have a user interface, but the fragments discussed in the scope of this book do all have fragments.

CREATING FRAGMENTS

To create a fragment, you extend the `Fragment` class or one of its subclasses (`Dialog Fragment`, `ListFragment`, `PreferenceFragment`, or `WebViewFragment`).

Most of your knowledge of working with activities is applicable to working with fragments, with a few notable exceptions. First, many of the utility methods you might want to use are not provided by the fragment superclass, and fragment is not a `Context` object. To get a `Context` object, call the `getActivity()` method. It will return the activity that your fragment is currently attached to. You can use that to call the method you need from a `Context` object. Note that the method can return `null` if the fragment instance isn't currently attached to any activity.

The second big difference is that you cannot call the `setContentView()` method to set the fragment's user interface. Instead, the fragment's user interface is created using the `onCreate View()` method. You must override the method and return the user interface view from that method.

FRAGMENT LIFECYCLE

Fragments have similar lifecycle methods to activities. You can use them to stop and start functionality the same way you do with activities. For the full lifecycle method specification, you should take a look at the Android documentation at `http://developer.android. com/guide/topics/fundamentals/fragments.html`.

The important lifecycle methods within the scope of this book are `onCreateView()`, whereby you create your fragment's user interface and the `onActivityCreated()`, which is called after the `onCreateView()` when the parent activity is created. That is a good place to initialize components that require a `Context` object.

ADDING FRAGMENTS TO LAYOUTS

Fragments alone are not very useful. You must add them to layouts. There are two ways to do this. The simplest way to place fragments on a user interface is to use an XML element in a layout file. The `fragment` element can be placed anywhere in any layout file where you would place any other user interface components. Its size and location is defined the same way as other user interface components. You define the fully qualified class name of the implementing `fragment` class and that's all. Whenever the layout is displayed by any activity, the fragment is automatically initialized and the user interface is placed on the screen. Your fragment must implement a constructor without any parameters for this to work properly.

The following code example shows you how to define a `fragment` element:

```
<fragment
  android:id="@+id/<id goes here>"
  android:layout_width="match_parent"
  android:layout_height="match_parent"
  class="<fully qualified class name of the fragment class>" />
```

You can also add fragments dynamically to layouts from your code by using the `FragmentManager` class.

FRAGMENTMANAGER AND FRAGMENTTRANSACTION

`FragmentManager` and `FragmentTransaction` are the helper classes you can use to add, remove, and replace fragments in your activities. To acquire a `FragmentManager` instance, you call the `getFragmentManager()` method in your activity.

You can change the fragments in the user interface by using transactions. A *transaction* is an atomic group of operations that are executed together. With fragment transactions, you can define multiple operations—such as replace multiple fragments—that are executed simultaneously. To create a fragment transaction, you must begin the transaction and then define all the actions. Calling `commit` on the transaction will execute it.

Usually when replacing or adding fragments to/from code it makes sense to add a dedicated frame layout into your layout XML as a placeholder for the fragments. This makes it easier to define the size and location of the fragment.

The following source code shows a very simple example of replacing a fragment in a container:

```
FragmentTransaction ft = getFragmentManager().beginTransaction();
ft.replace(R.id.<container id>, <fragment object>);
ft.commit();
```

Tip: Replacing fragments isn't the only option you have. The fragment transaction also allows you to add, remove, show, and hide fragments. For the full specification of the fragment transaction, see the Android documentation at `http://developer.android.com/reference/android/app/FragmentTransaction.html`.

Fragment Transitions

As with activities, when fragments are replaced they can also display transition animations. The animation is set to the fragment transactions. You can set fully custom animations using the `setCustomAnimations()` method to define enter and exit animations in the same way you would define activity transition animations. You can also use `setTransition()` to set one of the default transition animations.

Fragments and the Back Stack

By default fragment transactions don't affect the back stack. You can, however, easily add any transaction to the back stack by calling `addToBackStack()` with the fragment transaction. The operating system takes care of the rest. When the user presses the Back button a reverse operation automatically executes.

Tip: To ensure maximum flexibility of your fragments, take care to build each fragment in a scalable manner. Use the layouts and best practices introduced earlier in this book. If each of your fragments is scalable alone it means that the user interfaces built using the fragments are scalable and will easily adapt to layout changes.

FRAGMENT AND ACTIVITY ARCHITECTURE

The way you build interaction between your activities and fragments defines how flexible the user interface will be. Fragments are modules of the user interface, but they should also be modular in your code. The less the fragments have to know about other fragments and even about their parent activities, the more flexibly you can use them in different user interface configurations.

The most important rule to follow is that fragments should never communicate directly with each other. All communication should always go through the activities. If they must communicate directly, you will be forced to always display them at the same time, which forces undesired coupling in your architecture.

To be most flexible you can create an interface that defined communication from your fragment to the activity. By doing this you can use the fragment in any activity that implements the interface, and you're not tied into just one activity.

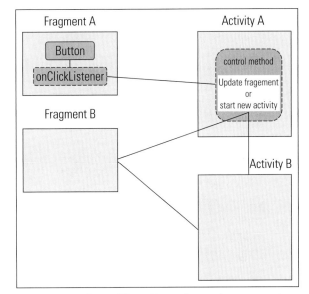

ACTIVITIES CONTROL THE FLOW AND LAYOUT

Activities have been controlling your app flow before fragments appeared and should remain controlling them. Whenever a control in a fragment needs to update other parts of the user interface, the fragment should call the parent activity. Figure 16-1

Figure 16-1: Example control flow architecture from one fragment to another, using a parent.

shows an example control flow. In this example, the user presses a button in fragment A that affects the user interface beyond the fragment itself. The control is sent to the parent activity, which decides based on the current layout whether a new activity needs to be launched or an existing fragment needs to be replaced or updated. A structure like this guarantees that you can use fragments A and B in the same activity or in separate activities.

Using Fragments on Older Devices

Fragments were introduced to the Android platform in the Android 3.0 Honeycomb release (API level 11). Using them on projects that target older platform versions is possible but requires few small code changes. You also need to import the Android support package to the project. Read more about support package in the Android documentation at `http://developer.android.com/sdk/compatibility-library.html`.

First, all the activities that handle fragments must extend the `FragmentActivity` class from the support package instead of the activity class. Second, you need to make sure that you refer to classes in the support package instead of the Android package whenever using any fragment related classes.

It is very easy to accidentally refer to a class from a wrong package when writing the code. The Lint tool, which is integrated to the Android Eclipse plug-in, will warn you if you are using classes that are not available on all devices your app is targeted to. These warnings are worth paying attention to as they can prevent runtime crashes on older devices.

ISOLATED FRAGMENT FUNCTIONALITY INCREASES MODULARITY

To keep your code clean and modular, you should keep the fragments' internal control managed by the fragments themselves. There's no need to give control back to the activity class when updates are made internally in the fragment and do not affect the rest of the user interface. Fragments that populate their own data and handle their own user interface updates are much easier to place in the user interface. The activities managing them need only to create them and place them into a layout and everything is done.

MIGRATING EXISTING APPS

Hundreds of Android apps were built before any Android tablets were announced. Android versions 2.3 and older didn't really support building truly responsive user interfaces anyway. It is very likely that you have old apps on Google Play or in some other stores that do not yet have a tablet layout and have not been build using the fragments. The question is what to do with these applications. Should you try to update their user interfaces slowly toward a more responsive approach to support tablets or fully redesign the user interface from scratch?

MOVING SLOWLY: AN ITERATIVE APPROACH TO NEW DESIGN

If you work for a company that has commercial software in the market, it is likely that the product management team is unwilling to invest in a full redesign and reimplementation of your app. Full redesign and implementation takes time and resources away from maintaining the software. In this kind of situation I recommend working slowly towards the responsive user interface. You can start by identifying the possible fragments in the old user interface, and sketch a possible large screen layout based on them. Doing the design and validating it with user testing can show whether the old interface can be turned into a responsive approach. If the results are negative it might not be worth spending the time needed for a gradual transformation, as it will probably be in vain.

Once you have identified the possible fragments, you can start turning them into fragments one by one. You can simply replace your activity's layout with a fragment where possible. Also move the independent functionality to the fragment to make reusing it easier later.

You can do the slow one-by-one replacement of the fragments while updating the user interface and fixing any bugs. The user interface won't change at all during this phase. Also, because there are no visible changes in your user interface all automated user interface testing should still work; you can easily verify that you haven't accidentally broken anything. You will most likely have to reimplement your unit tests however.

At some point your app is either fully or nearly fully transformed into the new fragment technology. You can now start experimenting with different layouts and creating activities that manage the responsive user interface. At this point it is probably also easier to take the last steps toward supporting larger screens, as the investment is considerably smaller and safer.

GET IT OVER WITH: FULL REDESIGN AT ONCE

Of course, if your app design isn't good enough for making a slow transformation, you might need to do a one-off redesign. Before you jump into doing that, remember to utilize your old app in usability testing to find out what the users really do with your app. Having an old app version can be very valuable in the design process for understanding real user needs. From there, the redesign is like building a new app.

LOOKING AT AN EXAMPLE APP

This section looks at an example app that ties in everything from this and from the previous chapters. This simple app demonstrates how to reuse fragments and lay them out in different configurations, as well as how to manage the communication between the fragments and activities.

The app function is simple. Users can select a color from three provided choices. After the selection, the users see the color and can then choose to see more information about it.

Scan the QR code with your Android phone to open the companion app and try out a functional example.

APP DESIGN

Let's start exploring the app design from the phone interface wireframes. This is probably something you'll be doing for your own app, too. Phones are still the most important target group for most apps and probably will be for a long time in the future.

The phone app consists of three screens. Figure 16-2 shows the wireframes. The user will press one of the buttons on the first screen to select a color (color picker screen). That selection will open up a second screen with that color shown (color screen). Pressing the button on the second screen will take user to the last screen, which contains textual information about the selected color (color info screen).

Now, taking that design to larger screen the first step is to look at smaller tablets and how to better utilize the available space. On a smaller tablet, you can nicely fit two of the screens together. For this available space, I've created two screens that unify two of the three phone screens into one. Figure 16-3 shows how this would look on a portrait tablet.

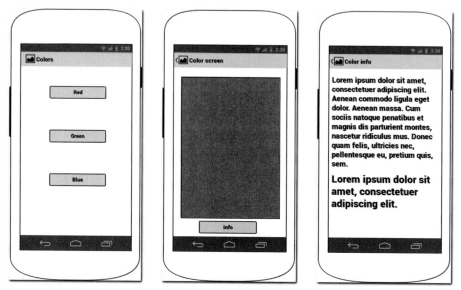

Figure 16-2: The example app smartphone screen design wireframes.

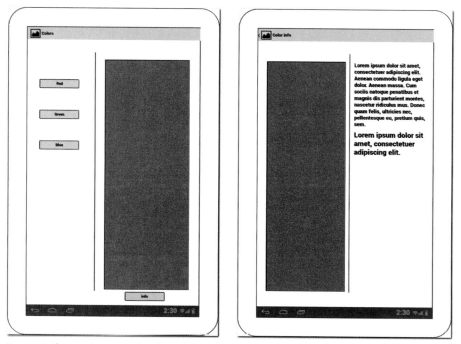

Figure 16-3: The example app two-column layout design wireframes.

The two-column layout is not optimal for larger 10-inch tablets. For a larger tablet, I've created a three-column layout that unifies all the three phone screens into one (see Figure 16-4). Note that the button on the color screen is not needed in this design, because the info text is always visible.

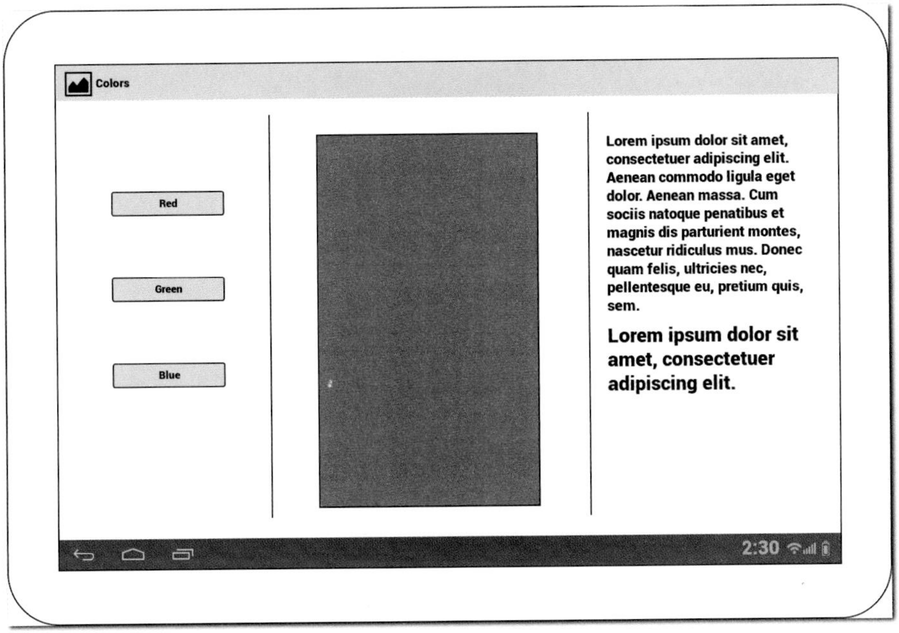

Figure 16-4: Example app with three-column design wireframes.

BUILDING THE PHONE USER INTERFACE WITH FRAGMENTS

In this state it is easy to see that there clearly are three fragments in this design. Each of the phone design screen forms one design. When you're starting to build the app (whether or not you plan to support larger screens in the first release), it makes sense to build these three screens using fragments. Each one of the screens is an activity.

Color Picker Screen

Let's look at the activity and the fragment of the color picker screen.

Activity

The color picker screen activity at this point sets a simple content layout that only points to the fragment. See the following example code:

```
<FrameLayout
   android:id="@+id/color_picker_frame"
   android:layout_width="300dp"
   android:layout_height="match_parent" >

   <fragment
      android:id="@+id/color_picker_fragment"
      android:layout_width="match_parent"
      class="com.androiduipatterns.smashingandroidui.
               examples.responsive.PickColorFragment"/>
</FrameLayout>
```

The activity class (`ResponsiveExampleActivity`) has one extra method that is called from the fragment to handle the color change as well as constants defining the colors:

```
public static final int COLOR_RED = 0;
public static final int COLOR_GREEN = 1;
public static final int COLOR_BLUE = 2;


public void setColor(int color) {
   Intent intent = new Intent(this, ResponsiveExampleColorDetailsActivity.class);
   intent.putExtra("color", color);
   startActivity(intent);
}
```

Fragment

The `PickColorFragment` class uses a simple layout that displays the buttons in a linear layout.

```
<?xml version="1.0" encoding="utf-8"?>
<LinearLayout xmlns:android="http://schemas.android.com/apk/res/android"
    android:layout_width="match_parent"
    android:layout_height="match_parent"
    android:gravity="center_horizontal"
    android:orientation="vertical" >

    <Button
```

```
            android:id="@+id/responsive_example_red"
            android:layout_width="100dp"
            android:layout_height="wrap_content"
            android:layout_margin="10dp"
            android:text="Red" />

  <!-- the other buttons -->

</LinearLayout>
```

In the `fragment` class code, the only method that is implemented is the `onCreateView` where the fragment layout is set and the button listeners are initialized.

```
public class PickColorFragment extends Fragment {

    @Override
    public View onCreateView(LayoutInflater inflater, ViewGroup container,
            Bundle savedInstanceState) {
        View view = inflater.inflate(R.layout.responsive_example_color_picker,
                container, false);
        Button redButton = (Button) view
                .findViewById(R.id.responsive_example_red);
        redButton.setOnClickListener(new View.OnClickListener() {

            @Override
            public void onClick(View v) {
                ((ResponsiveExampleActivity) getActivity())
                        .setColor(ResponsiveExampleActivity.COLOR_RED);
            }
        });

        //.. listeners for the other buttons

        return view;
    }
}
```

Figure 16-5 shows the activity being displayed on a phone screen.

Figure 16-5: The example app's color picker screen on a phone screen.

Color Screen and Color Info Screen

The other two screens, shown in Figures 16-6 and 16-7, are built the same way. The layout the activity uses points to the fragment and the fragment creates a scalable layout that is placed on the screen.

FROM PHONE INTERFACE TO TWO- AND THREE-COLUMN INTERFACES

Now to the interesting part—making this phone interface responsive and ensuring that the design scales up nicely to larger screens. Because the interface is already fragment-based, the job of converting this interface to work on a larger screen is much easier.

Figure 16-6: The example app's color screen on a phone screen.

Figure 16-7: The example app's color info screen on a phone screen.

Layouts

As you can see on the wireframe designs, the first activity can have any of the three layouts—a one-column phone screen, two columns on a small tablet screen, or three columns on a large tablet screen. The first thing to do is to build these three layout files. The first one is already done in the previous phase and it is placed in the `res/layout/resource` folder. That is the safest layout, and it is the one that is going to be used if nothing else is better.

To add the other layouts, you need to create two more layout folders and add resource qualifiers to them in order to define the minimum screen width. The values used in the example code are based on my evaluation of what looks best in one-, two-, or three-column layouts.

For the two-column layout, I created a `res/layout-w550dp` folder (which is used when the available width is at least 550dp). Then I created a layout XML file with the same filename used in the phone layout with the following content:

```xml
<?xml version="1.0" encoding="utf-8"?>
<RelativeLayout xmlns:android="http://schemas.android.com/apk/res/android"
    android:layout_width="match_parent"
    android:layout_height="match_parent" >

    <FrameLayout
        android:id="@+id/color_picker_frame"
        android:layout_width="300dp"
        android:layout_height="match_parent"
        android:layout_alignParentLeft="true" >

        <fragment
            android:id="@+id/color_picker_fragment"
            android:layout_width="match_parent"
            android:layout_height="match_parent"
  class="com.androiduipatterns.smashingandroidui.examples.responsive.
            PickColorFragment" />
    </FrameLayout>

    <FrameLayout
        android:id="@+id/color_frame"
        android:layout_width="300dp"
        android:layout_height="match_parent"
        android:layout_alignParentRight="true"
        android:layout_toRightOf="@id/color_picker_frame" >
    </FrameLayout>
</RelativeLayout>
```

Note that only `PickColorFragment` is defined in this layout. The second fragment is added dynamically from the activity code. The layout has an empty frame layout as a fragment container that you can easily use from code to change the fragments whenever the user selects a color. Figure 16-8 shows how this layout looks on a tablet in portrait mode.

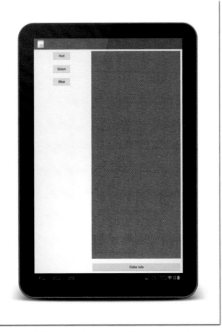

Figure 16-8: The example activity with a two-column layout.

For the three-color layout, I add the `res/layout-w1200dp` folder (used when the available width is at least 1200dp) and a layout XML file, again with the same name, that has a three-column layout:

```xml
<?xml version="1.0" encoding="utf-8"?>
<RelativeLayout xmlns:android="http://schemas.android.com/apk/res/android"
    android:layout_width="match_parent"
    android:layout_height="match_parent" >

    <FrameLayout
        android:id="@+id/color_picker_frame"
        android:layout_width="300dp"
        android:layout_height="match_parent"
        android:layout_alignParentLeft="true" >

        <fragment
            android:id="@+id/color_picker_fragment"
            android:layout_width="match_parent"
```

```
            android:layout_height="match_parent"
            class="com.androiduipatterns.smashingandroidui.
                    examples.responsive.PickColorFragment" />
    </FrameLayout>

    <FrameLayout
        android:id="@+id/color_frame"
        android:layout_width="300dp"
        android:layout_height="match_parent"
        android:layout_toRightOf="@id/color_picker_frame" >
    </FrameLayout>

    <FrameLayout
        android:id="@+id/color_info_frame"
        android:layout_width="300dp"
        android:layout_height="match_parent"
        android:layout_alignParentRight="true"
        android:layout_toRightOf="@id/color_frame" >
    </FrameLayout>

</RelativeLayout>
```

As with the two-column layout, only `PickColorFragment` is added to the layout file. The other two fragments are added dynamically from the code into the frame layout fragment containers. Figure 16-9 shows how this layout looks on a large tablet screen.

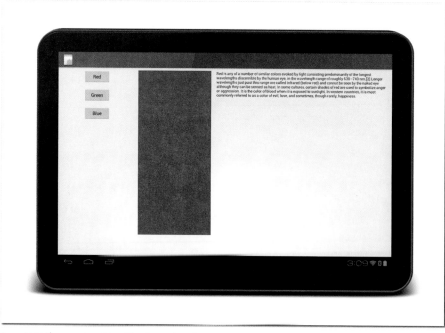

Figure 16-9: The example activity with a three-column layout.

Because all these layouts use the same filename but are placed in different folders, the operating system will take care of using the correct layout in correct devices.

Activity

The activity needs to be changed to manage all the different layouts. Although the operating system already chooses the correct layout automatically on runtime, the activity still needs to react correctly to user interactions. The first step is to make the activity aware of which layout is currently used. You can do that by adding control constants and checking which fragment containers are available.

```
private static int LAYOUT_ONE_COLUMN = 1;
private static int LAYOUT_TWO_COLUMN = 2;
private static int LAYOUT_THREE_COLUMN = 3;

private int currentLayout = LAYOUT_ONE_COLUMN;

    @Override
    protected void onCreate(Bundle savedInstanceState) {
        super.onCreate(savedInstanceState);

        setContentView(R.layout.example_fragment_layout);

        View colorFrame = findViewById(R.id.color_frame);
        View colorInfoFrame = findViewById(R.id.color_info_frame);

        // determine which layout is in use so the actions can be
        // redirected correctly
        if (colorInfoFrame != null) {
            currentLayout = LAYOUT_THREE_COLUMN;
        } else if (colorFrame != null) {
            currentLayout = LAYOUT_TWO_COLUMN;
        } else {
            currentLayout = LAYOUT_ONE_COLUMN;
        }

    }
```

Another change you must make is to the `setColor` method. Right now, it launches an activity (when on a phone), replaces one fragment (for the two-column layout), or replaces two fragments (for the three-column layout).

```java
public void setColor(int color) {

    if (currentLayout == LAYOUT_THREE_COLUMN
            || currentLayout == LAYOUT_TWO_COLUMN) { // just change
                                                     // fragments

        ColorFragment colorFragment = (ColorFragment) getFragmentManager()
                .findFragmentById(R.id.color_frame);
        if (colorFragment == null || colorFragment.getColorShown() != color) {

            if (currentLayout == LAYOUT_THREE_COLUMN) {
                colorFragment = ColorFragment.newInstance(color, false);
            } else {
                colorFragment = ColorFragment.newInstance(color, true);
            }

            FragmentTransaction ft = getFragmentManager()
                    .beginTransaction();
            ft.replace(R.id.color_frame, colorFragment);

            // info only shown on three-column layout
            if (currentLayout == LAYOUT_THREE_COLUMN) {

                ColorInfoFragment colorInfoFragment =
                    (ColorInfoFragment) getFragmentManager()
                        .findFragmentById(R.id.color_info_frame);
                if (colorInfoFragment == null
                        || colorInfoFragment.getColorShown() != color) {

                    colorInfoFragment = ColorInfoFragment
                            .newInstance(color);

                    ft.replace(R.id.color_info_frame, colorInfoFragment);
                }
            }

            ft.setTransition(FragmentTransaction.TRANSIT_FRAGMENT_FADE);
            ft.commit();
        }

    } else { // launch other activity
        Intent intent = new Intent(this,
                ResponsiveExampleColorDetailsActivity.class);
        intent.putExtra("color", color);
        startActivity(intent);
    }

}
```

One More Activity

The other two-column screen is still missing. That screen should be shown when the user presses the color info button on the two-column layout. To make the screen accessible, you need to add another method to the previous activity that is handling the color info button press. This method is called from the color fragment when the user presses the button. In this case, you don't need conditional statements, because the Info button is visible only if the app is in the two-column layout.

```
public void setColorDetailsSelected(int color) {
    Intent intent = new Intent(this,
            ResponsiveExampleColorDetailsActivity.class);
    intent.putExtra("color", color);
    startActivity(intent);
    overridePendingTransition(android.R.anim.fade_in,
            android.R.anim.fade_out);
}
```

The same activity also starts when you're using the one-column phone layout. This means that you need to make this other activity responsive as well. That activity will be used only in the one- and two-column layouts, so you need to add only one extra layout. Figure 16-10 shows how this two-column layout is rendered. This is the same activity you saw in Figure 16-6.

Figure 16-10: The second example activity with two-column layout.

OLDER ANDROID VERSIONS

The example you've seen in this chapter uses the newer qualifier that is available only on Android 3.2 or newer as well as the fragment APIs, which are only available on Android 3.0 and newer. To make this example backward compatible, you need to use the support package for all fragment-related classes, as explained earlier in this chapter.

When it comes to the layouts, you have two choices. Folders with qualifiers that are not understood by the runtime are simply ignored by the system. In this case it means that older devices will always use the single-column layout. Often that is good enough as a large majority of Android tablets run Android 3.2 or newer. If you want to bring the responsive user interface to older devices, you can use the old size qualifiers (`-large`, `-xlarge`). Unfortunately, they are not as fine-grained as the new ones. If you end up using both the old and the new qualifiers, you should avoid copying your layouts, and use the include and merge elements introduced in Chapter 13.

SUMMARY

Android provides great tools for implementing responsive user interfaces. You can create modular user interfaces using Android fragments and dynamically let the operating system pick the correct layouts using the Android Resource Manager. Modular and independent fragments can easily be reused in different layout configurations while letting activities handle the workflow control.

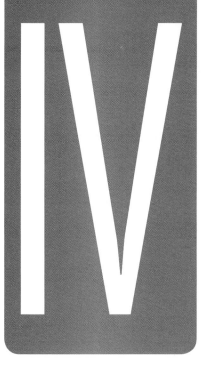

ANDROID UI DESIGN PATTERNS

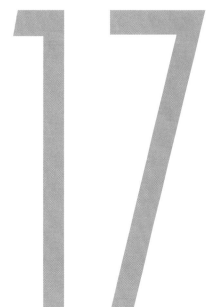

INTRODUCTION TO USER INTERFACE DESIGN PATTERNS

A DESIGN PATTERN is a well-thought-out solution to a common problem. In your everyday life as well as in your work, you likely run into the same problems over and over again. In many cases, you may have found solutions that work and then repeat the same behavior patterns whenever you encounter the same problems again. People also tend to share such solutions with others.

Design patterns provide a way to formalize the same approach to help designers with their professional challenges. The "gang of four," in their book *Design Patterns,* were the first to utilize the design pattern approach in the software realm. If you are a software developer, you are probably familiar with this book.

Design Patterns introduced multiple software design patterns that described commonly known problems in building software and solutions for solving them. These patterns are now commonplace in developer language. You hear developers talking about *singletons* and *factories* when they talk about software architecture and design. These design patterns not only give them proven solutions to their problems but also provide a very powerful communication tool. Having commonly used names for design patterns allows developers to communicate complex solutions in one or two words.

USER INTERFACE DESIGN PATTERNS

User interface design is less formal than writing code or designing software architecture. But still in design the same design problems reoccur. This is especially true when you're designing software for small screens of mobile devices, which add further constraints to the available solutions.

In the time of this writing, Google Play has more than 500,000 apps—many with great user interfaces and many with poor user interfaces. By viewing thousands of different solutions to common problems, you can see which solutions have worked and which have not. By studying other apps, you'll start to see good user interface design patterns as well as bad ones.

DESIGNING THE DESIGN

The first chapters of this book talked about user goals and scenarios and understanding the user's need. Then, the following chapters talked about tools you can use to build the interface once you know what your users want. This part, the user interface design patterns, is what you use when you need to organize the components of your designs. Design patterns can help you form a concrete design based on the user's needs.

It is good to remember that user interface design isn't an exact science, so user interface design patterns are much more like foundations for solving problems than complete out-of-the-box solutions. They can sometimes be applied directly, but more often than not they should be adapted to the needs of the particular user interface being designed.

WHEN TO USE AND WHEN NOT TO USE DESIGN PATTERNS

A design pattern should never be applied if you don't have a compelling reason to do so. You should never try to solve a problem that doesn't exist. For example, the side navigation Android user interface design pattern—which is very widely used—does not work with every app. If the app in question shows the next departures of a nearby bus stop, for example, the design probably should not have side navigation. Figure 17-1 shows an example app that is using side navigation well. There is much more about side navigation in Chapter 19.

> Tip: Never use a design pattern if it doesn't solve a problem you have! Even if you have an exact problem described in a pattern description, design patterns don't always work in every app. It's always wise to evaluate the use of any design pattern in the context of your app.

Figure 17-1: Evernote's use of side navigation is justified, as the app has more a complex structure.

Source: Evernote Corporation

BENEFITS OF USING UI DESIGN PATTERNS

There are many benefits of knowing the platform and its common design patterns.

DON'T REINVENT THE WHEEL

Design patterns don't emerge overnight. They have evolved through many iterations. The solutions that form design patterns have been vigorously tested by thousands of designers and developers and used by thousands of users. The solutions that have survived as design patterns have been found to work in multiple different apps in the real world. Some of the solutions have been tweaked and refined by highly skilled designers over time. The benefits of using solutions like these are evident. You get to build on top of a solid foundation.

PLATFORM CONSISTENCY

Solid foundations aren't the only benefit of using user interface design patterns. The user interface design patterns also bring consistency to the Android platform. Users know how Action Bars and side navigations work, and they don't have to learn your app's user interface separately. Even complex user interfaces are easy to use if they are consistent in all, or most, of the apps on the platform.

LIBRARY SUPPORT AND READY COMPONENTS

Another notable benefit of using UI design patterns is the library support. Some of the design patterns are going to find their way into the Android core libraries and Google's support library. Using those components guarantees quality of the components. But many of the design patterns won't be supported by the core libraries. Fortunately, there are multiple third-party library projects, many of them Open Source, that aim to fill the gap. It is always better to use a library that has been tested and is being maintained than to build your own. Just remember to contribute your changes back to the community!

DESIGN PATTERNS IN ANDROID DESIGN GUIDELINES

Android design guidelines list some design patterns as well. You should take a look of the listing in the Android design website at `http://developer.android.com/design/patterns/index.html`. Some of the design patterns listed in this book are the same as in that website. When I talk about a design pattern that's listed in the Android design guidelines, I give you a link to the web page.

> *Tip: There are a lot of bad designs out there. Chapter 21 covers bad user interface designs by explaining what not to do. These common solutions are bad for the user experience. I'll explain why they're bad as well as give you an alternative solution that is better.*

USER INTERFACE DESIGN PATTERNS FOUND IN THIS BOOK

As mentioned previously, a design pattern is a proven solution to a commonly occurring problem. I have kept the same approach in this book. For each of the design patterns, I start with the problem description after a short overview. After describing the problem I talk about the available solutions. The solution describes the design pattern and usually also gives examples of apps. The solution is an abstract description of how the user interface works. It doesn't tell you how to implement it, although sometimes you might have a really good idea how you would implement it intuitively. The solution part of a user interface design pattern is like a developer goal. Your goal is to make the user interface work the way the solution describes.

PHONES, TABLETS, AND RESPONSIVE DESIGN

One of the important themes in this book is the responsive design that makes your apps work well on small phone screens as well as on large tablet screens. For each design pattern in this book I describe how to use it on small and large screens. Some of the design patterns can be used directly without any modifications, but some of them need to be adapted and in some cases even discarded when the user interface moves from a small screen to a large screen.

EXAMPLE APPS

The example apps included in this book represent a good implementation of the design pattern. I encourage you to download and experiment with the apps I mention. However, the app design is moving so fast that some of the designs you see mentioned here might have been changed by the time you read this book. In all of the cases there are many other apps you can find to see the same design pattern.

Note that I don't want to encourage you to copy the example app's design directly. Each design pattern should be adapted to your needs; it is very unlikely that your app has exactly same needs as the examples shown here. Take time and evaluate the examples and other apps you find, and make your own design.

EXAMPLE CODE

For some of the design patterns, I also include source code examples to help you get started; however, many of them don't include any code. The reason for that is that many of the design patterns introduced in this book are well supported by multiple Open Source libraries. I have included links to the projects usually in github (`https://github.com/`), where you can find much better examples than the space in this book allows me to include. These Open Source libraries are valuable in the process of implementing your app. Many of them are backward compatible with older Android versions and allow you to skip some of the most difficult parts of Android development.

DESIGN PATTERN NAMING

The name of a design pattern is an important part of it. As I mentioned, a well-known design pattern is a powerful communication tool. A sentence like "should we use an Action Bar on this screen?" can communicate a lot of information without having to explain what an Action Bar is. Using these standard naming conventions allows the design team to communicate effectively.

This book uses the terms that have gained popularity with the Internet Android design community. Many of the design patterns have multiple names and I have included some of the other names in the description of the design patterns that do not have a well established name yet.

It is also worth noting that design patterns often do not use the names of the technical implementation components or classes. The class names and package names in the Android source code serve a different purpose than design pattern naming. A design pattern name should refer to the problem it solves, combined with the solution. A technical class name, on the other hand, is typically used to describe the functionality.

USER INTERFACE DESIGN PATTERN CATEGORIES

This part of the book is organized into three user interface design pattern categories and one chapter on bad design patterns (called *anti-patterns*). The categories are loosely organized but hopefully will help you find the designs you need. The user action design patterns all have something to do with user interaction with the app. Layout and navigation design patterns can help you solve layout and scalability problems. The data design patterns can help you organize your data to make it easier for users to understand. Some of the design patterns could probably be in more than one of the categories.

SUMMARY

User interface design patterns can help you move from an idea toward an app. It's very likely that other designers have wrestled with the same problems you are encountering, so it makes sense to use these same solutions, which have already proven to work. You should, however, always be critical and make sure that the solution you are applying is solving a real issue you have. Do not add design patterns to your app design just because others are using them.

USER ACTION DESIGN PATTERNS

THIS CHAPTER INTRODUCES and explains the user action design patterns. These patterns can help you solve issues related to presenting and performing user actions. Some of the design patterns are very commonly used and are an integral part of the Android platform (like the Action Bar pattern), whereas others are much more rare and solve more obscure problems.

The user action design patterns discussed in this chapter include the following:

- The Action Bar pattern
- The Quick Actions pattern
- The Action Drawer pattern
- The Pull-to-Refresh pattern
- The Swipe-to-Dismiss pattern

USING THE ACTION BAR PATTERN

The *Action Bar* is the styled top bar of a user interface view that consists of the app icon and the contextual action buttons. It can also optionally contain an overflow menu as well as some navigation options. The Action Bar is one of the defining user interface design patterns of the Android user interface language. This design pattern has been around for a long time and has become one of the most recognizable components of the Android user interface.

PROBLEMS ADDRESSED

The Action Bar pattern can potentially be a solution to multiple different problems, each of which is discussed in the following sections.

Important Contextual Actions

Mobile apps have many actions that users can perform on any screen. Some of these actions are important and are used often. These actions can be, for example, sending an email from the compose screen or showing a new note on a note taking app's list screen. These important actions need to be instantly accessible and their placement in the user interface must be intuitive and consistent.

Corporate Logo

Presenting the corporate logo or brand in an app somewhere is very important to most companies. The user interface is often covered by components that are relatively difficult to customize or at least would cause a lot of additional design, implementation, and quality assurance effort to manipulate.

Sense of Location

Users should always have a clear understanding of where they are in the app structure and be able to clearly understand the significance of the information they are presented. On a small phone screen, it can be difficult to include navigation aids like breadcrumbs or navigation menus with the location highlighted.

SOLUTIONS

The Action Bar pattern is a dedicated area at the top of the screen that is visually separated from the rest of the user interface. The height of the Action Bar is typically the height of a single clickable icon plus the margin. The Action Bar is usually present on all screens through-out the app.

Action Bar Components

The Action Bar has four sections (see Figure 18-1). Note that you don't have to use all of them. Your app might not require all of the possible functions. The left side of the Action Bar is reserved for the app icon. The app icon has three possible functions. It can take the users to the app front page, take them one level higher, or open the side navigation menu (more about side navigation design pattern in Chapter 19). When the app icon is used to navigate to a higher level, it is called the Up button and is displayed with a companion icon, sometimes called up *affordance*, indicating the up functionality. In some cases, the app icon doesn't have to have any functionality.

The second part of an Action Bar is the view control. In Figure 18-1 the view control is just a simple label and doesn't have any interactive functionality. I'll talk more about the navigation aspect in Chapter 19.

The action buttons are shown on the right side of the Action Bar. Any actions that do not fit to the Action Bar or are low priority or rarely used are moved into the action overflow menu.

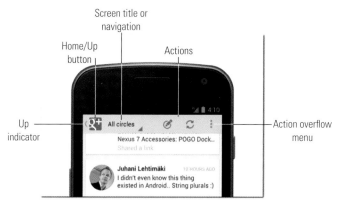

Figure 18-1: Action Bar components.

Source: Google

Action Bar and Corporate Brand

Color selection of the Action Bar background in combination with the app icon (or any other icon that is used in the Action Bar) provides a very distinguishable application brand without having to customize other components.

Figure 18-2 shows a good example of the Action Bar design pattern. The TED app uses the Action Bar to give the app a recognizable TED branding by using its colors and icons. The app also shows three actions available to the users on the screen.

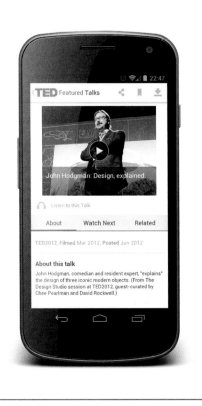

Figure 18-2: Good use of the Action Bar design pattern by the TED app.

Source: TED Conferences

Official Design Guidelines

The Action Bar design pattern is very well defined in the Android design guidelines documentation. I recommend reading it to get Google's point of view of this design pattern at `http://developer.android.com/design/patterns/actionbar.html`.

CONSEQUENCES

The Action Bar provides a consistent place for the most important actions. By using a common component in multiple applications, users learn to expect the functionality and find it easy to use. If the applications consistently provide the functionality, the app user interface does not have to be relearned. Users can utilize the knowledge established in other apps. This makes users more comfortable with the app's main functionality, thus improving the overall user experience tremendously.

ADDITIONAL FEATURES

There are few user interface features that relate to the Action Bar design pattern without being part of the pattern itself. These additional features, discussed in the following sections, can be added to the Action Bar and are often seen as part of the same design.

Up Button

The app icon is often used as an Up button. The Up button concept can be fairly complex and sometimes difficult for the users to understand. The problems arise when the Up button is confused with the Back functionality. The Up concept is, however, part of the Android design guidelines and worth noting. The Up button should always take the users to the parent screen in the app hierarchy, regardless of how the user ended up at the current screen. The Up functionality is indicated with a small left caret symbol. You can read more about the Up navigation from the Android design guideline page online at `http://developer.android.com/design/patterns/navigation.html`.

Extra Navigation Controls

The Action Bar is sometimes used as a container for navigation controls. The two common navigation controls are the dropdown spinner navigation list, such as the one shown on the Google Maps app in Figure 18-3, and the use of tabs, such as those shown on the YouTube app in Figure 18-4.

LARGE SCREEN ADAPTATION

The Action Bar adapts to larger screens very easily. The larger horizontal space makes it easier to fit all the components on the Action Bar. The Action Bar is often slightly taller on a tablet device than on a phone, so it looks more visually balanced. Figure 18-5 shows how the TED app's Action Bar looks on a tablet device. This is the same screen shown on the phone in Figure 18-2.

The increased space of larger screen or landscape layout allows you to add components like navigation tabs (see Figure 18-4), expand labels, and move some of the actions from the action overflow menu to the Action Bar.

Many of these adaptations are provided by the Action Bar libraries or the Android SDK. You'll read more about implementation options in the technical implementation section later in this chapter.

CONSIDERATIONS AND CRITICISMS

The Action Bar, although a very common design pattern, isn't without criticism. There are few things to consider when implementing an Action Bar design.

Figure 18-3: The Google Maps app uses the dropdown spinner navigation as part of the Action Bar.

Source: Google

Figure 18-4: YouTube apps places tabs in the Action Bar when the device is in landscape mode.

Source: Google

Figure 18-5: The TED app and Action Bar on a larger tablet screen.

Source: TED Conferences

Reach

The Action Bar contains the most important functionality and is located at the top of the screen. As smartphone displays grow in size, it is increasingly more difficult for users to use their phones with one hand and especially to reach the top part of the screen.

Wasted Screen Real Estate and Hiding

Another issue with the Action Bar has been its persistent nature. In some apps screens need to be fully dedicated to the content, and there's no room for the Action Bar. Apps like video players and ebook readers are good examples of this. The Action Bar is often hidden until the user taps the content to make it visible again. Although this interaction has become pretty common, it can still cause discoverability problems.

Icon-Based Actions

The actions on the Action Bar are most of the time associated with icons. Icons, especially on touch screens, are often not very intuitive. Users cannot hover over an icon to get a helpful tooltip if the meaning of the icon is unclear.

Google added action tooltips, which can be shown by long-pressing the Action Bar icon (see Figure 18-6). Although this can be helpful for some users most of the users do not know that they can long-press icons to get this tooltip. You should not rely on this to help your users, but you should definitely provide this functionality in your Action Bars. As time passes, more users are likely to find out about this feature. In any case the most important thing is to make sure that your Action Bar icons are descriptive and intuitive to your users!

VARIATIONS OF THE ACTION BAR PATTERN

There are some common variations on the standard Action Bar pattern that have become commonplace; several of them are covered in the following sections.

Split Action Bar

As a response to the limited space in the Action Bar as well as the reach problem, a split Action Bar concept has emerged. The split Action Bar adds another bar of actions to the bottom of the screen. There are a few variations of this concept. Sometimes the bottom Action Bar functions as an extension of the top Action Bar, and the actions that do not have enough room to be shown on the top Action Bar are placed on the bottom. In this case the overflow action menu should be placed on the bottom Action Bar instead of the top right.

Another way to split the Action Bar is to leave the app icon in the top Action Bar and move all its actions to the bottom part. This solves the reach issue but creates inconsistency in the Android system. Figure 18-7 shows an example of a split Action Bar that lists the functions in the bottom bar.

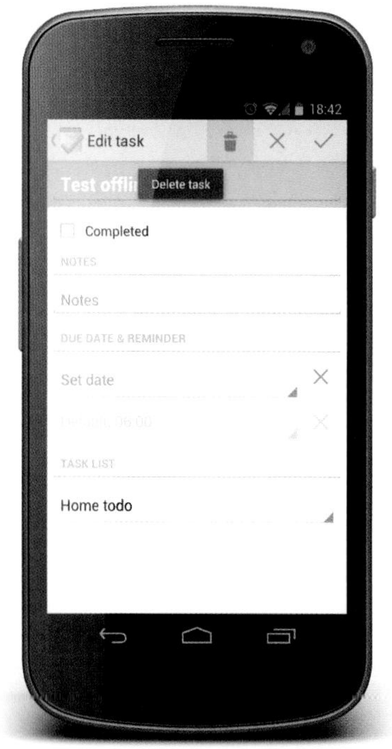

Figure 18-6: An example of tooltip help in the Tasks app, which you access by long-pressing an icon on the Action Bar.

Source: Tasks App

Figure 18-7: Evernote uses the split Action Bar.

Source: Evernote

It is very important to make sure the split Action Bar adapts correctly to orientation changes. Reserving top and bottom bars in landscape mode is not acceptable. When a split Action Bar screen rotates, the Action Bar should switch to single top Action Bar mode.

Contextual Action Bar Mode

In some screens, the user can manipulate individual items instead of just performing actions. In these situations, a so-called contextual Action Bar mode or action mode is often activated. It causes the Action Bar to show actions that relate to the selected items. Action mode is discussed more in the quick actions design pattern section later in this chapter.

WHICH ACTIONS TO SHOW?

Since the space for actions is limited you must carefully consider which actions you want to place in the Action Bar and which ones to leave in the overflow action menu.

Your first priority should be to include actions that are contextual to the screen and are very frequently used. A good example of this is the send action on an email compose screen. The second priority is actions that might not necessarily be contextual but address some of the most common use cases. In an email application, for example, the compose email action on the app landing screen should be visible on the Action Bar.

Adaptive Action Bar Actions

Different phones and tablets and different screen orientations have differing amounts of space for actions. Your app's Action Bar should adapt to different screen sizes the same way as the rest of the user interface. Based on the importance of these actions, you should classify them in three categories:

- Always show on the Action Bar
- Show on the Action Bar if there is space
- Never show on the Action Bar

Most of the actions you deal with should be classified in the "if space" category. Only very general actions, like general settings, should be placed into the "never show" category.

TECHNICAL IMPLEMENTATION

Since the Action Bar is a very well-established design pattern it has good support for implementation. It is one of the few complex components that has been added as part of the Android core SDK.

SDK

Support for the Action Bar was added to the Android SDK at the release of Android 3.0 Honeycomb, and support for the phone Action Bar was added to the Android 4.0 Ice Cream Sandwich release.

If your app targets only Android 3.0 or newer you can simply use the Action Bar provided by the SDK. It gives you a lot of functionality out of the box. It automatically adapts to larger screens and screen orientations as well as manages the shown actions based on the definitions you give to the action items. It also provides the long-press tooltip functionality and allows you to turn the app icon into an Up function.

For the full specification and guide for using the SDK's Action Bar you should read the Android documentation at `http://developer.android.com/guide/topics/ui/actionbar.html`.

ActionBarSherlock

If you have a project that supports older Android versions, there is a very good Open Source third-party library that you can use. The library is called `ActionBarSherlock`, and it is maintained by Jake Wharton. The library allows you to bring the Action Bar functionality to all Android versions starting with Android 2.1. The library is implemented well and uses the same API call and styling parameters that the SDKs Action Bar uses. This means that you don't have to relearn everything to use the `ActionBarSherlock` library. The library also automatically uses the native Action Bar when available.

Download and read the documentation for using `ActionBarSherlock` from the project website at `http://actionbarsherlock.com/`.

Theming

You have a large set of parameters you can use to create Action Bar themes. You can use solid colors or user background images for color themes. It's best to use nine-patch images for backgrounds.

Drawing all the required assets can be a long process. There are tools that make it easier. For example, you can use an Action Bar style generator website created by Jeff Gilfelt to generate all the graphics based on numerical color values. The site also generates all the required XML files for you. You can find the generator at `http://jgilfelt.github.com/android-actionbarstylegenerator/`.

USING THE QUICK ACTIONS DESIGN PATTERN

The Quick Actions design pattern helps you create a user interface for actions that affect only one or a few items on the screen. This design pattern is most often used with list screens or other screens that show multiple items.

PROBLEMS ADDRESSED

Apps often have screen where they display multiple items like emails, notes, and to-do items. Users need to be able to perform actions only on items they want to be affected. Operations like delete, edit, and move require users to select the items explicitly.

With mouse-operated user interfaces, users are used to right-clicking items they want to manipulate individually. On touch screens that approach is not possible, so an alternative must be found.

SOLUTION

This design pattern contains multiple solutions to this problem. Each solution works best in certain. The first one, the contextual Action Bar, is the preferred solution but is not applicable if the application doesn't use the Action Bar design pattern. It can also sometimes be cumbersome compared to the other solutions—the dropdown menu and custom overlay. The contextual Action Bar is the only one of the solutions that supports bulk operations that can be performed on multiple selected items.

Note that there is a related anti-pattern, called Swipe Overlay Quick Actions, covered in Chapter 21.

Contextual Action Bar

The Contextual Action Bar is an extension to the Action Bar pattern introduced previously. This is also the recommended solution in the Android design guidelines. The Contextual Action Bar is sometimes called the Action Bar action mode. The Gmail app uses the Contextual Action Bar to display actions that the users can perform when email list items are selected (see Figure 18-8). The Action Bar style changes and the actions provided there apply to selected items only. The top-left icon on the Action Bar changes into a Done icon that the users can use to cancel. The Android back button also cancels this mode.

 Scan the QR code with your Android phone to open the companion app and try out a functional example.

When using the Contextual Action Bar, you should indicate clearly that the list items are selectable. Often the best solution is to add a checkbox to the list items. List items with checkboxes allow users to select multiple items easily and edit their existing selection. When using checkboxes in list items that are themselves active selection components (such as when users can tap a list item to move to the item details screen), you must make sure that the checkbox area is large enough. Making only the checkbox itself the hit area will lead to user confusion and frustration. It is a good idea to make the portion of the left end of the list item a hit area for the checkbox as well.

Long-pressing a list item should also select the item.

Read more about contextual Action Bar from the Android design guidelines at `http://developer.android.com/design/patterns/actionbar.html#contextual`.

Dropdown Menu

The dropdown menu can be used to present options for individual list items when no bulk operations are needed and the available operations are difficult to explain in the Action Bar icons. The Google Play Music Player app (see Figure 18-9) shows a good example of acceptable use of the dropdown menu quick actions.

Dropdown menus do not allow users to select more than one item at a time. However, you have much more space to explain the actions. In my opinion, you should use a dropdown menu only if the contextual Action Bar is not suitable.

Figure 18-8: The Contextual Action Bar is used in the Gmail app.

Source: Google

Figure 18-9: Using dropdown quick actions in the Google Play Music Player app.

Source: Google

Be sure to indicate that users can open the menu by using the Android's dropdown menu symbol on your list items. That symbol will visually indicate that a menu is available. Users can then open it by tapping the menu indicator or long-pressing the list item.

Custom Overlay

The third option is use a custom overlay to present quick actions to users. Although this is not the standard way of showing quick actions and might require more development work, the result can be very stylish. The TouristEye app shown in Figure 18-10 uses this approach. The TouristEye app doesn't have that many quick actions, and they also don't need any bulk operations. This custom overlay solution is very non-intrusive and offers users easy access to the actions. Note the use of the indicator icon, which triggers the custom overlay.

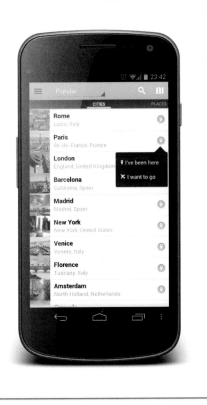

Figure 18-10: Nice use of custom overlay to show quick actions in the TouristEye app.

Source: TouristEye app

CONSEQUENCES

Providing an easy and consistent way for users to perform actions is very important. If users are forced to navigate to separate screens in order to perform actions, the application will start to feel cumbersome. Using these common design patterns will also help users understand the functionality of your app more easily. They won't have to spend time figuring out how to perform their desired actions.

LONG-PRESS

Long-press has become a standard gesture on touch screens. It replaces the right-click on pointer devices. Users are used to right-clicking components they want to manipulate individually. You should make sure that you provide long-press as a way for doing the same. Whichever of the previous solutions you choose to implement, make sure the long-press always brings up the quick actions.

LARGE SCREEN ADAPTATION

All of these solutions adapt to large screens very nicely. Contextual Action Bar uses the added screen real estate to show the actions nicely (see Figure 18-11 for an example). The other quick action alternatives do not require any alterations for the larger screen and can be used the same way they are used on smaller screens.

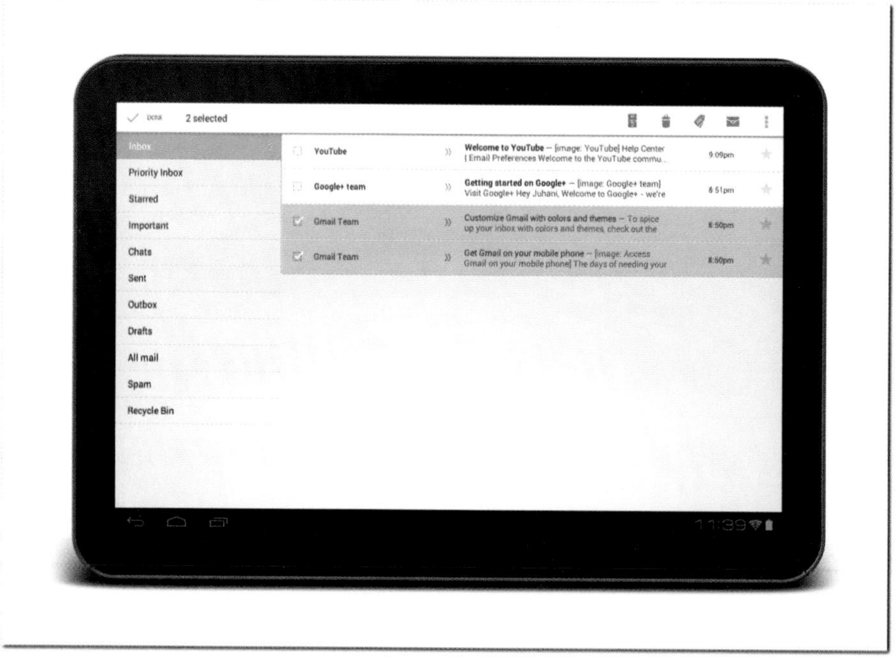

Figure 18-11: The Gmail app contextual Action Bar on a tablet.

Source: Google

CONSIDERATIONS AND CRITICISM

The way quick actions are presented has changed as the Android design has evolved. You might still see the old pre-ICS style quick actions in apps, although the new Android standards make them look outdated and you should not use them anymore. Prioritizing the contextual Action Bar makes it easier for you, from both a design and implementation point of view.

An important consideration when designing quick actions is that—regardless of which approach you take—you should always avoid hiding the selected items. You should also make it very clear to users which items are going to be affected by the actions. See Chapter 21, which covers anti-patterns (or bad designs), for more information about this.

TECHNICAL IMPLEMENTATION

Depending on the solution you've chosen, the implementation can be very straightforward or somewhat complicated.

Contextual Action Bar

The Contextual Action Bar implementation is supported in the Android SDK as well in the `ActionBarSherlock` library. Most of the heavy lifting is done by the framework or library code.

When working with `ActionBarSherlock`, you only need to provide an `ActionMode.Callback` implementation that is used to display the contextual Action Bar. See the following code example for a simple implementation skeleton:

```
private final class ExampleActionMode implements ActionMode.Callback {
    @Override
    public boolean onCreateActionMode(ActionMode mode, Menu menu) {

        menu.add("Example action 1").setShowAsAction(
                MenuItem.SHOW_AS_ACTION_IF_ROOM);

        return true;
    }

    @Override
    public boolean onPrepareActionMode(ActionMode mode, Menu menu) {
        return false;
    }

    @Override
    public boolean onActionItemClicked(ActionMode mode, MenuItem item) {
        // react to selections
        mode.finish(); // end action mode
        return true;
    }

    @Override
    public void onDestroyActionMode(ActionMode mode) {
    }
}
```

To start the action mode, you simply call `startActionMode` provided by the activity and give your action mode as a parameter:

```
startActionMode(new ExampleActionMode());
```

Dropdown Quick Actions Menu

For dropdown quick actions, you must implement a dropdown spinner user interface component. This spinner should take care of displaying and handling the actions. See the dropdown spinner user interface component for more implementation details in Chapter 11.

Another option for implementing a dropdown menu is to use `View.registerFor ContextMenu()`. See the Android documentation for more details and examples: `http://developer.android.com/guide/topics/ui/menus. html#FloatingContextMenu`.

Custom Overlay

Custom overlay is the most complicated implementations of these three alternative quick actions approaches. Fortunately, there are Open Source libraries you can use as starting point for your implementation. A library called New Quick Actions 3D is one of them. You can find the instructions and source code for the project from githib at `https://github.com/ lorensiuswlt/NewQuickAction3D`.

USING THE ACTION DRAWER DESIGN PATTERN

The Action Drawer design pattern is not commonly used, but still discussed in this chapter because the problem is commonly occurring and the solution can be very powerful. It saves space on-screen but still provides controls to users when they need them. This design pattern is sometimes called the *sliding drawer,* after the technical implementation in the Android SDK.

PROBLEMS ADDRESSED

On small smartphone displays, screen real estate is very limited. Designers must carefully consider which actions should be shown to users on-screen and which ones will be hidden behind menus or other structures. Hiding menus or other screens can make them hard to find and make the app feel difficult to use.

SOLUTION

Action drawer is a view that contains user actions and controls that aren't fully visible on the screen by default. Usually a handle component is shown to users, which they can use to expose the view. The opened drawer view covers the user interface either partially or fully without moving the user into a new activity. The Winamp app uses the action drawer to show additional playlist controls when the user needs them. In Figure 18-12, the action drawer is closed and only a handle to open it is visible. In Figure 18-13, the action drawer is open and is covering the underlying user interface.

Figure 18-12: Winamp app uses the action drawer to hide additional player controls. In this screen the action drawer is closed.

Source: Nullsoft

Figure 18-13: Winamp's action drawer opened to expose additional player controls. This is the same screen as Figure 18-12.

Source: Nullsoft

The action drawer should be opened when the user taps the handle or drags it open. The action drawer should be closed when the user taps the handle or drags it close. The Back button should also close the action drawer.

CONSEQUENCES

Having secondary actions hidden frees space for primary functions and makes the user interface less cluttered. An action drawer is a very simple concept to understand and discover. An action drawer also maintains the user's position in the user interface and is unlikely to confuse users as to the context of app navigation.

LARGE SCREEN ADAPTATION

It is unlikely that you'll need an action drawer on a larger display. You should design your large screen user interface in a way that the actions that are hidden on a smaller display are visible on the large screen.

CONSIDERATIONS AND CRITICISM

Android design in general has shifted away from this design pattern; apps are more often using the Action Bar overflow menu. The overflow menu is very pervasive and is often much more familiar to users than an action drawer. To justify using an action drawer, the components placed there must be more complex. For example, in the Winamp app's case, the seek bar cannot be part of an overflow menu as the overflow menu can only contain simple text items.

You should also make opening the action drawer as smooth and easy as possible. The drawer should open immediately and follow the user's drag gesture immediately. It is also important to make the handle component look like it opens the action drawer to make it intuitive to users.

TECHNICAL IMPLEMENTATION

Android SDK provides a user interface component for implementing an action drawer easily. The sliding drawer component was introduced in Chapter 11. For more information about the implementation, refer to the chapter or to Android documentation online at `http://developer.android.com/reference/android/widget/SlidingDrawer.html`.

Note that the sliding drawer implementation allows only for creating drawers that open by pulling from the bottom upward. There are third-party libraries that can be used to implement drawers that open in other directions.

USING THE PULL-TO-REFRESH DESIGN PATTERN

Pull-to-refresh is a more controversial design pattern and has not been fully accepted as suitable for the Android platform. It is more prominent on the iOS than on Android devices even though its origins are not platform specific. It is also covered by a software patent owned by Twitter. Twitter has publicly announced that they intend to use the patent only as a defensive tool and sue anyone with this patent only if they are being sued first, but anything written in this book should not be taken as legal advice, and you should consult your company's lawyers instead.

The pull-to-refresh pattern adds functionality to your list components by allowing users to refresh lists. They can pull down the list when it's scrolled all the way to the top.

PROBLEMS ADDRESSED

Refresh is a very common action that usually must be provided to users especially when you're displaying dynamic data. The refresh function often appears as a button on the Action Bar, which is valuable and limited screen real estate.

When users need to use the manual refresh very frequently, it can be annoying to constantly reach for the Action Bar on top of the screen.

SOLUTION

To save room and allow users to manually invoke the refresh functionality, users can pull the list down beyond the top item. Figure 18-14 shows an example sequence. The user moves the list all the way to the top and then pulls it down. An additional user interface component is placed above the list, giving the user feedback of the action. Once the user releases the drag gesture, a loading indicator is placed above the list. Once the refresh operation is finished, the loading indicator disappears and any new items are added to the list.

Figure 18-14: Different states of pull-to-refresh when user pulls down the list.

Source: Twitter

Note that pull-to-refresh works only on lists that have the most recent items placed on the top. If the list is not ordered, the gesture does not make sense.

CONSEQUENCES

Pull-to-refresh allows users to easily invoke the list refresh from any point on the list user interface. Pulling the list downwards is a very natural interaction as that is the normal way users interact with list components. If a user wants to see what is on top of the top-most item, pulling it down is the intuitive gesture.

LARGE SCREEN ADAPTATION

Pull-to-refresh works well on large screens. In most cases, there's no need to modify the functionality when moving to larger screens.

CONSIDERATIONS AND CRITICISM

Pull-to-refresh has been criticized for not feeling like an Android design feature. It has been associated with the iOS bouncy list border effect, which doesn't exist on the Android platform. My opinion is that pull-to-refresh is platform-independent and having bouncy list border effects is not necessary or related.

Discoverability is a real concern with pull-to-refresh. It's not visible on-screen before users try to perform the pull gesture. Some developers have suggesting using a small indicator on top of the list, but this hasn't gained significant penetration yet.

TECHNICAL IMPLEMENTATION

There are few Open Source libraries that implement the pull-to-refresh feature for the Android platform. In my experience the best one is the Android-PullToRefresh library by Chris Banes. You can download the library project as well as see more details about how to use it from the github page at `https://github.com/chrisbanes/Android-PullToRefresh`.

The library project is implemented in a very smart way, extending the Android list view. That way, you can use all the functionality from the Android list view. Instead of using the default `ListView` in your layout code, you must use the list view class provided by the library project. The following layout code shows an example:

```xml
<?xml version="1.0" encoding="utf-8"?>
<LinearLayout xmlns:android="http://schemas.android.com/apk/res/android"
    android:layout_width="fill_parent"
    android:layout_height="fill_parent"
    android:orientation="vertical" >

    <!-- The PullToRefreshListView replaces a standard ListView widget. -->

    <com.handmark.pulltorefresh.library.PullToRefreshListView
        android:id="@+id/pull_refresh_list"
        android:layout_width="fill_parent"
        android:layout_height="fill_parent" />

    <TextView
        android:id="@android:id/empty"
        android:layout_width="wrap_content"
        android:layout_height="wrap_content"
        android:layout_margin="5dp"
        android:text="List is empty" />

</LinearLayout>
```

You can add a simple listener to the activity or fragment code that will receive an event when users pull down the list:

```
pullToRefreshView = (PullToRefreshListView) getActivity().findViewById(R.
```

```
  id.pull_refresh_list);
pullToRefreshView.setOnRefreshListener(new PullToRefreshListView.OnRefreshListener() {
  @Override
  public void onRefresh() {



    new GetDataTask().execute(); // do refresh in background.
  }
});
```

To remove the list-loading indicator, you need to let the list item know that the `refresh` operation is complete with the following simple call:

```
pullToRefreshView.onRefreshComplete();
```

USING THE SWIPE-TO-DISMISS GESTURE

Swipe-to-dismiss is a way for users to get rid of individual items shown on-screen. This is a new and emerging design pattern that is likely to become more common in the future. It has a somewhat limited area of use due to some gesture conflicts.

PROBLEMS ADDRESSED

For long lists of notifications or similar content, users might want to get rid of the items individually instead of clearing them all at once. Users can use individual delete with the quick actions design pattern introduced previously, but it can be cumbersome, as it requires selecting the item first and then performing the action.

The problem of not being able to quickly dismiss items is emphasized if the app in question generates data automatically. Automatically generated data, whether the data is events from other systems or something else, can lead to too much information being presented to the users. In situations like this, users must be able to easily dismiss the items they are not interested in while keeping the others.

SOLUTION

Android 4.0 Ice Cream Sandwich introduced few changes to the Android notification system and to the multi-tasking system. Notifications and recent apps are now both shown as lists. If users want to get rid of any of the individual items in either list, they can simply drag the item they want to get rid of to the left or right. This effectively throws the item outside the screen. Figure 18-15 shows how Android notifications can be swiped to dismiss.

At the release of the Android 4.1 Jelly Bean, Google introduced a new Google service called *Google Now*. This is the first app that utilizes this pattern in an app instead of in a system service. The app is a single list of cards that can be dragged outside the screen to get rid of them (see Figure 18-16). Note that in this app as well as in the notifications, the item that is being swiped away follows the user's finger. This makes the gesture more pleasant and easier to discover.

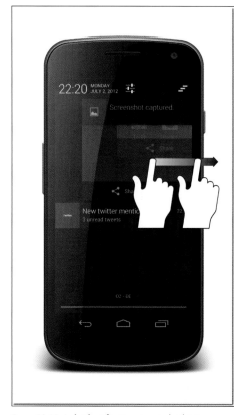

Figure 18-15: Android notifications since Android 4.0 use swipe to clear individual notifications.

Source: Android

Figure 18-16: Google Now allows users to swipe individual notifications.

Source: Google

CONSEQUENCES

Swiping is an intuitive gesture for getting rid of things. It corresponds to real-world actions. People tend to swipe things away from their view when they don't need to see them. Users can also intuitively try this gesture as it is being used on other similar functions on the platform. It's easy to find and pleasant feeling, as it corresponds to the real world.

ADDITIONAL FEATURES

There are many ways you can design this gesture to make it easier to understand. You can, for example, apply an increasing transparency or other effect when the user is moving it further away from its original place.

LARGE SCREEN ADAPTATION

On larger screens, it doesn't always make sense to require users to swipe the item all the way off the screen. You must make sure that you use a transparency effect or something similar to clearly communicate to your users how far they have to swipe to dismiss the item. The Android multi-tasking menu is a good example of this. The multi-tasking menu is placed on the left side of the screen, but users can still remove recent apps from the list by swiping them to the right a few centimeters.

CONSIDERATIONS AND CRITICISM

Although swiping might be good, it is also already reserved for a lot of different functions in the Android user interface. Recall, too, the difficulties of detecting a swipe versus a drag to pan. Swiping is also very commonly used to switch between workspaces on tabbed user interfaces (more about workspaces in the Chapter 19).

TECHNICAL IMPLEMENTATION

At the time of this writing, the technical implementation of this design pattern requires large amounts of code using the Android framework classes, including property animations. Including the full example here would be too cumbersome. There are, however, Open Source projects that provide this functionality. Therefore, I recommend you search github for "swipe to dismiss" to find the best project. One project that might help you is the SwipeToDismiss-NOA project by Jake Wharton, based on work of Roman Nurik. You can find it from the github at `https://github.com/JakeWharton/SwipeToDismissNOA`.

SUMMARY

User action design patterns can help you create designs that users can easily interact with. These design patterns vary, from handling individual items to executing batch operations on multiple items to app operations like refresh. Of all the patterns discussed in this chapter, the Action Bar pattern is the most important and has become a standard component in almost all Android apps.

NAVIGATION AND LAYOUT DESIGN PATTERNS

NAVIGATION AND LAYOUT design patterns help you display information on-screen in a way that's intuitive, familiar, and easy for users to learn and use. These patterns help you arrange information based on how it's related to other information. The layout design patterns discussed in this chapter include the following:

- Stacked galleries
- Dashboards
- Workspaces
- Split view
- The Expand-in-Context pattern
- Side navigation

USING STACKED GALLERIES

A stacked gallery provides you with a way to present multiple sources of independent information on the same screen while giving users an easy way to navigate through any one of them.

PROBLEMS ADDRESSED

Apps that aggregate data from multiple sources or apps that contain multiple categories of information often require that users navigate between views to get an overview of the content in each category or source. If the content is separated on different screens, it takes users much longer to navigate through them.

SOLUTION

By presenting stream or category content in independently scrolling gallery components, an app can offer users a compromise between the amount of information shown from each stream and an overview of all the content. The Pulse app is a good example of using stacked galleries to show user streams. Figure 19-1 illustrates how the categories can be separately scrolled with a horizontal drag gesture. Only one of the categories scrolls horizontally a time. This allows users to get a good overview of all the items in one category. Figure 19-2 shows how all the categories can be scrolled up and down by dragging vertically. This allows users to get a good overview of the latest items in all categories.

Figure 19-1: The Pulse app uses stacked galleries. Users can scroll each category separately by dragging.

Source: ALPHONSO LABS

Figure 19-2: Users can scroll the whole interface up and down by dragging and exposing more categories.

Source: ALPHONSO LABS

CONSEQUENCES

Providing users with an easy way to navigate and browse through categories as well as within a category can be very powerful simple user interface when this kind of navigation is needed. All the interactions are easily understandable and don't need explanations. Dragging on a touch screen device is one of the best gestures to use due to its intuitiveness.

ADDITIONAL FEATURES

Each of the categories can be combined with the pull-to-refresh design pattern introduced in Chapter 18. Pulling a category to the left can be used to expose a pull-to-refresh indicator and trigger an individual category refresh.

LARGE SCREEN ADAPTATION

Stacked categories scale up very well to larger devices. This is because the component expands in both directions, fully utilizing the extra screen real estate horizontally and vertically. Figure 19-3 shows the Pulse app on a tablet screen.

Figure 19-3: The Pulse app utilizes a larger tablet screen without having to add new components to the screen.

Source: ALPHONSO LABS

TECHNICAL IMPLEMENTATION

You can implement a stacked gallery user interface easily by using the Android standard components. To build it you should create a scroll view that holds a linear layout with the gallery components for each category. The scroll view will take care of vertical scrolling and each gallery component is independently scrollable horizontally.

> Tip: If, while implementing this, you run into problems of components locking into scroll modes—for example the scroll view preventing the galleries from scrolling— you might want to try a non-locking implementation of the scroll view. You can find an example implementation from here: `https://github.com/Cyanogen-Mod/android_packages_apps_Email/blob/ics/src/com/android/email/view/NonLockingScrollView.java`.

USING THE DASHBOARD

The dashboard is one of Android's oldest user interface design patterns. At some point this design pattern was one of the official recommendations from Google, but that is no longer the case. The dashboard is a landing screen that contains large icons leading to the app's functionality.

PROBLEMS ADDRESSED

Mobile apps can be overwhelming, especially to first-time users. Users are sometimes confused by information on the first screen and can easily miss functionality that isn't clearly presented. Competition in the mobile app market is fierce and a confusing or overwhelming first experience can lead users to abandon your app and search for alternatives.

SOLUTION

A dashboard screen is the app's landing screen. This screen is designed to be simple. This screen does not have much information on it but instead has links to the app's functionality. The functions have traditionally been presented as large icons fitting up to six of them on the screen. The number of functions presented on this screen is very important. Any number beyond six is very likely to add to confusion instead of solving it. Of course, not all apps have that many functions, and it is not necessary to use that many icons on the screen. Think of the dashboard screen as a showcase for your app's hero functionality. Each of the icons on the dashboard screen should take users directly to a logical part of the app.

Although the original guideline for dashboard was very simple, it has evolved to be something more. For example, the Aldiko reader app added a secondary part to the dashboard, providing the user with a direct link to the books in addition to the four icon links (see Figure 19-4). The Songkick app, on the other hand, is using the dashboard design patterns but fully redesigned the visuals to match the Android 4.0 guidelines (see Figure 19-5).

Figure 19-4: The Aldiko reader app uses a dashboard that is pretty close to the old style dashboard with small modifications.

Source: Aldiko

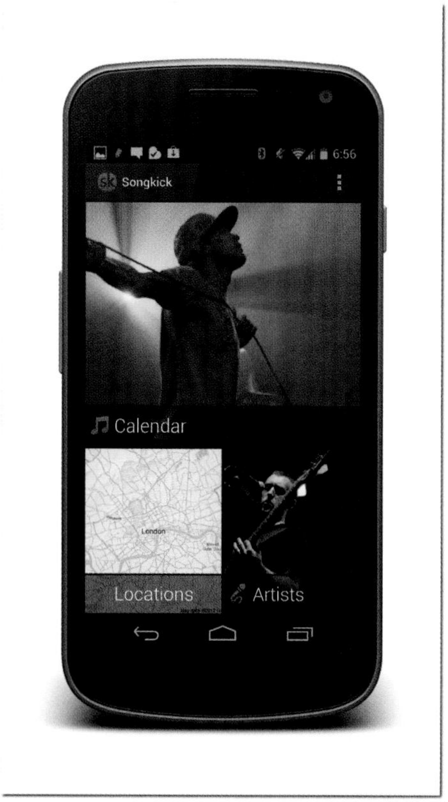

Figure 19-5: The Songkick app uses a dashboard that has a modern look.

Source: Songkick

CONSEQUENCES

A dashboard makes the app's first user experience friendlier. The user gets a good overview of the app's functionality as well as an easy navigation approach.

> *Tip: A dashboard can also serve as a place for displaying updated information and notifications to the users. Many apps that use a dashboard have used an informa-tion bar on the bottom of the screen to display such information. You might display, for example, sync status or the latest updates to the app.*

LARGE SCREEN ADAPTATION

The dashboard design pattern does not scale up to a larger screen that well. If you want to use the same concept on larger screens, you must be creative with it and think about ways you can bring part of the app's content to the landing screen. Don't ever simply stretch out your dashboard to a larger tablet screen size!

The Aldiko reader app (see Figure 19-6) uses a dashboard on its tablet design as well. Aldiko utilizes the added screen real estate by making the bookshelf larger and showing more content on it. The screen is still very welcoming, without wasting space.

Figure 19-6: The Aldiko reader app's dashboard is part of its tablet-landing screen.
Source: Aldiko

CONSIDERATIONS AND CRITICISM

The dashboard design pattern has recently been removed from multiple high-profile apps. The main reason is that it makes it slower for users to access the app's actual content. Many apps that have a clear main function make the main function the app's home screen.

The side navigation pattern, which is introduced later in this chapter, is slowly replacing the use of the dashboard in many apps. It solves a very similar problem.

VARIATIONS

You've already seen two very different variations of this design pattern in the figures shown in this section. This design pattern is visually very weakly defined. Customizing the idea and creating visually pleasing dashboards require good visual design skill. A dashboard can be a hero screen of an app and provide a great brand experience. If you choose to implement this design pattern in your app, I recommend that you experiment with it and not settle for the simplest alternative.

TECHNICAL IMPLEMENTATION

You can manually build the layout or use the standard Android layouts. Grid layout, for example, can be a very good solution, but it is available only on newer Android versions. It requires you to create two layouts—portrait and landscape versions. There are layout classes available that take care of the work for you. One of them is available with the 2011 Google I/O app. Dashboard was used in the Google I/O 2011 app, but was removed in the 2012 app. The `dashboard` layout class is included in the book's companion app source code. If you include the `layout` class in your project, you can then simply define the `dashboard` layout as part of any layout in your app. See the following layout XML as an example:

 Scan the QR code with your Android phone to open the companion app and try out a functional example.

```
<com.google.android.apps.iosched.ui.widget.DashboardLayout
        android:layout_width="fill_parent"
        android:layout_height="fill_parent" >

    <Button
        android:id="@+id/button_examples"
        android:layout_width="wrap_content"
        android:layout_height="wrap_content"
        android:drawableTop="@drawable/section_icon"
        android:text="Examples" />

<!-- … more buttons here … -->

    <Button
        android:id="@+id/button_more_functions"
        android:layout_width="wrap_content"
        android:layout_height="wrap_content"
        android:drawableTop="@drawable/ic_launcher"
        android:text="One more function" />

</com.google.android.apps.iosched.ui.widget.DashboardLayout>
```

Tip: The `dashboard` layout has a known bug that might affect you and cause layout issues. You might want to get a patch to that issue from http://code. google.com/p/iosched/issues/detail?id=19.

USING WORKSPACES

Workspaces are screens that are linked to make navigating between them very easy. This is one of the most important and widely used design patterns on the Android platform.

PROBLEMS ADDRESSED

Apps often have much more content, functionality, and data than that can fit on a single screen. Allowing users to view all of that information can be difficult, especially when users are forced to navigate up and down in screen hierarchy to move from one set of functionality or data to another. To make your apps useful and intuitive, your users must be able to directly move between screens.

SOLUTION

Tabs have been a solution to this problem even before there were cell phones. Although it is possible to use simple tabs on the Android platform, you should take your tabbed user interface one step further. The exact solution depends on the number of screens in the construct. If you have only a few screens (such as three or fewer), tabs are a good solution. Tabs don't work as well with a larger number of screens.

The following solutions are similar but visually slightly different. This is due to the fact that the tabbed user interface can be used only with a limited amount of tabs. The title strip, on the other hand, can be used with a much larger amount of content. Both solutions enable users to navigate between tabs or views using the swipe gesture. The use of the swipe gesture eliminates the need for users to reach the Tab bar. Users can control the tab selection from any point of the user interface when using the swipe gesture.

> Tip: It is important to think of workspaces as part of the same screen and not as separate screens. Users do the same. They do not expect the Back button to move them to the previous workspace.

Workspaces are referred to as *swipe views* in the Android design guidelines; see `http://developer.android.com/design/patterns/swipe-views.html`.

Tabbed User Interface

Tabs are a very familiar concept. The tabs on the Android platform have additional features not seen on other platforms. Android tabs are always located at the top of the screen. Bottom tabs are not used on Android. The reason for this is that top tabs adapt much more flexibly to different screen sizes. On other platforms like the iOS, bottom tabs are often used to make it easier for users to operate them. On the Android platform, tabs can be changed by using the swipe gesture, so top tabs are as easy to use as bottom tabs.

The tab's visual presentation is unique on the Android platform. You should follow its common theme in your apps. Black square tabs with gray icons feel and look wrong on Android and should not be used. The tabs used in Android apps usually do not have icons on them, but they can have, and they use a solid background color and a line at the bottom part of the tab to highlight the selected tab. Figure 19-7 shows a simple tabbed user interface—this Google I/O 2012 app uses tabs to separate two different categories of information. Users can move between the two by tapping on the non-active tab or swiping.

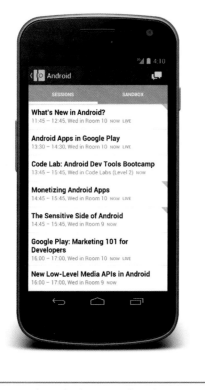

Figure 19-7: The Google I/O app uses tabs on this screen to separate Android sessions and sandbox presentations in the event.

Source: Google

Tabbed user interfaces play well with the Action Bar design pattern. Figure 19-8 shows an example of tabs being merged into the Action Bar as space allows. This saves a lot of space on-screen, especially in landscape mode.

Figure 19-8: The same screen presented in Figure 19-7, but this time in landscape mode, where the tabs are merged into the Action Bar.

Source: Google

Title Strip

Using the title strip provides a way to implement a very similar interface as the tabbed interface, but without a limitation on tabs. With this approach, the tabs are replaced with a title strip. This title strip always shows the current selection and available selections to the left and right. The Google Play app shows a good implementation of a title strip (see Figure 19-9).

CONSEQUENCES

Easily accessible content with a consistent swipe gesture support can make apps feel light and easy to use. The swipe gesture is a very natural and pleasant gesture on touch screens and fits to this pattern perfectly. Workspaces are present on Android in many places, from home screens to application launchers. Apps that use the same approach to present content are intuitive to users.

LARGE SCREEN ADAPTATION

Tabs are as much present on large screens as on small screens. They are very often merged into the Action Bar. Title strips also work on large screens and often do not need to be modified. However, on a large screen, using a title strip might look bad as it only shows three titles and therefore leaves a lot of empty space. It's probably best to consider prioritizing tabs over title strips on case-by-case basis.

CONSIDERATIONS AND CRITICISM

Swiping between content is a very good gesture, but once it is used in that context it is reserved for it and cannot be used in any other function. That is why workspaces containing horizontally scrolling components can cause problems. Is the swipe gesture meant to scroll the content or move to the next tab or view? In situations where content must be horizontally scrollable, using the workspaces design pattern might not be the best option.

Figure 19-9: The Google Play app uses a title strip to provide users with very easy access among app categories.

Source: Google

TECHNICAL IMPLEMENTATION

Technical implementation of this pattern is very straightforward using the Android SDK or available third-party libraries. The Android ADT (the Eclipse plug-in) helps you create your activity to support both tabs and a view pager. When creating a new activity using the new activity wizard, you can select from templates. View pager is the technical concept that is used to provide a container for swipable containers. The view pager is also part of the support package so you can use it even when targeting older Android versions.

To fully support the tabs in older versions, you can use ActionBarSherlock, which supports embedding tabs in the Action Bar when in landscape mode.

 Scan the QR code with your Android phone to open the companion app and try out a functional example.

View Pager

You can find the `ViewPager` class from the support package, which implements the work-spaces as well as the swipe gesture support. You can combine it with `PagerTitleStrip` class or `PagerTabStrip`, which you can find from the support package as well, depending on if you are implementing tabs or a title strip. There are also good third-party implementa-tions like the `ViewPagerIndicator` project, which you can find from `http://viewpagerindicator.com/`.

USING SPLIT VIEW

Split view is a layout design pattern for showing information side by side. This pattern is often used as the cornerstone of responsive design when moving from smaller smartphone displays to larger tablet displays.

PROBLEMS ADDRESSED

Forcing users to navigate to another screen to show more information can make the app seem slow and awkward. This is especially true with larger screens, where there's enough room to show more details about selected items.

SOLUTION

A user interface design pattern called "overview besides details" has been used on desktop apps as well as on the web to make it easier for users to see more information about selected items. This is commonly used with lists of items. The additional details are shown on the same screen. Users understand the relationship between the two parts of the screen easily as long as the right part of the user interface, the details part, is extending the details shown in the left part of the user interface, the overview part.

Smartphone screens are often too small to utilize this pattern, but it is a very good approach for tablet user interface design. For example, the Google RSS Reader app utilizes this pattern in its tablet design (see Figure 19-10).

Split view is referred to as *multi-pane layouts* in the Android design guidelines; see `http://developer.android.com/design/patterns/multi-pane-layouts.html`.

Figure 19-10: The Google RSS Reader app on the tablet uses split view to show a list of the user's reader items as well as the details of the selected item.

Source: Google

CONSEQUENCES

A screen that utilizes the split view design pattern allows user to navigate between items and their details effortlessly. This design pattern provides a massive benefit over having to navigate to another screen for such details. It's also been in use for years and is familiar to users.

SMALL SCREEN ADAPTATION

This pattern is very rarely used on smartphone screens. To accommodate the same information on smaller devices, you most likely need to create two separate screens. This principle was explained in more detail in Chapter 15.

VARIATIONS

Split screen designs can vary a lot. They should always maintain the same relationship between the selected item and the details content. A great example of a very different visual approach is the Google I/O 2012 app (see Figure 19-11).

Figure 19-11: The Google I/O 2012 app uses a split view on the tablet to show the conference sessions and their details. The visual implementation is different from the normal split view, but the concept is the same.

Source: Google

TECHNICAL IMPLEMENTATION

For technical implementation of this pattern you should use the Android layouts and fragments. See Chapter 16 for technical implementation details.

Note that the Android Eclipse plug-in allows you to create an Android project from a template using the new Android project wizard. The wizard builds a framework for the template. This construct is called the *master-detail template* in the wizard.

USING THE EXPAND-IN-CONTEXT PATTERN

Expand-in-context is a simple yet powerful design pattern that can make your user interfaces less overwhelming as well as save screen real estate. The idea of this design pattern is to show only a smaller portion of the selected content and allow users to easily expand the section to see the rest.

PROBLEMS ADDRESSED

Sometimes one screen is too small to fit the information you want, without making the user interface feel cluttered, overwhelming, or forcing users to scroll almost endlessly to reach the bottom of the screen.

In many cases, the content is dynamic or user-provided and its length isn't known beforehand. If a single screen contains this type of content, it can be difficult to design the page structure in a consistent way.

SOLUTION

The solution to this problem is to show the content only partially and hide the rest. The Google Play app uses this pattern to make it easier for users to see all the information about an app without having to scroll through the very long scroll views. In the app details screen, each app in Google Play has multiple information fields with user content, like description and what's new. There's no way of knowing how long an app description will be, for example. It could be possible to solve this issue by using some kind of pop-up windows containing the data, but pop-up windows are usually interruptive and irritating.

A much better solution is to make the content sections a fixed size by default and allow users to tap to expand them to full size without leaving the screen. Figure 19-12 shows a single app's information page opened in the Google Play client. The description section is visible and so is the Reviews section. In the bottom right corner of the description section, you can see a small indicator arrow pointing down. It tells the users that there is more content in this section than what is currently visible.

When the user taps anywhere in the description, the section extends and the entire content is shown (see Figure 19-13). Note that the user is still on the same screen.

Figure 19-12: The Google Play app showing one app's details screen. The description section is a fixed size no matter how long the app's description is.

Source: Google

Figure 19-13: The same screen as in Figure 19-12, but the user has tapped the description section to open it.

Source: Google

CONSEQUENCES

When you build your user interface using sections that expand in context, the interface will be a constant size even when you're displaying dynamic and user generated content. You can design your interface without worrying about extremes.

Making the content expand in context instead of forcing users to open another screen or a pop-up helps the user interface feel easy to use. Users don't lose their sense of location when data expands in context like this.

ADDITIONAL FEATURES

In some cases it makes sense to allow users to collapse the expanded content. They should be able to do this by tapping the container again. The indicator arrow should rotate around and point upwards if collapsing the section is possible.

It is also worth noting that this pattern is being used in the Android 4.1 Jelly Bean notification to allow users to expand notifications. As tapping on notifications is already reserved for activating them, Google has decided to use a two-finger swipe as the primary gesture to expand and collapse the notification content (although other gestures work as well). This two-finger swipe gesture might become popular in the future, but it isn't there yet.

LARGE SCREEN ADAPTATION

Large screens have more space so this design pattern isn't that useful on them. You can automatically expand such sections on large screen devices. If showing the content fully on a tablet display is not possible, however, you might utilize this design pattern there, too.

TECHNICAL IMPLEMENTATION

To implement an expandable section, you must make sure that the content in the session is dynamically laid out and that you can change the parent container's size without causing problems. The implementation requires hard-coding the section size when it is closed and listening for the tap event to expand.

 Scan the QR code with your Android phone to open the companion app and try out a functional example.

USING SIDE NAVIGATION

Side navigation is replacing the use of the dashboard design pattern on many Android apps. It provides more direct access to different sections of the app than a dashboard does. This design pattern is shown as a side navigation panel that can be pulled out from the left side of the screen.

PROBLEMS ADDRESSED

In larger apps, there often are multiple logical sections of the app where users navigate deeper into the screen hierarchy. Accessing other parts of the application can be difficult if users must first navigate all the way to the top level of the dashboard to dive into another section.

SOLUTION

The side navigation approach has very similar functionality to the dashboard. In fact, many apps have recently replaced their dashboard implementation with a side navigation. The side navigation is a sliding panel that can be opened from the left side of the screen without leaving the current screen. Opening the side navigation doesn't alter the user's back stack. To indicate that fact, a small portion of the screen is still visible on the right side of the side navigation panel.

Perhaps the best implementation example available is the Prixing app. The app implements both the side navigation and gestures to open it very well. The app allows users to open the side navigation from any screen. It is always available to users by tapping the Action Bar's left button. The app also provides a secondary way to open the side navigation—using the bezel swipe (see Figure 19-14).

CONSEQUENCES

Without having to launch the app to the dashboard screen, users can access the content directly. The app's landing screen can be the most used content screen instead. Users also get a good understanding of the app's functionality by viewing the side navigation.

In-app navigation also becomes easier, as users no longer have to navigate all the way to the dashboard to access other parts of the app. The side navigation provides consistent and easy-to-understand direct navigation.

Figure 19-14: The Prixing app is a great example of a well-implemented side navigation design pattern. Users can access the side navigation from any screen by using the Action Bar's top-left button or by using the bezel swipe gesture.

Source: Prixing

ADDITIONAL FEATURES

Some apps, like Evernote, take the side navigation one step further by providing more than just navigation in the side panel (see Figure 19-15). However, you should be careful not to overwhelm users with additional features in the side navigation panel. The panel must remain clean and easy to use.

LARGE SCREEN ADAPTATION

Side navigation can be used on larger screens, but sometimes it is not necessary. You might be better off designing the screens to show the same information your side navigation shows constantly, without hiding it.

CONSIDERATIONS AND CRITICISM

The side navigation pattern is still changing, and there are many different implementations of it. One big difference, particularly in Google's apps, is that the side navigation is accessible only from the root screen of each app section. Google uses the Up button in its design to navigate up from all other screens. It also uses the same Up button to open the side navigation once the section's root screen is reached.

Although I'm not a fan of the approach Google has taken due to the lost direct navigation, it is something you might consider for platform consistency. At the time of this writing, the side navigation pattern has not yet appeared in the official design guidelines, but Google has hinted that it might be added soon. If that is the case by the time you're reading this, you should definitely take into account what the design guidelines advise.

VARIATIONS

In addition to Google's Up button approach mentioned previously, different implementation use different ways to open the side navigation. Many apps use the top-left Action Bar icon, whereas others use different forms of swipe gestures. Note that a gesture should never be the only way to open the side navigation! In my opinion, the bezel swipe is the best gesture to be used here. It will not break other swipe gestures used in the app, and it is intuitive due to the way that side navigation is presented.

Figure 19-15: The Evernote app includes actions like creating new notes as well as some status information in the side navigation panel.

Source: Evernote Corporation

TECHNICAL IMPLEMENTATION

As the design pattern itself is still evolving so are the libraries implementing it. At the time of this writing, there are multiple Open Source libraries that have started to implement this design pattern, but none of them is fully complete. Take a look at the SlidingMenu project, which you can find in github at `https://github.com/jfeinstein10/SlidingMenu`.

SUMMARY

Navigation and layout design patterns help you find good ways to layout and organize your app's user interface on both smartphones and tablets. Navigation design patterns like the side navigation bring user interface consistency to apps running on the Android platform. This helps Android users intuitively understand your user interface and know how to navigate between screens and sets of related data.

DATA DESIGN PATTERNS

HANDLING AND SHOWING data requires that you consider many factors, from both a performance and a usability point of view. In many apps, accessing the data is the user's goal. Users want to see or modify a certain piece of information. If your app shows or manipulates data poorly, your users won't be happy.

This chapter covers data-related user interface design patterns. It is worth noting that these are not data structure or data architecture design patterns; it doesn't cover correct usage of databases or caches. There are other books that are better for that. This chapter covers data design issues from the user interface perspective.

The data design patterns discussed in this chapter include the following:

- Dynamic lists
- The image placeholder pattern
- The non-forced login pattern
- The drag-to-reorder handle

USING DYNAMIC LISTS

The dynamic list is one of the most common components in Android apps. They also are fairly complex from both a user interface point of view and from a code point of view. Android has great support for lists; it can automatically optimize memory usage and even recycle view objects for you. You must consider how much data you need to show in one list and how users can access more data when they need to.

PROBLEMS THAT LISTS SOLVE

The list has a limited number of items in it. When you're handling real-world data like social network update statuses or online store item catalogs, however, the amount of data will be much larger than can be shown in a single list. You need to design your lists so it's easy and intuitive for users to view more items.

SOLUTION

A dynamic list can automatically load more items without users having to explicitly request more. Whenever a user scrolls the list to a point where there are no more items available, a dynamic list will loading the new items automatically. To let users know that more options will appear automatically, you should include an indicator at the end of your list. The Twitter app does this perfectly (see Figure 20-1). The app is often so fast that the users don't even see the loading indicator; the list just feels endless.

CONSEQUENCES

Loading more items only when they're needed makes your app more responsive; you can show the list much faster, as you don't have to wait for a long download first. The automatic download trigger, which is activated when users reach the end of the list, makes it effortless for users. They don't have to think about it or even notice it.

Although it's often enough to start loading new items when the last item becomes visible, you can also tweak the loading triggers if it is likely that your users are going to load more items in your app. You can, for example, start the load process in the background when another item other than the last one becomes visible. Depending on your app, users might not ever see the loading indicator, and they'll simply feel that the list has everything loaded already.

Figure 20-1: The Twitter app automatically starts downloading
new items when users reach the end of the loaded items.

Source: Twitter

LARGE SCREEN ADAPTATION

The dynamic list design pattern works on large screens as well as on smaller screens. You don't
have to make any changes to it.

VARIATIONS

If your list-loading process is very slow or uses a lot of data (or for some other reason should
not be triggered automatically), you can use a manual trigger instead. You can add an extra
list item to the end of your list with appropriate controls so users can start loading additional
items.

Note that this manual option should be used only if there's a very good reason not to use the
automatic option.

TECHNICAL IMPLEMENTATION

There are few specialized third-party library components that are built to implement the dynamic list design pattern. It's a good idea to quickly search github before you start to implement your own functionality, especially if you need something more complex. For example, `cwac-endless` is one of the projects that implement this design pattern. You can find it at github (see `https://github.com/commonsguy/cwac-endless`).

It is, however, possible to implement this design pattern using Android components. You simply need to add an `OnScrollListener` listener instance to your lists. The Android system will then notify the listener automatically when the list ends and you can invoke methods to load more items.

Here's a short example code for the `OnScrollListener` `onScroll` method implementation. It calculates whether new items should be loaded. Note that the event can be fired multiple times as the last list item becomes partially visible. You must prepare and handle it and trigger the loading process only once.

```
public void onScroll(AbsListView view, int firstVisible, int visibleCount,
                     int totalCount) {
    if(firstVisible + visibleCount >= totalCount) {
        // load more items here
    }
}
```

USING THE IMAGE PLACEHOLDER PATTERN

Making your interface feel fast and responsive is very important and can sometimes be difficult when you use large images or have images that are loaded over the Internet. In these cases, it's better to use a local placeholder image initially, while your slow images load, in order to make the user interface operational as quickly as possible. Note that a splash screen or a blocking loading indicator is not a good solution to this problem. In fact, splash screens are covered in the anti-patterns chapter (see Chapter 21).

PROBLEMS THAT THE IMAGE PLACEHOLDER PATTERN SOLVES

If your interface has images that are large or loaded over the network or Internet, they can cause your app to become less responsive and slow. Making users wait for images to load before you allow them to interact with your interface is not acceptable.

SOLUTION

Whenever you need to show images that take some time to load, you should show a local placeholder image first. Render the user interface and activate the user controls and then load the images in the background. The local placeholder image should be good enough in case the connection fails. The user interface must be usable even when no images are loaded. The placeholder image should also be lightweight, so that it's rendered quickly. The Gigbeat app uses placeholders in its user interface, so it's ready to be used immediately (see Figure 20-2).

Figure 20-2: The Gigbeat app uses placeholder images so the user interface can be used immediately.

Source: Gigbeat

CONSEQUENCES

Using lightweight local images makes the interface immediately usable. Your users will be much happier if they can start using the app without waiting. Using placeholder images also make the app usable when users are offline.

LARGE SCREEN ADAPTATION

There is no difference on a large screen compared to smaller screens with this design pattern.

TECHNICAL IMPLEMENTATION

The best way to go about implementing this design pattern is to use a third-party Open Source library. There are multiple libraries you can use and if one of these libraries doesn't support your use case, you can easily find others that will. You can also modify the existing libraries to add features you need.

One of the lightweight libraries that can help to get you started is called `UrlImageView Helper` (see `https://github.com/koush/UrlImageViewHelper`). This library loads images based on URLs and can cache them. It automatically replaces your placeholder images when the real image is done loading. You don't have to use custom image views. You simply pass the target image view, the remote image URL, and a placeholder image to the helper class and it takes care the rest automatically. It even checks the cache before triggering a download in the background. The following short code sample is all you need to write when using this library:

```
UrlImageViewHelper.setUrlDrawable(mImageView, drawableURL, R.drawable.placeholder);
```

USING THE NON-FORCED LOGIN PATTERN

Forcing your users to log in to your app before they can see any parts of the interface is extremely bad practice. Instead, your app should allow the users to explore the app before it forces them to log in or create an account.

PROBLEMS THAT THIS PATTERN SOLVES

It's not uncommon for an app to have server-side functionality that requires users to log in to a system before using it. The apps might be extensions to already existing systems (for established users), for example. But if new users search Google Play and your app is featured or trending in the Google Play, these new users might try to install the app from this approach. Your app will then launch directly to a login screen. Most of the potential new customers are likely to be turned off and leave.

SOLUTION

Do not force users to log in. Let unidentified users try your app's features and experiment with it before forcing them to create an account or sign in. You might think that your app is useless without an account but the reality is that most apps are not. Your app might not be at its full potential without an account, but potential users can form an opinion and determine whether they should take the time to create an account.

Think of ways you can provide local caching or access to public information, or maybe even provide an example account for potential users so they can see what your app is all about—all without having to create an account.

The Catch notes app does this very well. When the app launches for the first time, it prompts users to log in to the app but also provides users with an option to continue to use the app without an account (see Figure 20-3).

Figure 20-3: The Catch notes app shows this screen when it starts. It invites users to log in but also provides a link for non-logged-in use.

Source: Catch.com

Once the users have started using the app without an account, they can keep on using the app. However, all of the sync features are not available. The user's notes are saved in local storage and synced later if they decide to log in to an account. The app also discretely reminds users of the features that can be enabled with an account on the app's landing screen (see Figure 20-4).

Figure 20-4: Once the user starts to use the app in non-logged-in mode, the app shows information on the app's landing screen encouraging the user to log in.

Source: Catch.com

CONSEQUENCES

If you let your users experiment with your app without creating an account, you are likely going to gain new customers. Users who find your app through a mobile app market are more likely to stick with it if they see more than just a login screen.

LARGE SCREEN ADAPTATION

When you use this design pattern on large screens you have an even better opportunity to promote the benefits of creating an account. You can show features that are disabled on the screen. However, never make disabled features look like they are enabled. If users press a button on your user interface, it should be active. It's not good practice to use a pop-up window to inform the users that the button they just tapped isn't active and they need to create an account. It is better to make the unavailable features look disabled and explain that creating an account will enable them.

CONSIDERATIONS AND CRITICISM

In some cases, creating a functional app without forced logging means a lot more work. As with everything, you need to perform a cost-benefit analysis as to whether it's best to create non-forced logins. At the very least, you should allow new users to see parts of the user interface without any functions. Do not block users from the login screen.

> *Tip: A simple variation is to create a demo account and provide an easy way for users to log in to it. You might want to make the account read-only to avoid privacy and license agreement issues.*

TECHNICAL IMPLEMENTATION

Technical implementation of this design pattern depends on your app's functions. It's best when your app is set up to work in offline mode and then sync data when users are online. You might be able to utilize the same mechanism for unregistered users as well.

USING THE DRAG-TO-REORDER HANDLE PATTERN

The drag-to-reorder handle design pattern allows users to reorder list items. This pattern is most commonly used in lists, but it can be applied to similar constructs.

PROBLEMS THAT THIS PATTERN SOLVES

In lists where order matters, users should be allowed to manually reorder them. Many gestures are already reserved on lists, such as the long-press to trigger quick actions and dragging to scroll the list. Forcing users to select and then move the items using some kind of separate controls is too cumbersome and can lead to bad user experiences.

SOLUTION

Adding a handle to lists that can be reordered is a nice, clean way to allow users to manipulate your interface. Users can grab the handle to move the items around easily, with a simple and intuitive gesture.

The Tasks app implements this design pattern very well. The Tasks app's developers added a drag-to-reorder handle to the list item's right side (see Figure 20-5). The handle is easy to understand due to its graphical representation. Once the user touches the handle part of a list item, the item immediately indicates to the users that they have selected the correct item (see Figure 20-6). When the users drag their fingers, the list rearranges itself on the fly. This makes it clear to users what would happen in each state if they were to drop the item. It is very important to indicate the new order during the gesture.

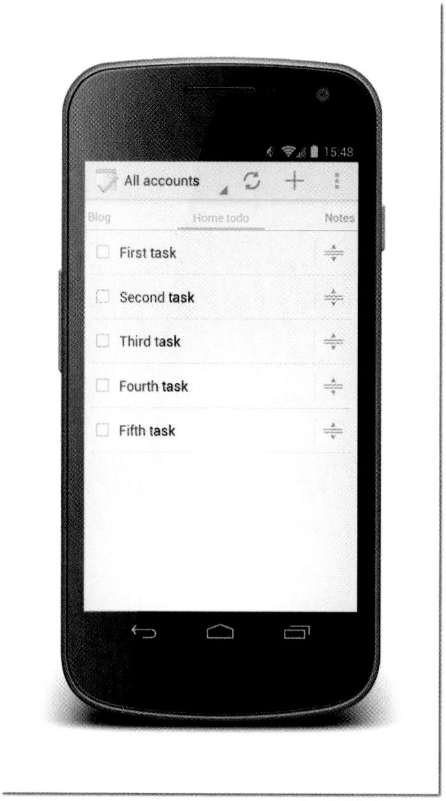

Figure 20-5: The Tasks app has a handle on each list item. The visuals clearly indicate where users can grab an item.

Source: Tasks App

Figure 20-6: When users touch the drag handle on a list item, the list item is immediately highlighted and starts to follow the user's gesture.

Source: Task App

CONSEQUENCES

When you implement this feature, your users can effortlessly order the list items without having to think about conflicting gestures and complicated interactions. Keep in mind that the dragging handle does consume some of the screen real estate available for your list items.

LARGE SCREEN ADAPTATION

The same approach works on larger screens as well. You just need to be mindful of the list item sizes. Do not make the lists too wide and the dragging handle too far from the list content. Otherwise, it will be difficult to keep the list item visually consistent.

VARIATIONS

You can change the style of the dragging handle in different ways. In the Tasks app, the handle is an icon representing the function, whereas in other apps a different metaphor is used. You can, for example, make it look like a handle or a rougher surface that encourages users to grab it.

TECHNICAL IMPLEMENTATION

There are several Open Source libraries that you can use to implement this functionality. You can use these libraries as a basis for your own implementation. My recommendation is to use a library called `DragSortListview`. You can get it from github at `https://github.com/bauerca/drag-sort-listview`.

SUMMARY

The data user interface design patterns introduced in this chapter can help you handle data-related problems in your apps. You should always be conscious of the ways your users are going to interact with your data. Your goal should be to think of ways to make data manipulation easier, transparent, and even automatic.

CHAPTER

USER INTERFACE DESIGN ANTI-PATTERNS

USER INTERFACE ANTI-PATTERNS are bad—but common—solutions to commonly occurring problems. All of the anti-patterns described in this chapter are relatively common, and you'll see them in apps that are currently distributed in Google Play. I don't show real-life examples of the bad designs because I have no intention of shaming any developers, well-known and not. I'm sure you have seen instances of these anti-patterns and probably even have apps that use them on your phone. It is also worth noting that an app that uses some of these anti-patterns should not automatically be seen as badly designed. Such app designs might be flawed in one place, but are still excellent in other respects.

As with user interface design patterns, user interface design anti-patterns do not apply in every situation. If your app has certain exceptions and constraints, these anti-patterns might after all be an acceptable solution, or maybe your only recourse. Suffice it to say that it's always better to avoid these anti-patterns if at all possible, but keep in mind that there are exceptions to every rule.

The user interface anti-patterns discussed in this chapter include the following:

- The splash screen
- The tutorial screen
- The confirmation window
- On-screen Back button
- Menu button
- Hiding the status bar
- Swipe overlay quick actions
- Using non-Android designs

AVOID USING THE SPLASH SCREEN

The splash screen is a loading screen that appears while the app's interface is loading. It typically shows the logo and company name and is a full-screen image that sometimes includes a loading indicator.

This is not a new device. Splash screens have been used on desktop computers for a long time. If you're an Android developer, you have most likely seen a splash screen used when the Eclipse or IntelliJ IDEA is launching.

PROBLEM BEING ADDRESSED

The process of loading an app's user interface can take a fair amount of time, especially when the app contains a lot of heavy graphical assets and components loaded over a network connection. Indicating to the users in some way that the app is loading is better than having the screen appear black and unresponsive.

WHY A SPLASH SCREEN IS A BAD SOLUTION

With desktop operating systems and applications, the splash screen is a pretty standard and acceptable design approach. This is due to the large size of desktop applications (they take a long time to load) as well as the nature of how applications are used on desktop computers. Computer desktop games, IDEs, and programs are typically used for hours in one go. The same is not true on a mobile phone. Apps are used in short bursts, sometimes for a few seconds. Therefore, it is important to load your app as soon as possible. Including a splash screen will make it slower. First, loading the splash screen itself takes extra time. Most apps implement a minimum time for a splash screen to be seen. Remember that your app should include features only if they help your users reach their goals. There is no mobile phone goal that is helped by using a splash screen.

BETTER SOLUTION

Instead of using a splash screen, try to make your app's landing screen lightweight and void of heavy graphical elements that must be loaded before the interface is functional. Utilize design patterns like the image placeholder pattern introduced in Chapter 20. Your goal should always be to allow users to start using your app as soon as they open it. Even a few seconds of delay when opening your app can lead to a poor user experience, especially if your app is the kind they might use for 10 seconds at a time.

EXCEPTIONS

Games are a good example of apps that can get away with using splash screens without losing users. Try to avoid it, even with games if possible, but it can be more difficult to do so than in normal apps due to the heavily customized and graphics-heavy user interfaces in many games.

AVOID USING THE TUTORIAL SCREEN

Tutorial screens appear when users first open an app. They explain the app's available functionality and screens. They usually contain instructions on how to open menus, find functions, and perform gestures.

PROBLEM BEING ADDRESSED

Learning to use an app and learning the user interface can be difficult at first, especially when the app uses non-standard user interface components or gestures. The tutorial screens try to explicitly tell the users where the features are and how to access them.

WHY IS THIS A BAD SOLUTION?

Although it might sound like a good idea, the tutorial screen is actually counter-productive. When users start your application for the first time, they do not have any understanding of your app's user interface, functionality, or context.

Users are also more interested in using your app instead of reading text or looking at tutorials. They just want to see the UI and start using it. It is also very difficult to know which of your users are new and which ones are just reinstalling the app after changing to a new device or using a secondary device. Those users are going to be extra annoyed by tutorial screens that are forced on them.

BETTER SOLUTION

Of course, the best solution is to make your app so easy to use and intuitive that no tutorials are needed. That's not always possible. You should, however, make sure that your app's main user interface and core functions do not need any tutorials. Make sure users can just jump in and start using the main screen.

You still might have to explain how the more advanced features are used. It's better to incorporate your tutorial screen into your app instead of showing it upon launch. Once your users have become familiar with the app's user interface, it is much easier for them to learn new features.

All user help should be available on request once the users are familiar with the user interface. User help should also be presented in the right context. The Evernote app has done a great job work implementing its tutorials. Users can at any point open a list of available tutorials (see Figure 21-1). When a tutorial is selected, it is shown in right context for users to understand easily what it means (see Figure 21-2).

Figure 21-1: Evernote displays its tutorials in a list whenever the users want to see them.

Source: Evernote Corporation

Figure 21-2: When a user selects one of Evernote's tutorials, an overlay on the live user interface shows the help functionality.

Source: Evernote Corporation

AVOID USING THE CONFIRMATION WINDOW

The confirmation window is typically a pop-up dialog box that confirms users actions. You've probably seen thousands of these before. Many of them are used to ask the users questions and confirm their actions.

PROBLEM BEING ADDRESSED

These windows help prevent users from accidentally performing operations that are irreversible. Users might accidentally delete a file or discard edits they've made in a text document.

WHY IS THIS A BAD SOLUTION?

Users do not always read what a dialog box says. In many cases, they simply tap yes for any question presented to them. This is learned behavior from years of using apps that abuse pop-ups and confirmation dialog boxes.

A pop-up confirmation window is the easiest way to try to move the responsibility of accidental operations from the developers to the users. However, forcing a user to tap an OK button doesn't relieve the design and developer team from responsibility if users mistakenly lose their data or perform actions they don't want to.

BETTER SOLUTION

Every action should be reversible. Try to provide an Undo for all operations instead of confirmation windows. The Gmail app does this brilliantly. When a user deletes an email, the app deletes it but provides an easy way to undo this deletion (see Figure 21-3).

EXCEPTIONS

There do exist operations that are truly irreversible. Still it is worth trying to find alternatives before reverting to a confirmation window. Sending email is a good example of an irreversible operation as once the email is in the receiver's email box you cannot change it. Even in this example you should try to make sure that the users will not send the email accidental by organizing your user interface in a way that it is very clear how the email is sent and avoiding user interface component placements that can cause confusion or accidental taps.

AVOID USING THE ON-SCREEN BACK BUTTON

The on-screen Back button is a part of the app's user interface that brings the user back to the previous screen. It is common to see these buttons on apps that have been directly ported from the iOS. On the iOS, apps must have a Back button.

Figure 21-3: The Gmail app provides users with an easy undo
if they delete an email by accident.

Source: Google

PROBLEM BEING ADDRESSED

Users need to be able to navigate back to the previous screen when they navigate in the app's
screen hierarchy.

WHY IS THIS A BAD SOLUTION?

All Android devices have a Back button. Some of them are software Back buttons, and some
of them are hardware buttons. Adding an extra Back button to the app user interface is
counter-productive. The back stack can already be confusing to users, especially when
combined with the Up button concept. If you add an on-screen Back button, your app's users
will probably confuse it with an Up button. If the button then works as a Back button instead
of an Up button, it is likely to cause confusion.

BETTER SOLUTION

You can rely on Android's Back button and the Up button to handle all the required backward and upward navigation in your app. Do not add on-screen Back buttons to your app. Also, make sure that your Up button doesn't look like a Back button. Try to use the Action Bar's up affordance without modifying it. It can already be fairly confusing to users and making it look like a left arrow is likely to add to that confusion.

AVOID USING THE MENU BUTTON

Before the release of Android 4.0 Ice Cream Sandwich, all Android phones were required to have a hardware menu button. The menu button opens a context menu on screens that have a menu set.

PROBLEM BEING ADDRESSED

Not all actions can be addressed in the user interface. Users need to have access to advanced contextual actions on top of the visible action on the screen.

WHY IS THIS A BAD SOLUTION?

From a user interface design point of view, the early Android phones had two large design flaws. First, you had to hold down the Home key to access multitasking. The second flaw was the use of the hardware menu button. The problem with a hardware menu button is that users cannot tell if the menu is available. Not all screens and apps use the context menu, so users have to guess. The only way to find out if it's active is to press it. It goes against all usability guidelines to force users to do that.

BETTER SOLUTION

In the Android 4.0 release, support for software buttons was added and the requirement for a menu button was removed. In the new guidelines, the menu concept is gone altogether, and it is replaced with the Action Bar design pattern combined with the overflow action menu. You should use this new guideline instead of the old menu concept.

AVOID HIDING THE STATUS BAR

Android allows your app to hide the status bar (the top bar with notifications, clock, and so on). It is quite common to see reading apps, for example, hiding the status bar.

PROBLEM BEING ADDRESSED

Hiding the status bar leaves more on-screen space for the actual content. This can be especially true when the content is large blocks of text, such as with an ebook reader.

WHY IS THIS A BAD SOLUTION?

Android notifications are visible to users only in the status bar. These notifications are not accessible if the status bar is hidden. If user is using an ebook reader app that hides the status bar when they're reading a book, for example, they can still hear the notification sound. The user has no way of telling whether the notification is important or not if the status bar is not visible. The only way for her to know is to go back to the home screen and check the notification. If the status bar was visible, she could simply dismiss the notification if it wasn't important.

It is also important to realize that hiding the notification bar also prevents users from seeing the time. That can be annoying and counter-productive.

BETTER SOLUTION

Try to avoid hiding notification bars. Users use their phones to pass time while waiting for a train or bus. During that time, each notification might be significant and hiding the status bar in your app will make it much more difficult for users to react to notifications. Remember that yours isn't the only app running on the user's device.

EXCEPTIONS

Apps playing full-screen video in landscape mode have often a good reason to hide the status bar. Having the status bar visible with full screen video would ruin the video experience. Google's YouTube app has dealt with this issue by showing the video in full-screen landscape mode without the status bar, but including the status bar when the video is viewed in portrait mode.

AVOID USING SWIPE OVERLAY FOR QUICK ACTIONS

Some apps use a swipe gesture to activate quick actions in list items. See more about quick actions design pattern in Chapter 18. Users swipe the list item to expose a quick actions panel that replaces the list item.

PROBLEM BEING ADDRESSED

Apps often have screen where they display multiple items like emails, notes, or to-do items. Users need to be able to perform actions only on items they want to be affected. Operations like delete, edit, and move require users to select the items explicitly.

On mouse-operated user interfaces, users are used to right-clicking items they want to manipulate individually. On touch screens, this approach is not possible. An alternative must be found. Note that this is the same problem that the quick actions design pattern handles effectively (see Chapter 18).

WHY IS THIS A BAD SOLUTION?

There are three reasons why this approach should not be used in Android apps. First, this gesture is very difficult to discover. It is not a standard way of activating a quick action on the Android platform, so users are unlikely to know about it. Second, the swipe gesture already serves a different purpose on the Android user interface—it is used to switch between workspaces (see more about the workspaces design pattern in Chapter 19) or removing items using the swipe-to-dismiss user interface design pattern.

The third and possibly biggest problem to this approach is that the quick actions panel replaces the actual list item. This means that users immediately lose context to their actions. When you replace the row in your list that the actions apply to, you have removed the most important part of the user interface that should be visible.

BETTER SOLUTION

You should use the solution outlined in the quick actions design pattern in Chapter 18. It is much better to allow your users to see the available actions without hiding the actual content these actions are going to perform. That way, users remain aware of the context and can perform the actions with greater confidence.

AVOID USING NON-ANDROID DESIGNS

The importance of designing for the Android platform specifically and not applying a design that was originally made for another smartphone platform is sometimes difficult to communicate to your project's stakeholders. Bad decisions might lead to a situation where a design that is not suitable for an Android device ends up being used anyway.

PROBLEM BEING ADDRESSED

Good design requires skill and time. Using a design that was already created for a different platform might sound like a good way to save time and money. Some people think that all smartphone platforms are the same, and, therefore, all touch screen designs are interchangeable. This is not true.

I've also heard arguments about maintaining brand consistency among smartphone platforms and, therefore, keeping a one-to-one design approach across all platforms.

WHY IS THIS A BAD SOLUTION?

Unfortunately, all the large smartphone platforms are different. Android has its own design guidelines that you should follow. Users have certain expectations of how apps work and they will expect your app to work within these basic paradigms or otherwise will find it frustrating and difficult.

The argument about brand consistency over platform consistency is also flawed. Users rarely own more than one smartphone, particularly ones running on different operating systems, at the same time. Users will, however, have multiple applications on their phones. Your app will be one of many. If your app differs from the general experience, it is much more likely to be abandoned and rated poorly.

BETTER SOLUTION

It is worth investing in correct design from the beginning, even if your client or company already has a successful app on another platform. Android has the largest mobile operating system and, therefore, can offer your project a lot more visibility and more new customers. You only get one chance to launch a first impression.

EXCEPTIONS

The web is a platform that spreads across operating system limits. Each of the large mobile operating systems has a browser capable of rendering modern web applications. If your client doesn't want to invest into application design for a platform-specific app, you might be better off targeting mobile web browsers instead. Users have different expectations of an app's functionality when it runs inside a web browser. Your app can look similar on the iOS and on Android, for example, as long as users access it through a web browser.

SUMMARY

Anti-patterns are design approaches that you should avoid in your apps, even though you will see many examples of them on current Android apps. There are better ways to handle these problems, but sometimes it requires more work and design investment. You must perform a cost-benefit analysis on a case-by-case basis. In some cases, the cost of implementing the better design might actually be less. Always keep in mind the user's goals—what do your users want to achieve when using your app? Don't create user interfaces that just look cool or are great on other platforms. Create a good Android user experience and your users will be happy. In addition, your app will receive better ratings and more downloads.

INDEX